UNBROKEN THREAD

UNBROKEN

AN ANTHOLOGY OF PLAYS BY

THE UNIVERSITY OF MASSACHUSETTS PRESS   AMHERST

THREAD

ASIAN AMERICAN WOMEN

 EDITED BY ROBERTA UNO

Copyright © 1993 by The University of Massachusetts Press
All rights reserved   Printed in the United States of America
LC 93-21858   ISBN 0-87023-856-6 (paper)
Set in Sabon by Keystone Typesetting, Inc.
Printed and bound by Thomson-Shore
Library of Congress Cataloging-in-Publication Data
Unbroken thread : an anthology of plays by Asian American women /
edited by Roberta Uno.   p.   cm.   Includes bibliographical references (p.).
Contents: Introduction — Paper angels / Genny Lim — The music lesson /
Wakako Yamauchi — Gold watch / Momoko Iko — Tea /
Velina Hasu Houston — Walls / Jeannie Barroga — Letters to a student revolutionary /
Elizabeth Wong — Appendix: Plays by Asian American women.
ISBN 0–87023–856–6 (paper : alk. paper).
1. American drama—Asian American authors. 2. American drama—Women authors.
3. Asian American women—Drama. 4. Women—United States—Drama.
5. Asian Americans—Drama. I. Uno, Roberta, 1956–
PS628.A85U53   1993   812'.540809287—dc20   93–21858 CIP
British Library Cataloguing in Publication data are available.
Copyright notices for the individual plays appear on their title pages.

For Chinua and Mikiko

Acknowledgments
The editor wishes to thank
Hilary Edwards, Riki Hing, and Njeri Thelwell
for their assistance with research and manuscript
preparation for this volume.
Special thanks are also due to Len Berkman,
Dennis Carroll, Tisa Chang, Lee Edwards,
Eric Hayashi, Leonard Hoshijo, Randy Kaplan,
Sidney and Emma Nogrady Kaplan,
Bea Kiyohara, Bill and Yuri Kochiyama,
Wing Tek Lum, Mako, Yvonne Mendez,
Mariko Miho, Franklin Odo, Chieko Tachihata,
Fred Tillis, Richard Trousdell, Kiku Uno,
Ernest and Grace Uno and Shawn Wong for their
advice on and/or support of this project.

CONTENTS

❀

INTRODUCTION

❀

I am struck not with lines drawn between parents and children but how the parents' and children's lives flow into each other, how the father becomes the son and how the daughter is the mother. Thus, there is both change and continuity: there is no break, no incompatibility between "East" and "West." —Elaine Kim, "Not 'the Best of Both Worlds': Issues of Identity in Asian American Writing"

The six plays of this anthology represent some of the best dramatic literature written by Asian American women since the 1970s. Each is a groundbreaking work and addresses in its own way the experiences of Asians in America. Included are plays by pioneering writers Wakako Yamauchi and Momoko Iko, as well as works written by "second-generation" writers Genny Lim and Velina Hasu Houston and by younger writers Jeannie Barroga and Elizabeth Wong. All six playwrights are American-born daughters of Asian immigrants, and their voices span the genres of naturalism, impressionism, ritual drama, postmodern collage, and media-influenced episodic drama.

Although the plays are grounded in the individual cultural sensibilities of their Chinese American, Japanese American, Amerasian, and Filipino American authors, they speak of common experiences. The themes of isolation and captivity, both physical and metaphorical, run throughout. For the immigrants of Lim's *Paper Angels*, the immigration detention center on Angel Island in San Francisco Harbor is a prison from which they can see Gam Saan, the Gold Mountain. In *The Music Lessons*, a widow and her children toil on a remote farm that is dwarfed by an unending land-scape. *Gold Watch* takes place in the tumultuous days preceding the roundup and incarceration of Japanese Americans. The women of *Tea*, Japanese-born wives of American servicemen, are sepa-rated from their motherland and seek for themselves a sense of place in the heartland of America. The characters of Jeannie Bar-roga's *Walls* live constantly with the pain borne by survivors of the Vietnam War. In Elizabeth Wong's *Letters to a Student Revolu-tionary*, a Chinese woman and a Chinese American woman chafe against societies that confine them: one struggles against the lack of personal freedom in her country and the other grasps for meaning in a culture that both celebrates and abandons the individual.

Examining the themes of reconnection and freedom, the play-wrights focus less on the events of history than on the impact of those events in human terms. Yamauchi, Iko, Houston, Lim, Bar-roga, and Wong offer special insights into the lives, roles, and rela-tionships of Asian American women. These plays present images of Asian American women given flesh, whether they be the real wom-en behind media stereotypes or those whose portraits were never painted, like the tenant farmer or the newly arrived immigrant.

The common thread that runs through these plays is their au-thors' sensitivity to the lives of Asian Americans, particularly wom-en, in a changing world. That world might be as vast and on the edge of time as a California desert in the 1930s or as turbulent and momentous as Tiananmen Square in the spring of 1989. These are not women of classically heroic proportions. The scale of their lives is the ordinary; the situations they have been placed in are common to countless others. These are women who have endured immigra-tion detention centers, cultivated the earth, married in hopes of a brighter future, toiled at demeaning jobs in order to survive, or simply attempted to live an independent life. Their actions, con-fined mostly to personal decisions, only cumulatively contribute to a sense of triumph.

Silent or Silenced?

Watching war movies with the next door neighbors, secretly rooting for the other side. —From *"Yellow Pearl,"* lyrics by Chris Ijima and Nobuko Miyamoto

Paper Angels, The Music Lessons, Gold Watch, Tea, Walls, and *Letters to a Student Revolutionary* are arranged not in the order in which they were written or produced, but according to the histori-cal era each play addresses. In this way the collection represents not only a range of voices but also a chronology of Asian American experience reflected through Asian American women's eyes. The plays assert a presence, a participation, a point of view from a segment of America that has been traditionally viewed as silent.

That this silence has its basis in part in historical reality is undeniable. Asian women arrived on these shores in far fewer numbers than Asian men. Unlike African slaves, who were purchased as an investment which would increase in value through reproduction, Asians were originally imported as temporary labor. Thus the immigration of women was not encouraged. Among Chinese immigrants (who constituted the first major wave of Asian immigration beginning in 1840), only one of every twenty were women until the turn of the century.[1] The social conditions and laws encountered by Asian immigrants served to silence further this population. From exclusionary and restrictive immigration laws to statutes preventing landownership, intermarriage, or citizenship, to the internment of Japanese Americans during World War II, Asians have been relegated to the status of perpetual foreigners by legislation and social practice.

In contemporary times, women of Asian descent have been effectively silenced by the popular media. When seen at all, they are generally depicted as the exotic prostitute or geisha, the quiet, submissive servant or peasant, the treacherous dragon lady or villain, the comic buffoon, or the industrious model minority. Most prevalent is the Asian woman as ornament. From airline ads to panty hose and beauty cream commercials, the Asian woman is a smiling, nameless, decorative accessory.

In the American theater the silencing of Asians has been particularly consequential, not only because of their invisibility or marginalization, but also because of the distortion of their image by both stereotypical writing and the continuing, accepted practice of casting European American actors as Asians. The silencing of Asians in America through laws, social practice, and the media has cumulatively served to affect the psyche of Asians and non-Asians alike. The result is a willingness to accept and view Asians as silent, uncomplaining, and accepting of their lot.

Smashing the Mask

> *We must recognize ourselves at last*
> *We are a rainforest of color and noise*
> *We hear everything*
> *We are unafraid*
> *Our language is beautiful*
> *—From Janice Mirikatani's "Shedding Silence"*

The 1989 *Miss Saigon* controversy brought to the fore the ongoing battle by Asian Americans to interpret their own images in both the popular media and the stage. The national protest was a painful reminder of the lack of progress in the media for Asian American writers and performers. It echoed similar earlier protests, including the 1970 boycott of *Lovely Ladies and Kind Gentlemen* in Philadelphia, New York, San Francisco, and Los Angeles, and the 1980 outcry against a Hollywood remake of *Charlie Chan*. It not only raised the question of the substitution of a yellow-face adhesive taped actor for one possessing authentic epicanthic eyelids, but it also rejected the material itself—questioning whose writing is produced and what perspective, what point of view, the writer takes. Mary Suh and other critics pointed to lyrics like "Tonight I will be Miss Saigon / Tonight you'll be Miss Jumped upon / I'll win a G.I. and be gone / He'll screw you with your crown still on,"[2] in questioning the energy expended fighting for demeaning roles.

Through the painstaking uncovering of our early literature by King Kok Cheung, Frank Chin, Eric Chock, Arnold Hiura, Marlon Hom, Kai-yu Hsu, Yugi Ichioka, Lawson Inada, Elaine Kim, Amy Ling, Darrell Lum, Wing Tek Lum, Stephen Sumida, Shawn Wong, Stan Yogi, and others, we have learned that despite the popular myth of Asians as mute foreigners, nearly every facet of Asian American life has been written about by the people undergoing the experience. From the anonymous poetry of Angel Island, to the verse and memoirs of World War II internees, to short stories and novels by first-generation immigrants, Asians in America have documented their experience in this country in their mother tongues and in English.

That Asian American dramatic literature is a fairly recent development should come as neither paradox nor surprise. The publication of ethnic theater has commonly followed the emergence of prose, poetry, and fiction for very logical and practical reasons. Unlike poetry or fiction, which can be passed from hand to hand or duplicated relatively easily, writing for theater implies not only an audience, but production: performers, costumes, props, and, most important, a physical location in which to bring all of these elements together. In choosing to write for theater, the playwright must either imagine the possibility of production or be resigned to creating work that may never live off the page.

When we look to African American literature, we see the poetry of Phillis Wheatley and Jupiter Hammond and the memoirs of Oluduah Equiano and William Wells Brown preceding the appearance of theatrical writing by several decades. Even as William Wells Brown's antislavery melodrama *A Leap to Freedom* (1858) was written to be read from the pulpit and was never produced during his lifetime,[3] so it was with many of the early African American women playwrights. According to Kathy Perkins in *Early Black Female Playwrights*, "Many of these women . . . wrote plays not expecting ever to see them staged. . . . The few plays that were performed were usually put on by libraries, churches, schools, or clubs within the black community."[4] Asian Americans have followed this pattern of literary development—the poets who carved their dreams, anger, and fears in the walls of the Angel Island detention center in the early 1900s became flesh on stage some seven decades later. Asian American women's writing for the stage began as early as the 1920s with Gladys Li's *The Submission of Rose Moy* (1924), which dramatizes a Chinese American girl's rejection of an arranged marriage. Willard Wilson of the University of Hawaii Department of English encouraged a pioneering generation of Asian American playwrights through his playwriting classes and his collection of the best of these works in ten volumes of *College Plays*. He fostered the emergence of a new drama, focusing on the Asian experience in Hawaii, expressed in a uniquely Asian American dialogue. He urged the student of writing to "look around . . . to attempt to present life as it has impinged upon him and as he sees it."[5] Among the Asian American women playwrights who wrote during these early decades, finding publication in *College Plays*, *The Hawaii Quill Magazine*, and *Theater Group Plays*, are Gladys Li (*The Submission of Rosie Moy*, 1924; *The White Serpent*, 1924); (*The Law of Wu Wei*, 1925); Wai Chee Chun (*For You a Lei*, 1936; *Marginal Woman*, 1936); Bessie Toishigawa (*Nisei*, 1947; and *Reunion*, 1947); and Patsy Saiki (*The Return*, 1959; *The Return of Sam Patch*, 1966; and *Second Choice*, 1959).

Creating a Stage

As an actress in The World of Suzy Wong *and the* Basic Training of Paulo Hummel *I knew first hand the stereotypes that abound on Broadway and in Hollywood—of being at the whim of people who don't know my culture. There was no one writing roles for Asian women. We needed a structured, ongoing acting company. There was something about taking our destiny into our own hands, forging our own professional paths that was very empowering. We could decide what our real images are, what stories we want to tell. —Tisa Chang, Artistic Director, Pan Asian Repertory Theater*

For many Asian American writers in the mid-1970s the specific stimulus for choosing the theatrical form came from a particular element within the Asian American community. It was the Asian American actor, dissatisfied with the limited opportunities offered by the Hollywood motion picture and television industry, who served as catalyst for an Asian American theater. Central to this movement was the actor Mako, former artistic director of Los Angeles' East West Players, which he and a collective of actors founded in 1965.

For many years Asian American actors have felt themselves marginalized by the narrowly stereotyped and reductive presentation of Asian characters in the mainstream media industry. Even in those rare instances when one of these actors won a major role, subsequent film opportunities were meager. Although Mako had earned an Academy Award nomination in 1966 for Best Supporting Actor for his work with Steve McQueen in the film *The Sand Pebbles*, comparable substantive dramatic roles were not forthcoming.

Such was the experience of other accomplished Asian American actors including Sessue Hayakawa (best supporting actor nominee, *Bridge Over the River Kwai*, 1957), Miyoshi Umeki (best supporting actress, *Sayonara*, 1957), Haing S. Ngor (best supporting actor, *The Killing Fields*, 1984), and Pat Morita (best supporting actor nominee, *The Karate Kid*, 1984). Morita extended his role in sequels to the *Karate Kid* and is recognizable to most Americans in ads as Colgate's Wisdom Tooth, a combination of Confucius and Charlie Chan who promotes dental hygiene. Umeki's only major role following her Oscar was in the early 1970s as the housekeeper Mrs. Livingston on television's "The Courtship of Eddie's Father" with Bill Bixby. Haing S. Ngor has yet to follow his Oscar-winning performance with another comparable film.

For the Asian American actor, frustration became fuel for creative expression. In 1968 East West Players, aided by a two-year Ford Foundation grant, launched a national playwriting contest for Asian Americans. Wakako Yamauchi and Momoko Iko, members of a group of pioneering playwrights that includes Frank Chin and Ed Sakamoto, began their careers as playwrights as a direct result of their contact with East West Players.

Momoko Iko, a second-generation Japanese American (Nisei) living in Chicago, was writing fiction and had not thought about writing a play until she read about the East West Players playwriting contest in the Japanese American newspaper *The Chicago Shimpo*. She had been working on a novel which dealt in part with the internment experience. "I read the notice and thought hmmm . . . I'll see if I can turn a portion of the novel into a play. I'd been working with the story from so many different angles that the play came very quickly—I finished it in six weeks. I only really began to research playwriting when I decided to write that play."[6]

Of the resulting work, *The Gold Watch*, Mako observed, "Momoko's play was so hard to read, it was on onion skin paper and looked like the third carbon copy. It was impossible! But I was struck by the depiction of the Issei [first-generation] characters. There was a passion and a truth there. I had to go on reading it."[7]

Nisei Wakako Yamauchi was also a fiction writer. Inspired and encouraged by her friend, pioneering short-story writer Hisaye Yamamoto, Yamauchi wrote and published poetry and short stories in the Japanese vernacular press. "I had sent my work out and gotten rejected by all the mainstream publications—*Colliers, Saturday Evening Post, Redbook.* I had nearly stopped writing. I published an annual story in the Christmas issue of *The Rafu Shimpo* newspaper."[8] Yamauchi was invited in 1974 to publish her short story "And the Soul Shall Dance" in the groundbreaking anthology, *AIIIEEEEE,* which brought it to the attention of Mako, who persuaded her to adapt it for theater. "Actually I'm a playwright by fluke: I was asked by East West Players to adapt a short story into a play and was given a grant to complete it. I realized then how few people were writing our Asian American stories, and how few roles were open to our Asian American actors. I have been writing plays since then."[9]

An Unbroken Thread

I remember the first time I saw a play with Asian actors—Wakako's And the Soul Shall Dance *was on T.V. I sat in front of the television with tears running into my lap —Elizabeth Wong*

Playwrights Genny Lim, Jeannie Barroga, and Elizabeth Wong, who along with Velina Hasu Houston, Phillip Kan Gotanda, Jessica Hagedorn, David Henry Hwang, and R. A. Shiomi represent a second generation of Asian American playwrights, found their identification with playwriting natural because of the existence of an Asian American theater. Genny Lim observes, "If it hadn't been for the existence of East West Players and the Asian American Theater Company I don't know if I would have gone ahead and written a play because there would have been no place to have it shown."[10] Elizabeth Wong adds, "The first generation of writers gave me the courage to make the decision to be a playwright."[11] While opportunities have increased for Asian American playwrights and more are seeing their work developed and produced at mainstream theaters, it is the ethnic and multicultural theaters that have sustained the work, giving it continuity, building on past efforts, and, most important, producing the work despite changing theatrical fashion and fundraising trends.

Pan Asian Repertory, founded in New York City in 1977 by actress Tisa Chang, has produced fifty plays by or about Asians and Asian Americans. East West Players under the direction since 1990 of actress Nobu McCarthy has staged some one hundred plays. Hawaii's Kumu Kahua, under the artistic leadership of founding artistic director Dennis Carroll, has produced over one hundred works since 1971. San Francisco's Asian American Theater Company, headed by founding member Eric Hayashi, has specialized in the development of new works and has staged some ninety plays since it was founded in 1973. Seattle's Northwest Asian American Theater Company (formerly Asian American Exclusion Act), headed by Bea Kiyohara, has contributed nearly fifty productions since 1976. These theaters along with national competitions like the Ruby Schaar Yoshino Playwriting contest of the Japanese American Citizen's League, a biannual contest begun in 1986 to encourage works depicting the Japanese American experience, and the Seattle Group Theater's Multicultural Playwrights' Festival, an annual play development laboratory begun in 1985, have been the primary forces behind the identification, encouragement, and development of the Asian American playwright. Recently formed theaters such as Teatro Ng Tanan (Theater for the People) in San Francisco and Silk Road Playhouse in New York City are giving birth to a new generation of Filipino and Korean American playwrights respectively.

The existence of multicultural and ethnic theaters and the inroads made by playwrights such as Velina Hasu Houston, David Henry Hwang, and Phillip Gotanda into the regional and commercial theater arena are evidence of a formalization in American terms of theatrical traditions inherent to Asia which have crossed the Pacific embedded in the cultures of Asian immigrants. The theater that has become visible, through publication and production, outside of Asian immigrant communities is a natural extension of an ongoing cultural response to new situations and social developments.

In addition, a largely unwritten community-based theater has served to preserve a sense of original identity without remaining rigid or static. The traditional Chinese Cantonese operas which were enjoyed in the oldest Chinese communities of Seattle, New York, Los Angeles, San Francisco, and Honolulu are connected to the Kabuki and Noh performed by first- and second-generation Japanese Americans, as evidenced in photographs from the prewar and war period. Similarly, the dramatic performances that take place today in more recently arrived communities of Southeast Asians and South Asians are linked intrinsically to the scripts in this volume. They form part of a thread—albeit one that has been pulled, twisted, frayed, and retied—which marks the dynamic cultural response of Asians in America. This thread at times has been so fine as to seem invisible, stretching across an ocean, linking two continents, serving as a fluid lifeline, a cultural continuum. From Chin Moo of *Paper Angels*, who crosses an expanse of ocean at the turn of the century uncertain of her future, to Bibi of *Letters to a Student Revolutionary*, who reverses that Pacific Ocean passage in an encounter with her Chinese homeland, a continuing sense of cultural connection is established. In the process, Asian American playwrights have infused the American theater with new energy and vision.

Notes

1. Ronald Takaki, *Strangers from a Different Shore* (Boston: Little, Brown, & Co., 1989), 235.
2. Mary Suh, "The Many Sins of Miss Saigon," *Ms. Magazine*, July 1990, 63.
3. James V. Hatch and Ted Shine, *Black Theater U.S.A. Forty Five Plays by Black Americans 1847–1974* (New York: Macmillan Publishing Co., 1974), 34.
4. Kathy Perkins, *Early Black Female Playwrights* (Bloomington: Indiana University Press, 1981), 16.
5. Willard Wilson, *College Plays*, vol. 2 (Honolulu: University of Hawaii Press, 1946–47), 3.
6. Editor's interview with Momoko Iko, Los Angeles, 18 January 1983.
7. Editor's interview with Mako, Los Angeles, 15 January 1983.
8. Editor's interview with Wakako Yamauchi, Gardena, California, 18 January 1983.
9. *Newsletter* of the Yale Repertory Theater (January 1987), cover page.
10. Editor's interview with Genny Lim, San Francisco, 10 February 1991.
11. Editor's interview with Elizabeth Wong, New York City, 22 February 1991.

PAPER ANGELS

❀

GENNY LIM

The seeds that blossomed into Genny Lim's *Paper Angels* were planted in 1976 when Lim began work on an oral history project which would evolve into the book *Island: Poetry and History of Chinese Immigrants 1910–1940.* In 1970 Park Ranger Alexander Weiss noticed Chinese characters inscribed on the walls of the Angel Island immigrant detention center in the San Francisco Harbor which, earmarked for destruction, had stood abandoned for over two decades. When Weiss's superiors did not share his perception of the significance of the carvings he contacted members of the Asian American community. George Araki of San Francisco State University and photographer Mark Takahashi investigated the find, documenting the inscriptions in photographs which initially appeared in the Asian American newspaper *East West.*[1]

"It was a revelation when I saw it in *East West,*" says Lim, who immediately contacted a friend, historian Judy Yung, with the idea of doing something to disseminate the information.[2] Yung involved fellow historian Him Mark Lai and soon the three, Lai, Lim, and Yung, all descendants of Angel Island detainees, embarked on a project of translating the poetry and interviewing immigrants. "At first we thought it would be a pamphlet," says Lim of the small number of poems which had survived up to six decades in the deteriorating barracks. The magnitude of the project changed when, as word drifted out into the community about the research, two elderly gentlemen, Smiley Jann and Tet Yee, came forward with two separate collections of poems that they had copied off the walls during the tedious hours of their own detentions in 1931 and 1932.

"We were very lucky to get two different versions from people who had stayed at different times so we could make a comparison," said Lim of the nearly one hundred poems which, along with oral histories conducted by Lai, Lim, and Yung, would become the basis for the *Island* book.

The involvement in the Angel Island project submerged Lim in a process of personal and cultural reconciliation which would become a major theme of her later work as a playwright. "For all of us it was a process of reverse history—we had to interview people and piece it all together before we could come to some insight about our own personal family experiences. . . . I didn't understand why my parents were the way they were—traditional, protective, and closed-mouthed about their background. I'd always felt alienated from my parents until I started understanding their history and what they went through. It became a bonding experience for me."

Born in San Francisco in 1946, Lim was the youngest of seven children in a household with only one son. She grew up aware of her status as a woman, while also straining against traditional career roles. Her grandfather, who was of a peasant farming family, had been a sojourner in America. He became a merchant, running a general store on Washington Street in San Francisco's Chinatown. He returned to his home province of Kwangtung in China to marry, Lim's father consequently was also born in China. Chinese men in America returned to China to marry, if they could, not only because there were so few Chinese women in America, but also because they believed that the women raised in China would be more proper, traditional wives. Lim's father came to America as a boy and was a student in one of the first classes of English taught to Chinese boys at the Commodore Stockton School in San Francisco. Like his father he saved money to return to China to marry, however he returned to America with his bride. He worked as a cook, a laborer, and a migrant farm worker before saving enough money to buy a small sewing factory in Chinatown. Her mother worked as a seamstress and Lim, along with her siblings, was raised working in her parents' business.

"All the women in my family are strong because my mother is very matriarchal," says Lim of the woman who both ran a business and raised a large family in a new country. Yet despite the number of women in the Lim household Confucian values dominated. "We grew up knowing it was insolent to even question [our position as women]—the son carries on the family name, the daughters are married out and diminish that name." In *Paper Angels* Lim illustrates the internalization of Confucian values. The character Chin Moo states matter of factly, "You know, a good son is the backbone of a family. More precious than jade. But a daughter is an empty rice sack. She exhausts the family reserves."

From an early age Lim was exposed to the arts by her parents who loved the Chinese theater and would take the family to the operas which frequently toured Chinatown. Although she grew up in a household where a passion for music and theater existed, "it never occurred to me to be an artist because I didn't think for my culture it was a possibility. . . . immigrant parents want so desperately for their children to be secure economically they push you into a more conventional career. . . . They don't want you to become a doctor, maybe a teacher or secretary so that your chances of matrimony are higher. If you overachieve you might have a hard time finding a husband. If you underachieve, that's not good either. So the whole focus is on creating good marriage material. That was my parents' responsibility to their daughters—making us good marriage material."

The creative impulse in Lim led to a rebellion that took her to San Francisco State University where she studied theater arts in an attempt to achieve her first goal of becoming an actor. During the tumultuous 1968 boycott and student strike for ethnic studies she left with only a few credits remaining toward her degree and became a singer with a rock band called "Glass Mountain." She moved to New York City in 1969 and graduated from the School of Journalism at Columbia University before going to work for CBS News. It was while at CBS that she came back in touch with her Asian identity: "I felt very isolated working in a non-Asian environment." When she learned that Frank Ching of the *New York Times* was looking for Asian American writers to volunteer for the newly formed *Bridge* magazine, Lim jumped at the opportunity. What initially was relief from the isolation she felt working in the white world of journalism was to become a career which combined her artistic aspirations with her ongoing interest in the Asian presence in America.

In *Paper Angels* Lim explores a world peopled by those courageous individuals who in defiance of discriminatory immigration laws came to America in search of a better life. As the first major wave of Asians in America, the Chinese, beginning in the 1840s, had arrived as laborers to participate in the California Gold Rush, the building of the railroads, and as fishermen and farmers. While initially treated with curiosity and welcomed in the United States, they soon became the target of discriminatory laws and racist sentiments. As the Gold Rush ended and the railroad connected the East Coast with the West, the Chinese became the pawns of employers who used them to artificially depress the wages of white laborers and to break strikes. Growing anti-Chinese sentiment from labor led to the passing of discriminatory legislation including the Foreign Miners Tax, the Queue Ordinance, the Cubic Air Ordinance, the Laundry Tax, and laws that prevented intermarriage with Caucasians, denied naturalized citizenship, denied Chinese the right to testify against whites in a court of law, and segregated their children in public schools.[3]

These laws culminated in the 1882 Chinese Exclusion Act, the first national immigration legislation that targeted a specific nationality, and the first of several such laws directed at immigrants from Asia. The Chinese Exclusion Act kept out the common laborer while permitting the entry of merchants, students, and tourists only. The 1906 San Francisco earthquake was a windfall for hopeful Chinese immigrants because the ensuing fire destroyed municipal records, opening a loophole through which many Chinese entered.[4] New arrivals claimed to be sons of American-born Chinese—thus the grueling interviews, coaching books, and concept of "paper sons" which are central to *Paper Angels*. The assumption of a new identity for a wave of immigrants (it is estimated that each Chinese woman living in San Francisco Chinatown would have had to have borne eight hundred children to account for the number of new Chinese who immigrated after Exclusion)[5] had deep personal ramifications. In *Paper Angels* the character Lee cries out against a system that forces him to deny his humanity, "I am Lee Sung Fei, not this Moy Fook Sing or whatever his name is! I am from Shekki not Sunning. I am a scholar, not a merchant's son!"

Lim is emphatic that while the characters of *Paper Angels* are victimized by circumstance they are not victims. "For Westerners to become a hero you have to win or beat up or kill." Of her female characters Chin Moo, Ku Ling, and Mei Lai, women who potentially may follow in the footsteps of Lim's own mother, she adds, "Certain feminists would want the women of this play to triumph. I see that as a Western interpretation and definition of feminism—that women should have to take on the patriarchal value system and . . . conquer in the same way that Western heroes conquer. My characters are strong but they don't function like Western heroes."

Since writing *Paper Angels* in 1978, Lim's work in theater has come full circle back to performance. Her recent work has diverged from naturalism, expanding on the impressionistic sensibility that is present in *Paper Angels* and other early works. Her movement to interdisciplinary performance art comes from more than her background in acting: "English is not my inherent language. Even though I'm American born I come from a bilingual, bicultural context. The English language is limiting for me. To break out of that construct I integrate music, movement, voice, poetry and visual art which bring in the Cantonese feeling." To this end Lim's preference is to work collaboratively; with musicians Max Roach, John Jang and poet Sonia Sanchez she developed *XX*, produced in November 1990 for San Francisco's Festival 2000. With the support of a Rockefeller grant she is currently developing a new piece with performance and visual artist Guadalupe Garcia and choreographer Alleluia Panis.

Notes

1. Him Mark Lai, Genny Lim, and Judy Yung, *Island Poetry and History of Chinese Immigrants, 1910–1940* (San Francisco: Hoc Doi Chinese Cultural Foundation, 1980), 9, 10.
2. Editor's interview with Genny Lim, San Francisco, 10 February 1991.
3. Ron Takaki, *Strangers from a Different Shore* (Boston: Little Brown, 1989), 79–131.
4. Ibid., 234.
5. Ibid., 236.

PAPER ANGELS

A One-Act Play

(with a prologue and fourteen scenes)

GENNY LIM

CHARACTERS

LUM, an able-bodied peasant youth. He is bold and ambitious, temperamental and cocksure—an aggressive fighter with honest motives.

FONG, a cynical, mercenary, middle-aged peasant with a penchant for making money and surviving the system.

LEE, a high-strung young poet with naive delusions of life. He wants very much to be western.

CHIN GUNG, an old timer, with a taste for freedom and adventure, who's been in the United States long enough to cultivate American habits, but who's never lost his traditional Chinese values and outlook on life.

MEI LAI, the devoted young wife of Lee. She possesses all the virtues of an ideal Chinese woman. Patient and loyal, gentle and loving, graceful and considerate. Yet there is a profound sense of loss and insecurity underneath her complacency.

KU LING, a moody young peasant girl from extreme poverty. She is all alone in the world and she possesses all the qualities considered unacceptable to a well-bred Chinese girl: headstrong and rebellious, independent and unladylike. Her hostility is equal to her vulnerability.

CHIN MOO, an old village woman with a simple, practical outlook on life. At home in the Toisan hill country, she is a fish out of water in American society. Yet she is resilient and philosophical in response to life's demands.

MISS CHAN, a Christian convert, who carries out her duties as interpreter with distinction and objectivity. While she is sympathetic to the immigrants, her loyalty is to her job. Chan can be played by a male or there can be two interpreters, a male for the men, a female for the women.

INSPECTOR, a civil servant, who's come up through the ranks. His jurisdiction over immigration cases gives him a sense of power and authority. His job is a personal mission to stem the Yellow Peril.

WARDEN, a middle-aged middleman trapped by the system. He carries out the commissioner's orders and polices the day-to-day. He is frustrated by his dead-end position and afraid of his expendability.

GUARD HENDERSON, a working-class redneck who hates his job. He takes the immigrants' hostility personally because of blind patriotism and abuses his power.

MISS GREGORY, a Methodist missionary who has devoted her life to the saving of Chinese women's lives. She is fearless of the authorities because of the latitude they give her on the Island and fanatically determined to eradicate heathenism and prostitution.

PRODUCTION NOTE: The setting, in the round or quasi-round, should be suggestive of a dormitory room with sleeping berths attached to long poles extending from floor to ceiling. A makeshift clothesline strewn with laundry and personal belongings, here and there, to create the feeling of confinement and transiency. The proscenium setting can also be impressionistic and simple, with the men's and women's quarters dividing the stage.

PROLOGUE

A darkly lit dormitory. A voice-over audio of an interrogation is in progress as Chinese immigrants stand amid the berth poles with their cloth bundles and few personal belongings. They are suspended in silent postures of expectation, longing and fear. An interpreter translates and a typewriter is heard in the background.

INSPECTOR: How old are you?

INTERPRETER: *Nay gay daw suey?*

APPLICANT: *Yee sup.*

INTERPRETER: Twenty.

INSPECTOR: When were you born?

INTERPRETER: *Nay gay nien chut-sai?*

APPLICANT: *Bot ngut sup-chut, yut bot gow um nien.*

INTERPRETER: August 17, 1895.

INSPECTOR: Where were you born?

INTERPRETER: *Hai bien shu chut-sai?*

APPLICANT: *Chew Kai Choon.*

INTERPRETER: Chew Kai village.

INSPECTOR: What is your father's name?

INTERPRETER: *Nay-ga fu chun mut yeh meng-ah?*

APPLICANT: Chow Kee-Lung.

INSPECTOR: And your mother? What is her name?

INTERPRETER: *Nay-ga mo-chung neh?*

APPLICANT: Ng Shee.

INSPECTOR: What kind of feet had she?

INTERPRETER: *Kuey-yow mo jot guerk-ah?*

APPLICANT: *Jot guerk.*

INTERPRETER: Bound feet.

INSPECTOR: How many stairs are there leading to your doorstep?

INTERPRETER: *Nay di ook-kay moon chien you gay-day low tai-ah?*

APPLICANT: *Gow-ga.*

INTERPRETER: Nine.

INSPECTOR: How do you know?

APPLICANT: *Ngaw ji doh way li-mun ngaw yow sow gor.*

INTERPRETER: I counted them because I knew you would ask that.

INSPECTOR: Oh, so you were coached!

INTERPRETER: *Nay you law ga ji-ah?*

APPLICANT: *M'hai, m'hai, ngaw mo law gah ji-ah.*

INTERPRETER: No, no! That is not true. I was never coached.

INSPECTOR: How much did you pay for the coaching papers?

INTERPRETER: *Nay bay gay daw tchien may gaw di how gung ji-ah?*

APPLICANT: *Ngaw mo mai ga ji-ah!*

INTERPRETER: I did not buy any coaching papers.

INSPECTOR: Why are your hands trembling?

INTERPRETER: *Dim-guy nay-ga sow jin?*

APPLICANT: (*looking nervously at his hands*) *M'hai-ah.*

Fade out.

SCENE I

The men's dormitory. A low, continuous moan is heard from offstage.

LEE: Why does he do that?

FONG: Poor bastard. He's been on the Island three years now.

LEE: Three years! What happened?

LUM: (*jumping down from the bed*) He's driving me crazy. (*Moan grows louder.*) Shut up, you hear me, shut up!

CHIN GUNG: Oh, be quiet!

LUM: Why don't they lock him up!

FONG: Don't mind him. He's possessed by ghosts. (*Confidentially*) He got word four months ago his wife died back in China. He's convinced it's a trick to keep him locked up. (*Moan.*) He talks to his wife in the dining room, as if she was right there in front of him!

LUM: (*yelling at him*) Ngow gwei! Wake up, you fool! Your wife's dead! You hear? She's dead! (*The moaning becomes a hummed folksong.*)

FONG: You may as well tell a dream to an idiot.

LEE: I don't blame the poor fool. If China wasn't so weak, we wouldn't be excluded from coming. We wouldn't have to be Paper Sons.

LUM: I'm no Paper Son. My father was high-class—a genuine U.S. citizen. Owned the biggest gambling hall in Chinatown. That's right, he didn't have to go back to China to report any phony sons. He could buy off the immigration people any time he wanted to!

FONG: Liar.

LUM: Hey, would I kid you? My father was a big shot. Anytime there was trouble, they'd go to him. He could claim you were an Earthquake Son and you'd be an instant citizen.

FONG: Your father never had shoes!

LUM: (*making an obscene gesture at Fong*) And your father had to cut his feet to fit his shoes!

LEE: *Szu mien ch'u ko.* (*Goes to the wall and starts carving a poem.*) King Hsiang knew he was surrounded when he heard the songs of his people.

LUM: Ah, a Chinese poet in a western suit. (*He examines Lee's clothes.*) When you get out of this prison, you'll be mistaken for an American. (*Looks over Lee's shoulder.*) What's that you're carving? Your obituary?

LEE: A poem.

LUM: Poem? (*Laughs.*) How's this for a poem? (*Breaks into a childish sing-song.*)

> Pok dai-bay, cheong son gaw,
> Yun-yun wah-ngaw mo lo-paw!
> Tien-nyget yau tchien de chow fon-gaw!

> Pat your thigh, sing a song,
> Everybody says I have no wife!
> Let them laugh, it won't be long,
> In Golden Mountain, I'll buy three wives!

LEE: I said poem, not peasant drivel.

Lum grabs Lee by the lapel. Lee's coaching book drops to the floor. Lee hurriedly stoops to pick it up, but Lum beats him to it.

LUM: Why you son-of-a-dirty-snake, what are you doing with this?

LEE: It's none of your business!

FONG: (*looking around and checking the door to make certain no guards are in earshot*) What the hell's going on here?

LUM: (*accusingly*) He's got his coaching book here!

FONG: (*looking around*) Sh-h-h! Keep it down, keep it down.

LUM: Why didn't you get rid of it? Why didn't you memorize it?

FONG: Burn it! (*Lum stuffs it in a spittoon and burns it.*) Do you know what they'll do to you if they find it? They'll ship you back to China so fast!

LEE: (*defensively*) I'm the one taking the chance!

FONG: I can hide a note in an orange, a pork bun, but where are you gonna hide a whole damn book, huh? In your asshole? The next thing you know, we'll all get deported.

LEE: You hypocrite, I've seen you taking money for those coaching papers! I've seen the kitchen help sneaking you notes past the guards!

FONG: That's different! If I didn't slip the notes, some of you wouldn't get through one hearing! If people like you got your stories straight, I wouldn't need to sneak 'em in!

LEE: (*resentfully*) I am Lee Sung Fei, not (*Gesturing at the burnt contents in the spittoon*) this Moy Fook Sing or whatever his name is! I am from Shekki not Sunning. I am a scholar, not a merchant's son!

FONG: Not anymore, you're not!

LUM: See? The only people who exist (*Tapping his head*) are in here.

LEE: Lies, all lies!

LUM: Come on, Li-Po, this is just the beginning! You'll be living it up good in Chinatown—while us low class bums'll still be here singing our filthy peasant rhymes.

FONG: Stupid paper son. I don't know what the parents teach these days.

LUM: Hey, look at me, I'm big and strong,
　　Not skinny and ugly like my old friend Fong.
　　Let him laugh, let him sneer,
　　When I get rich, he'll still be here.

FONG: Those with the emptiest heads make the loudest noise.

LUM: (*squatting down on the floor as he sets up a game of pai-gow*) Let's play some *pai-gow*.

FONG: (*sniffing the smoke*) This place smells rotten.

LUM: It's your socks, Fong. From all those rotten eggs you eat. (*To Chin*) Hey, Chin Gung, wanna play? (*The old man ignores him.*)

FONG: Leave the old man alone. He doesn't want to play.

LUM: Today's my day. I can feel it in my bones.

LEE: (*standing alone by his wall carving*) It's been three weeks since I've seen my wife!

LUM: What I wouldn't give for a little female companionship right now.

FONG: I've been here a year this coming January sixth.

LUM: (*whistles*) I would rather kill myself than be stuck here that long!

LEE: (*to himself*) I want to get Mei Lai a western style house with a toilet that flushes and a stove that turns fire on and off. I'll take our son up to the highest hill on Gold Mountain and we'll fly the biggest dragon kite you ever saw to heaven!

LUM: When I get to the Big City, you know what I'll get? A wide-brimmed hat. The kind the rich white men wear. I'll walk down Chinese Street like some rich Mandarin and all the ladies will turn their pretty heads and whisper, "Who is that handsome fella?"

23

Genny

Lim

"Why, don't you know? That's brother Lum, a big-shot—made a killing in Gold Mountain. Yessir, big brother Lum—even the white folks call him 'Mis-tah Lum!' "

FONG: (*opens a newspaper*) Ask me, I think you're all dreaming! Hmph, you'll be lucky if you can wash a basket of dirty laundry and earn twenty-five cents! A big heart and an empty pocket will get you nowhere!

LUM: (*looking over Fong's shoulder and pointing at a photograph in the newspaper*) What's that?

FONG: That's the Panama Pacific International Expo in San Francisco.

LUM: Hey, I bet you those were the lights we saw the night the ship landed! Yeah, that's where I'd like to go! To the World's Fair (*Grabbing Fong's hat off his head*) in my fedora! (*Fong grabs it back.*)

FONG: (*hands Lum a piece of chicken he's warmed on the radiator*) Here, sink your teeth into something real! Daydreams are not gonna fill your belly. (*He picks up a towel.*) Anyone got a bar of soap?

LUM: I've been wondering where all the soap's gone. You scrounger, you probably stole a whole suitcase full!

FONG: (*angrily tossing the towel at Lum*) If you got no soap, just say so! Yes or no?

LUM: No!

FONG: (*mumbling as he begrudgingly joins Lum at pai-gow*) Damn kids these days, got no respect for their elders!

Light fades on gambling din and comes up on Chin Gung's bed. Lee leaves the group and walks over to Chin Gung.

LEE: Chin Gung . . . can you do me a favor?

CHIN GUNG: What do you want, boy?

LEE: You've been to Gold Mountain, will you teach me English?

CHIN GUNG: What for?

LEE: I want to become an American.

CHIN GUNG: And you think by speaking English you will become American? (*No answer.*) So you want to learn the language of the White Demons? (*No answer.*) When you want to start?

LEE: Now! As soon as I set foot in America, I will work hard to become a success. I will make my family proud.

CHIN GUNG: Are you number one son?

LEE: Yes, I am. They worked hard just so I could come here. (*He pauses.*) Chin Gung, tell me, what is America like? Are the streets really paved with gold?

CHIN GUNG: (*laughs uproariously*) Paved with gold!

LEE: (*hurt*) If I am disrespectful, I apologize.

CHIN GUNG: (*wipes the tears of laughter from his eyes*) No, no, my son. I can't help laughing. For one moment, I thought I was looking into a mirror. Your smooth face, the fire in your eyes—yes, the fire. Look at these hands! I've shovelled enough tons of sand and turned enough pans of mud in my time. I've blasted through enough granite hills to know that this mountain is no mountain of gold. And I say all of you on this Island (*Gesturing*) will taste fool's gold. You know how I know? Because America is just (*Pointing to his head*) a faraway place in the mind—a piece of dream that scatters like gold dust in the wind.

LEE: Then why are you going back?

CHIN GUNG: Why? Because, my son, as you will learn some day, once a Gold Mountain boy, always a Gold Mountain boy. One foot in America, one foot in China . . . that's the sojourner passing.

Din of gambling can be heard as light fades out.

SCENE 2

Women's dormitory. Gregory, a Methodist missionary, is leading the women in song with the help of Chan, an interpreter. In spite of their unfamiliarity with the pronunciation and text, the women sing with gusto and animation.

WOMEN: My bonny lies over the ocean,
       My bonny lies over the sea,
       My bonny lies over the ocean,
       Oh bring back my bonny to me.
       Bring back, bring back,
       Bring back my bonny to me, to me.
       Bring back, bring back,
       Oh bring back my bonny to me.

GREGORY: Wonderful. You are all doing so much better. (*She looks at Chan for the Chinese word.*)

CHAN: *Ho-ho.*

GREGORY: (*to the women*) Ho-ho! . . . Oh, I haven't forgotten. (*She hands the women some candy, then addresses Mei Lai.*) I suppose you want a boy. Perhaps the lord will bless you. (*Flexes her arm to convey manhood.*) Well, that's all for today. *Joy-geen, joy-geen! Yeh-su oy-nay!*

WOMEN: Bye-bye, Missy!

CHIN MOO: Bye-bye, Missy Je-sus! (*To Mei Lai*) You are so lucky! I just checked the lunar calendar. If conceived on an even day, even month and even year, you will bear a son!

MEI LAI: Oh, I certainly hope so, Chin Moo! I already have a name for him—Yang Lee.

CHIN MOO: Ah, Curious One! You know, a good son is the backbone of a family. More precious than jade. But a daughter is an empty rice sack. She exhausts the family bin.

KU LING: (*acidly, seated on her bed*) The gods forbid a daughter with a stomach. She'll eat you out of rice and home!

CHIN MOO: (*ignoring her*) They say girls always favor their fathers and sons, their mothers.

MEI LAI: Are your children in China?

CHIN MOO: (*sadly*) I don't have children.

MEI LAI: (*embarrassed*) Oh. (*Cheerfully*) Yang Lee will be my first born.

KU LING: If it's a girl, you'd better drown her or sell her.

MEI LAI: (*admonishingly*) Ku Ling!

Sound of foghorn. Ku Ling crosses to the window.

KU LING: The ship's here.

MEI LAI: The witnesses have come in for the day.

CHIN MOO: Hmph! Is that all?

MEI LAI: It might be one of our relatives here and we can't even see them!

CHIN MOO: Tsk-tsk! It's no use wondering. When the melon's ripe, it will drop from its stem. When the time comes, we will each have our turn to testify—and we will each get our turn to leave.

KU LING: I have been here five weeks and others have come and gone in two!

CHIN MOO: Pah, five weeks! I have been on this Island for three months.

KU LING: How can you stand it?

CHIN MOO: What is three months compared to forty years? Forty long years . . . I was fifteen when I married and I was fifteen when my husband left me. He said, "I'm going to make my fame and fortune and I will come back for you!" So off he went to *Gum San*, this husband of six months!

MEI LAI: Did he come back for you as he promised?

CHIN MOO: When two persons are in love, they can live on water alone. Everyone said we were heaven's match. I was never happier. He taught me how to fish. We made baskets out of chicken wire with openings on top. We'd put chicken hearts, fishheads, worms and scraps inside and tie them to trees. Then we'd throw the traps into the river. By morning, we'd caught the plumpest, tastiest catfish, carp and crabs you'd ever sink your teeth in! (*Sighs.*) Then he got itchy feet. He had a burning desire to see the Beautiful Country. (*Sadly shrugs.*) So he left. He described everything he saw when he got there. But after awhile, the letters stopped coming. I let the incense grow cold in the burner, I left my hair uncombed. If you marry a dog, you must follow it. What could I do but sit at the doorstep and wait?

MEI LAI: (*thinking about Lee*) Did you ever give up hope?

CHIN MOO: The women used to get together and gossip about *Gum San*. They told me the women there were bold and shameless. They ran around with flesh exposed like boiled chickens. Truly demons who bewitched men's souls by staring into their eyes. They made the men drunk so they'd spend all their money. They'd sleep with them, so they'd forget their China wives. Before long, the only names the men could remember were theirs. (*In disgust.*) Home? Forget about home!

MEI LAI: I don't know what I'd do if I couldn't see Lee again.

CHIN MOO: When my mother-in-law died, I returned to my native village. I was ready to live out the rest of my days alone. (*Pauses.*) Then one day there was a knock on the door. Who could it be? I opened the door and there was my husband! Home after forty years! We both just stood there and stared at each other. I said, "Bick Hop," that was his name, "You have chicken skin and crane hair!" He replied, "You're no chickadee yourself!"

MEI LAI: I like happy endings.

KU LING: You wouldn't catch me burning incense for forty years!

MEI LAI: (*shocked*) Ku Ling, what a thing to say! A wife must always remain faithful.

KU LING: Hmph, to be faithful is to be foolish! Better to drown oneself in a pond than live in such misery!

MEI LAI: For shame, Ku Ling! You had better mend your tongue before it is too late.

KU LING: Too late for what?

MEI LAI: For you to remain a virtuous Chinese girl. (*Sarcastically*) There is a name back home for girls with unbound feet who wander.

KU LING: Madam, your feet are not exactly tiger-lilies. One can see they are big enough to do a bit of wandering on their own.

MEI LAI: Mark my words, Ku Ling, you will come to a bad end!

KU LING: The trouble with all of you is you have no spirit! You come all the way across the ocean, dragging your useless kitchen gods and superstitions. You remind me of ox tails. Swinging back and forth from the behind, without a head or a brain!

CHIN MOO: (*seizing Ku Ling violently by her clothes*) I ought to tear your skin off!

KU LING: (*snapping away, holding back angry tears*) You can all sit and rot here with your prayer-sticks. I'm not going to wait. I'm getting out of here, do you hear me?

Henderson, a guard, enters with Chan.

HENDERSON: (*shouting*) Sai-gai! Sai-gai! Good news! Good news! (*A bustle of excitement among the women.*)

WOMEN: Who is it? Who is it?

HENDERSON: Chang Li Ti! (*Makes sign language.*) Get your things together. You're leaving. Hurry up! (*The women clap their hands excitedly and chatter as an imaginary woman leaves.*)

CHAN: Fie die jup ho sai yeh. Seng fow-la!

The women bid farewell to Chang. Ku Ling withdraws to the window, weeping.

MEI LAI: (*notices her crying and goes to her*) Ku Ling, you mustn't cry every time someone leaves.

KU LING: I wish I was dead.

MEI LAI: (*touches her on the shoulder*) Don't say that! You are lucky to come!

KU LING: (*turns to face Mei Lai*) I hate this place. I hate the way the guards look at us. So this is *Gum San*! The land of barbarians. If I was a man and if I had a sword, I would kill them all.

MEI LAI: You say what your heart feels, but if you allow yourself such thoughts, you will lose hope.

KU LING: When I was six, my father used to tell me a story about a girl named Fei Shan. Her parents were killed by bandits. So she vowed one day to avenge their deaths. Fei Shan went to a mountain convent and studied martial arts under a master swordswoman. Soon she could wield a spear as straight and strong as any man, move as swift as a sparrow and strike with a fist hard as steel. One day, bandits attacked the convent. When Fei Shan returned, she saw a bandit raping one of the nuns. It was the very same man who had killed her parents! Crazed, she beheaded him with one stroke of the sword. Soon after she marshaled a great army to rid China of foreign aggressors. Fei Shan died a great leader of her people.

MEI LAI: That's a beautiful story.

KU LING: It's a fairy tale. You like fairy tales, don't you, Mei Lai? (*Mei Lai, hurt, ignores her.*)

Henderson enters.

HENDERSON: Chow! Chow!

The women rise in one group and exit. Fade out on women and fade-up spot on Fong.

FONG: If you want to be a Gold Mountain boy you got to pay the price. For one thousand dollars, you can be a merchant, a doctor, a teacher, an official . . . but no laborers, according to the Chinese Exclusion Act. That's why I'm here. On account of the law. Now that their railroad's built, their factories are humming, and the harvest is in, it's time to kick us coolies out by our butts! What can you do? I always make the best of a bad situation, you know? I figure, why try to fight the demon? He's got the power.

I've been in this wooden cage over a year now. I seen 'em come and go. I can tell you how many coaching notes have slipped

29

Genny

Lim

through my fingers without ever getting caught. Kitchen helper goes home, picks up the note at the Canton Flower Shop and brings it back on the morning boat. He puts the note in a dish and serves the dish to me. I, in turn, give it to the right party—for a slight service fee, of course. If it wasn't for me, some of the fellas would still be rotting here—like me.

Fade out.

SCENE 3

Interrogation room. The Inspector is pacing around. Chin Gung is seated.

INSPECTOR: Where in the village is your house located?

CHIN GUNG: From the south, fifth row, fifth house.

INSPECTOR: Is that a regulation five room Chinese house?

CHIN GUNG: Yes.

INSPECTOR: Any outside windows in it?

CHIN GUNG: No.

INSPECTOR: Are there any skylights?

CHIN GUNG: Four skylights and an open light well.

INSPECTOR: What are the floors made of?

CHIN GUNG: All dirt.

INSPECTOR: What type of material is your house made of?

CHIN GUNG: Clay.

INSPECTOR: Who lived in the house with you?

CHIN GUNG: My wife.

INSPECTOR: Anyone else?

CHIN GUNG: No, no one else.

INSPECTOR: Are you sure?

CHIN GUNG: Yes, certain.

INSPECTOR: Earlier, your wife testified that her mother-in-law also inhabited the house. Surely if you really are man and wife, you would know who lived in your own house!

CHIN GUNG: I know what the problem is. You are right. My mother also lived in the same house. But she died five years ago. So that when I came back she was not there.

INSPECTOR: What do you know! The old man's got an answer for everything. Did you raise any chickens?

CHIN GUNG: Yes.

INSPECTOR: How many?

CHIN GUNG: It depends. If the hen hatches, we have more. If we kill one chicken, we have less.

INSPECTOR: Is there a dog in the house.

CHIN GUNG: No, no dog.

INSPECTOR: How is it then that your own brother says there is one?

CHIN GUNG: Oh, that dog. But we ate it before we left.

INSPECTOR: Do you have any children?

CHIN GUNG: No.

INSPECTOR: How come there were no children?

CHIN GUNG: (*sighs*) Because we were only married six months before I came here. (*Sadly*) My wife did not conceive in that time.

INSPECTOR: It says here you returned to China four years ago. Why did you go back?

CHIN GUNG: To see my wife.

INSPECTOR: Why are you returning to America?

CHIN GUNG: Why do I come back? I come back because America is my home now—not China. I am old now. I will be buried here. This is my country.

Fade out as the Inspector exits; fade-in spot on Chin Gung.

CHIN GUNG: Oh, we laid that railroad track from sun up to sun down. The white boss said, "If they'd had you Chinaboys, they could've built Rome in a day!" It was the kind of work that made you strong as an ox. By the end of the day, you could pass out and drop ten thousand feet and never even wake up! There was this fella—Tong, that was his name. He laid the dynamite. We called him Spider cause he was so thin and wiry. All the other boys yelled and signalled with the rope like crazy when they lit the fuse. But not

Spider. He wanted to beat that mountain. You could hear him picking away with his axe, singing and chipping through the shale at the same time. (*Operatic wail.*) "Ah-ah-ah-h-h . . ." Chink, chink!

I was the anchor on the pulley. Spider didn't signal. By the time I realized something was wrong, it was too late. I screamed, "Pull, pull!" The gunpowder exploded. I fell. I never let go. I saw Spider's body shoot up through the blast of flying rocks and smoke, like a puppet . . . his straw hat chasing his head. (*A sobering revelation.*) I believe the son-of-a-gun never meant to signal.

Fade out.

SCENE 4

The women are filing out of the dining hall behind the matron. They pass the men, who await their turn to enter. There is whistling, flirting, and general commotion as the men try to get the women's attention.

LUM: (*pointing at Ku Ling*) *Ah Fong, nay tai, jow hai kuey-la!*

FONG: (*pointing at Chin Moo*) *Aw. Kuey?*

CHIN MOO: (*spotting Chin Gung*) *Ai-ya! Ah-gung-ah! Ah-gung-ah!*

FONG: (*pointing at Mei Lai*) *Ah, kuey jun-hai lieng-wah!* Beau-ti-ful!

LEE: Mei Lai! *Mey diemmah? Mo see-mah. Bee-Bee diem mah? Sun tai ho mah?*

MEI LAI: *Ah-Fei-ah! Ah-Fei-ah!*

Lee bolts from the group and dashes over to Mei Lai. They embrace. Henderson swiftly pulls the couple apart.

The men enter, seating themselves on benches around a long wooden dining table. Henderson is stationed behind them near the door. The kitchen-helper carries a tray to the table. He sets each dish on the table, while the men talk.

LEE: *Ki-eye!* Bastards!

FONG: Calm down! That was a stupid thing to do.

LEE: I only wanted to talk to her. She's my wife.

LUM: I don't blame you. I would have done the same thing.

FONG: You're stupid, too.

LEE: What right do they have?

FONG: You boys never think. They could have beaten you.

LUM: The Weaver Maiden and the Cowherd. Separated by the Milky Way.

The kitchen-helper nudges Fong.

KITCHEN HELPER: Fong Wah Hung. *How-gung-chi!*

The men turn to look at Fong. Fong looks discreetly from side to side, then rises and takes a dish from the helper. A slip of paper falls to the floor from under the dish; the guard spots the paper and rushes over. Fong picks it up; the guard seizes it from him, knocking him aside.

HENDERSON: What's this, old man?

LUM: *Mo-bay-kuey!* (*Lum pounces on Henderson from behind. The other men join in. The paper drops to the floor. A whistle blows.*)

FONG: *Law-di-ji, fie-dee! Fie-dee!*

Fong grabs the paper and stuffs it inside his shirt pocket as the other men riot.

Black out.

SCENE 5

Men's dorm. Fong is cutting Lum's hair.

FONG: In my case, I had such a lousy witness, he got everything all mixed up! Said my father wasn't married the year I was born. So of course they figured I couldn't be his real son if he wasn't even married then! It's stupid little things like that that trip you up— that drive you crazy!

LUM: Think of it this way—you'll get rich (*pointing at his head*) doing this.

FONG: Ah, what good is gold in hell?

LUM: I saw that girl on the ship. She had dark eyes, soft and sad. The minute I laid eyes on her I wanted to marry her.

FONG: I never think about girls.

LUM: I wanted to talk to her, but they wouldn't let me. So I gazed at her from a distance.

FONG: Everyone knows what happened to her on that ship. Unless you like white man's leftovers, forget her.

LUM: (*spinning around and grabbing Fong's scissors*) Don't say that!

The others turn to see what's going on.

FONG: Take it easy, take it easy! I'm not your enemy. (*Hands him the mirror.*) Here.

LEE: What day is it today?

LUM: What difference does it make?

CHIN GUNG: When you get to my age, one day rolls into another like a snowball.

FONG: It's Monday! I know because I mark off the days on my calendar. (*Holds up a Chinatown wall calendar.*)

LUM: (*grabbing it*) What kind of calendar is that? (*Lee joins to look.*)

FONG: Hey, fellas, don't bend it! My uncle sent it to me from San Francisco Chinatown. It's a western calendar with the Chinese dates on the right hand side of the English numbers.

LUM: But the numbers go backward!

FONG: From left to right, left to right.

LUM: Right to left, that's the way it's supposed to be!

FONG: What do those barbarians know? I hear they even eat the side of a cow raw!

LEE: Who told you that?

FONG: Sure, don't you know anything? They just chop off big hunks off the cow while it's alive, slap it on the table and eat.

LUM: (*frowning*) They tear it apart with their hands like cave men?

FONG: Numbskull, do you think they use chopsticks?

LEE: Don't they even use soy sauce?

FONG: Soy sauce? They don't even know what soy sauce is! (*With disgust*) Soy sauce.

The door clangs. The inmates look and see Henderson entering with the Warden and Chan. Henderson has a shiner and assorted injuries.

HENDERSON: (*pointing at Lum*) It was him, sir. He attacked first.

WARDEN: (*to Chan*) What is his name?

HENDERSON: (*tapping Lum*) Eh, you, what's your name?

CHAN: *Nay gew mut, meng-ah?*

Lum spits on the floor to show his contempt.

HENDERSON: I ought to smear that yellow face of yours all over the walls!

WARDEN: Knock it off, Henderson! (*To Chan*) Ask which one of them has the coaching paper.

CHAN: *Bien gaw yun yow how gong-ji?*

FONG: *Mo-yah! Mo-ji-yah!*

The others join in protest.

WARDEN: Tell them to shut up! Make them speak one at a time!

CHAN: *Mo-cho-wah! Nay-de yet-gor, yut-gor gong!*

CHIN GUNG: *Ngaw dey mo how gung chi-ya.*

CHAN: He says there is no coaching paper.

HENDERSON: He's lying! You Chinks know damn well there was a paper! (*The men continue to deny it.*) I saw it drop on the floor!

CHIN GUNG: Mistake, Officer. Please allow me to clear up misunderstanding. We have no coaching paper here. You may search our belongings but you will find nothing.

HENDERSON: Then what the hell was that paper that dropped on the floor?

CHIN GUNG: Ah, sir. I owe you an apology. I can explain. (*Takes a slip of paper from his pocket.*) I believe you are referring to this? (*Hands it to Henderson.*) I asked the cook to give me the name of a good herb doctor in San Francisco. I'm old and the body aches so much sometimes I can't sleep.

HENDERSON: You're lying old man. If that's all that was on the paper, how come they jumped me?

CHIN GUNG: I don't know. Young men have hot tempers. Perhaps they think you attack them for no reason. They are just young boys. Sometimes they get a little hot-headed.

HENDERSON: Sounds like a lot of cock-and-bull to me.

CHIN GUNG: Sometimes the truth appears furthest from the truth.

WARDEN: You have anything to add, Henderson?

HENDERSON: He's covering for them. You're not gonna buy the old Chinaman's story are you?

WARDEN: We have no evidence, Henderson.

CHIN GUNG: You are a wise man, sir.

WARDEN: You better tell your men they are subject to U.S. laws, not China's. We know notes are being passed into the barracks by some method and we intend to put a stop to it! I'm running a detention center. Any more injuries to my men will be dealt with accordingly. Henderson, take this man (*pointing to Lum*) to solitary.

HENDERSON: Yes, sir!

The Warden, Chan, and Henderson exit, Henderson dragging Lum, who struggles violently. He is finally dragged, kicking and screaming, by the hair, out the door.

LEE: Damn you, damn your country, damn your laws! They say eat, we eat. Get up, we get up. I've had enough. How long are we going to crawl and grovel? I'm ashamed to lift my head. I'm ashamed to be Chinese!

CHIN GUNG: You whining yellow bastard! How dare you call yourself Chinese! You think you can hide your skin inside those western clothes? Let me tell you something, schoolboy. While you were still sucking your mother's tit, thousands of young men like you gave their lives for China. Where were you during the Boxer Rebellion? Did you see them rape and kill your women? Did you defend China from foreigners? There is so much you don't know and you won't find it in your books!

FONG: (*bows to Chin*) Chin Gung, you saved my life. I am indebted to you always.

CHIN GUNG: We are all Chinese. You help me. I help you.

Fade out.

SCENE 6

The inmates, men and women, stand by the poles (as in the opening) suspended in time, looking straight ahead. It's as if they have been stripped naked, under surveillance, but their thoughts are what remain of themselves. The Inspector paces among them, referring to them in an objective interview manner. He occasionally gestures at them but for all intents and purposes, they are inanimate . . .

INSPECTOR: The Chinese question. It's my guess that a good ninety-five percent of the Chinamen coming through here are bogus. That's right. They come thinking they can pull the wool over the white man's eyes, figuring we can't tell 'em one apart from the other. And you know, for the most part, you can't! But I give 'em a run for their money. It's like outwitting a fox. Why the other day, this Chinaman comes to the hearing and I'll be damned if it wasn't the same Chinaman we'd deported three years ago! He was coming in under a whole new identity. I swear to god I recognized the little bastard. Why, I was the inquiry inspector who rejected his first entry application!

He was a smart little devil, too. We went back and forth. I was determined to trip him up and he was just as determined to toss every curve back. He was fast. Never flinched. Must've been no more than fourteen or fifteen. To tell the truth, I rather liked the little fella. (*Change of tone from amusement and near-admiration, to cold, dark detachment.*) But the law is the law. I have my job to do. You've got to have a system! Because if you don't, they'll take advantage and next thing you know, not only will you have droves of illegal aliens swarming into the country, but they'll be bringing over their wives, children, sundry aunts, uncles, and relatives, not to mention the little yellow ones they'll be propagating all over the U.S. I mean you've got to be systematic about it. If they're coming in fraudulently, we've got to do our best to keep them out!

Black out.

SCENE 7

Mei Lai and Lee on opposite sides of stage. Night. Thunder and rain.

MEI LAI: As a daughter, I have never questioned the wisdom of my father; as a wife, I am prepared to follow my husband; and as a mother, I will abide by my son's wishes. I have never known anything but hunger and poverty all my life. Now I have a chance.

Lee is writing to Mei Lai by the light of a candle.

LEE: My dear wife. Three weeks have passed since we parted at the dock. I dream of you mending my clothes, your head bent over your bag of colored patches . . . I count the days the river returns to the sea. Your devoted husband, Lee Sung Fei. (*He jumps up, crumpling the paper.*) Oh, what's the use. They will never let me get this to you.

Mei Lai hears the moans of Ku Ling and turns to her. Ku Ling moans and thrashes in her sleep, almost enacting the rape that continues to haunt her.

KU LING: (*almost incoherent*) Oh-h-h-h . . . let me go! Let me go! (*Her breathing grows heavier, as if being crushed.*) No, no, no-o-o! Don't—don't! Don't touch me!

MEI LAI: (*shaking her*) Ku Ling! Ku Ling!

KU LING: (*bolting up*) Wh-what happened?

MEI LAI: It's alright.

Mei Lai holds Ku Ling and cradles her like a baby.

KU LING: Did I talk in my sleep?

MEI LAI: It doesn't matter. You're safe now. Last night I dreamed I was walking along the beach. The waves grew higher and higher like dark mountains approaching shore. An old woman walked along dragging a cart. It was the old widow Lao Chu who lived down the road. She didn't see me. She squat down and with a rock began grinding a brick over a board. She took the fallen powder and stuffed it into her mouth. I walked over and looked in the cart. I saw the infant—Lao Chu's own granddaughter dead! She had delivered the baby, then drowned her. A daughter was just one more mouth to feed, one more woman destined to suffer.

Mei Lai holds Ku Ling as the rain falls.

Fade out.

SCENE 8

Men's dorm.

LEE: (*picks up newspaper*) Maybe the *Siu-Nin-Bow* [*Gold Mountain News*] can use a good writer . . . I'd like to start my own newspaper someday. I'll call it the *New Immigrant News!* (*Pauses.*) Chin Gung, you've lived on Gold Mountain a long time. What's it like?

CHIN GUNG: I remember when I first came here how big the city seemed. I was young and I wasn't afraid of anything. Chinatown was home. They warned us never to leave Chinatown because the white devils would stone you. I didn't believe them. One time I wandered past California Street and saw a group of white boys taunting a sing-song girl. She ignored them and kept right along on her bound feet. One of the boys ran up to her and snatched at her earring. Ripped it right off her ear!

An unruly and unshaven Lum enters, returning from solitary with Henderson, who pushes him inside and slams the door.

LUM: (*kicks the door, then turns to the men*) Hey you sons-of-hell, aren't you even going to welcome me?

FONG: Hey Lum, where you been?

LUM: To see your sister! How about a drink? And none of that cheap stuff!

FONG: What do you mean? This is *ng ga pei*! (*He passes the bottle around.*)

LEE: Other than your dog face, you haven't changed at all!

FONG: Just as stupid and loud as ever.

CHIN GUNG: (*grabs Lum and pats him on the back*) Good to see you, son.

LUM: It's good to be seen!

FONG: Sure, sure, enjoy.

They pass the bottle and the mood becomes festive, rowdy.

LUM: (*raising the bottle*) I want to drink a toast! (*They cheer loudly.*) To freedom!

FONG: Haven't lost your taste, eh?

LEE: What was it like?

FONG: Shut up, will you? This is a celebration!

CHIN GUNG: Another toast! To the opening of the World's Fair.

LEE: Do you think we'll get to see it?

FONG: Sure, sure. I'll send you a postcard from the Mark Hopkins.

LUM: Chin Gung, what are the women like in America? Are they very beautiful?

CHIN GUNG: (*chuckles*) The women . . . the women . . . long of thigh and short of temper! Oh yes, those sing-song girls could drive a Chinaboy crazy! I had my fill of them, too. Ol' Lilly tried to scratch my eyes out when I told her I couldn't take her home . . .

said I ruined her life. But how could you ruin a sing-song girl's life, I ask you? It was already ruined long before I ever came along! That's when she threw the pot of tea at me . . . (*The men laugh.*)

FONG: My uncle has already picked out a bride for me.

LUM: Is that why you left China?

FONG: No. They are waiting for me to become a rich man so I can send for her.

LEE: (*walks to window*) The fog's rolling in.

CHIN GUNG: Everybody says Ol' Chin is crazy. I've moved all around this country. After the rails, we followed the seasons—like geese, always looking for better climate, better conditions. I've picked lemons and artichoke. I've harvested walnuts with long poles and caught the falling nuts with sacks. I was a good cook so when the cook ran off, 'cause he couldn't pay off his gambling debt, I had to prepare the meals for thirty, sometimes as many as fifty men a day. I got so frustrated with my life, I gambled away all my earnings one day. The more desperate you are, the crazier you get. (*Pauses.*) I'll tell you one thing though, I know this land, I ache for her sometimes, like she was my woman. When I dig my hands into her flesh and seed her, something grows; when I water and fertilize her, she begins to swell. If you treat her with respect, she responds, just like a woman. A lot of whites don't know this. (*Pauses.*) You probably think I'm crazy, but I'm in love with this land. I want to die in America.

LUM: Not me. As soon as I strike it rich, I'm taking the first boat back home.

CHIN GUNG: I went to all this trouble bringing my wife with me this time. She waited forty years for me. Imagine that? Forty years. I figure she deserves something better than staring at the backside of a pig all her life. She's no young girl anymore. No, now she's a grandma and I'm a grandpa, except we got no grandchildren. That's not right, you know? Old people should have grandchildren. That way something of them lives on after they're gone. As for me, it's too late. (*Reminisces.*) Some of those sing-song girls were pretty nice. Especially Lilly. I could have married her. But how could I do that to my China wife, huh?

LUM: I would have. I would have married as many as I could afford.

CHIN GUNG: I know plenty of Chinaboys that did that but somehow I just couldn't. Boy, was she mad when I said I couldn't marry her! Missed me by just an inch with that pot of tea! Whew!

Fong strikes an operatic falsetto, grabs a kerchief from the laundry line and covers his head, using it like a Chinese wedding veil. They launch into a parody of a wedding ceremony. They kowtow three times to Lum who is acting as the father-in-law. The couple, Fong and Lee, re-enact the wedding night. Lee chases a coy and squealing Fong around the bed. The climax is reached when Lee finally captures Fong and unveils him. Lee falls back in shock at the grinning Fong.

The Warden, Henderson and Chan enter when the pandemonium reaches its peak. The men instantly stop clowning and signal to Fong, who is still mimicking the bride. He turns around unsuspectingly and comes practically nose to nose with the Warden's face.

HENDERSON: (*in heavy Anglo accent*) Chin Bick Hop. Who is Chin Bick Hop?

CHAN: *Bing gaw hai Chin Bick Hop?*

CHIN GUNG: (*with anticipation*) I am Chin Bick Hop.

WARDEN: Oh, you? According to your medical, you have a case of liverfluke—so you're not permitted to enter the U.S.

CHIN GUNG: (*shocked*) But—but I answered all the questions!

WARDEN: The hospital cleared your physical by error; otherwise, you wouldn't have even made it to the Board of Inquiry. (*He hands a letter to Chin Gung.*)

CHIN GUNG: But I answered all the questions . . .

WARDEN: Liverfluke cases are all deported without appeal. That's the rule.

CHIN GUNG: It's impossible! I'm no Paper Son. I've been here forty years. Forty years, you hear me?

WARDEN: (*genuinely*) Sorry, oldtimer.

The Warden, Henderson and Chan begin to leave. Chin Gung follows them to the door as he pleads.

CHIN GUNG: (*desperately*) But—but I'm a longtime Californ'! (*He looks for reassurance.*) There must be a mistake, eh?

WARDEN: I don't make the rules.

The Warden, Henderson and Chan exit. Chin reads the letter. The others circle around asking him what's happened, what's been said.

CHIN GUNG: Liverfluke worms. They can't do this to me. I'm a U.S. citizen!

FONG: Don't worry, *Ah Gung*, you can always appeal.

CHIN GUNG: They're sending me back to China. They might as well kill me.

LEE: There must be something you can do.

CHIN GUNG: What's going to happen to my wife? I dragged that poor old woman here for this?

FONG: (*putting his arm over Chin's shoulder*) Calm down, calm down, take it easy.

CHIN GUNG: You tell me. (*He looks at Fong helplessly.*) How does one lose face like a man?

FONG: No sense getting worked up over it, old man.

LUM: No skin off your nose, huh, Fong?

FONG: What's done is done! What can I do about it, huh? All of us have complications, appeals . . .

LUM: And who determines our appeals?

FONG: The United States government, of course. It's their country. It's their right.

LUM: Their right? Look at Chin! A returning citizen, been in this country forty years. Everybody knows if you want to get out of here fast you got to slip money to the authorities, right? It's a question of skin and money.

FONG: That's what I've been telling you all along! So what are you going to do about it?

LUM: My idea is to get out.

The lights dim as the men stare straight ahead in frozen postures which convey their differing attitudes. Henderson enters, watching the men like specimens through an imaginary partition of glass.

HENDERSON: I've been on this Island ever since it opened in 1910. I'm so sick of Chinamen, I could put a match to this place! Every time I walk into this stinking room, I feel a hundred slanted eyes boring into me like skewers. I know they despise me—because I despise them. They'd kill me if they could. One of these days, they just might try.

If I had my way, I'd ship the whole lot of 'em back to China. Goddammit, America is for Americans, they don't belong here! If they keep coming, there won't be any jobs left for decent white men. We've got to protect what's ours. The Chinamen are here to take what they can get. Do you think they give a damn about our country? Do you think they'd fight for Uncle Sam? Hell, no. If they want our jobs now, what do you think they'll want next? Our homes, our land, our money, our women? I got a daughter, you know? She's the most precious thing I got in this world. (*He stands next to Lum.*) If any slimey Chink every laid a hand on her, I'd cut off his balls!

Fadeout as Henderson exits; fade-in as men come to life.

LUM: I'll show you. (*He bangs on the door with his fists, yelling.*) Guard! Guard! (*He conceals a knife inside his clothing.*)

HENDERSON: (*voice from outside*) What the hell's going on in there?

LUM: (*still banging*) Help, help, somebody sick, hurry, hurry!

Henderson appears. After unlocking the door, he enters.

HENDERSON: All right, pipe down. Who is it?

LUM: Over here. (*Lum spins around and seizes Henderson in a hammerlock with the knife to his throat.*)

HENDERSON: You—you'll never get away with this!

LUM: Shut up! Get me a handkerchief and rope! (*The men help Lum tie up Henderson.*)

FONG: What are we going to do with him?

LUM: (*checks window and door to see if all's clear*) Lee, you wanna come with me?

FONG: You'll never make it, Lum!

LUM: It's time to put those mighty words into action.

FONG: Don't listen to him.

LUM: There's no more than ten miles between me and freedom.

FONG: If the sharks don't eat you first.

LEE: (*who has been struggling with himself*) I want to try it, too.

FONG: What—have you all gone crazy? You'll never make it! If you listen to Lum you'll end up dead. I warn you!

LEE: I'm a good swimmer.

FONG: You've got a family.

LUM: (*guiltily*) He's right, Lee. You're not coming with me.

FONG: I'm not going to let either one of you go. (*He rushes to the door.*) Guard!

LUM: (*pulls Fong back and shakes him*) Don't you understand?

FONG: (*sadly*) Young men are not afraid to die because they don't know how cheap life is.

LUM: Then why cling to it so dearly?

FONG: Because it's all I've got!

LUM: Then you will die small!

FONG: And what good is a big dead hero?

LUM: For me, there's no other way. (*Turning to go*) Look me up if you ever get to *Die-Fow*. Ask for Mister Lum! (*He looks around the room for the last time. Bows deeply to the men. They bow too.*) I'll write and tell you about the World's Fair! (*Grins broadly, then exits.*)

LEE: (*returns to his poem and reads*)
There are tens of thousands of poems composed on these walls.
They are all cries of complaint and sadness.
The day I am rid of this prison and attain success,
I must remember that this chapter once existed.

Fade out.

SCENE 9

Chin Moo is alone on one side of the stage, knitting a baby sweater. Chin Gung is seated on a chair, on the other side, knotting a rope. There is a pole to one side of him. The stage is dark except for alternating spots on Chin Moo and Chin Gung.

CHIN GUNG: I always thought life was a ladder. All you had to do was put one foot in front of the other till you reached the top. But all the time I thought I was climbing up, I was really going down . . .

CHIN MOO: (*amused*) Fifteen hundred dollars to live in the barbarian's prison. (*She shakes her head.*) Yet he calls this home. (*Shrugs.*) What was I to him all these years? Just a memory of China he tried to forget, but couldn't?

CHIN GUNG: . . . So cold up there. So quiet. I could've laid that track all the way from here to China!

CHIN MOO: Young boys, thirteen, fourteen year olds came on ships and worked in the gold fields, the railroads . . . They never returned. At night the women do not go to the bathroom for fear of seeing ghosts. Ghosts of all the people who have died here. When all's still, you can actually hear the walls breathing. You think, "It's only the wind!" But it's not. It's the sighing of spirits. Everytime the floor creaks, you say, "It's only the wood!" But it's human bones—stretched beneath the floorboards . . . (*She suddenly rises, as if to better sense a presence.*) This room is full of ghosts! (*She is facing Chin Gung as if looking directly at him but not seeing him.*)

CHIN GUNG: Where have all the years gone?

CHIN MOO: Two tons of bones piled on trains weaving through black mountains headed home for China.

CHIN GUNG: (*stands up on the chair*) I came on a ship full of dreams and landed in a cage full of lies. Sixty-years pissed away! I'm too old to travel anymore. I love this country. (*He places the rope around his neck.*) Whether or not you will have me, I am home.

Chin Gung kicks the chair over and hangs himself. We see his legs jerk in a spasm, then fall limp and dangle.

Fade out.

SCENE 10

Women's dormitory. Chin Moo hands Mei Lai the bright yellow baby sweater she's just completed knitting.

MEI LAI: Oh, Chin Moo, it's beautiful! Such a bright, bright yellow for my little Yang!

CHIN MOO: A brand new sweater for a brand new life!

MEI LAI: Thank you so much! (*She winces in pain.*)

CHIN MOO: Is it time?

KU LING: She should see a doctor.

The Warden enters with Chan.

WARDEN: Will Chin Bick Hop please come forward! Mrs. Chin Bick Hop!

Chin Moo comes forward with cheerful anticipation.

WARDEN: Mrs. Chin Bick Hop?

CHIN MOO: (*nodding happily*) Hai-hai!

WARDEN: (*to Chan*) You better break the news to her, Chan.

CHAN: *Chun si-nye, nay-ga sien-sahng cum-on gaw-jaw sun-la.*

CHIN MOO: (*confused*) *Mawt-ta wah? Choy? Nay gong mut-ah? Ngoi-ga thleen-sahn hai Chin Bick Hop.*

CHAN: *Hai-ah, ah Chun-sook. Cum-on, diew geng jee saht-la.*

CHIN MOO: *M'hai. Ngoi m'thleen nay-gong!*

WARDEN: Ask her if she wants his things.

CHAN: *Kuey mun nay seng law nay di seen sahng san di yeh mah?*

Chin Moo doesn't answer, but stands in shock. The Warden exits with Chan. The women try to comfort Chin Moo, but she is beyond comfort or communication. She takes several steps toward the door and collapses. Ku Ling and Mei Lai rush to her.

Fade out.

SCENE 11

The Warden, seated on a swivel chair at his desk, is on the phone.

WARDEN: (*in mid-conversation*) I didn't build those fly-traps, I inherited them. One crazy old Chinaman hangs himself—with his own rope. What the hell am I supposed to do? Confiscate all the damned rope in the barracks? . . . And for Chrissakes, keep those damned reporters off this island! (*Indicates letter in his hand.*) Listen to this report. "The lavatories and toilet rooms are poorly ventilated. The floors have no drains and the woodwork is soaked with urine and fecal matter. The offensive smell in these rooms is sufficient proof that they are failures from a sanitary standpoint. The amount of air space in these rooms is totally inadequate for the number of berths therein. Allowing five hundred cubic feet of air space to each individual, the larger rooms should accommodate 56 and the smaller ones 26 each. At present there are 204 and 192 bunks in the larger rooms and 60 each in the smaller ones. The spittoons in this building are dirty and fly-infested. The windows are barred and locked and there is only one exit for all four dormitories. Built of most inflammable material, destruction of the building in the case of a fire would be but a question of minutes. In a comparatively short time, these rooms will be unfit for habitation by reason of vermin and stench." I want you to begin fumigating those rooms! . . . And give me a quick run-down on the old China-man's wife. We'll have to nip this in the bud.

Fade out.

SCENE 12

Interrogation Room.

INSPECTOR: Is there a bridge in your village?

CHAN: *Nay gor chung your mo kue?*

CHIN MOO: *You, ngoi lai sui oh ga kell.*

CHAN: Yes. We stood on the bridge holding hands.

INSPECTOR: Is there a mountain near your village?

CHAN: *Nay-ga choon you m'your shan?*

CHIN MOO: *Sahn? Kuey moon mut-wah? Ngoi seung fon hui Hong Sahn?*

CHAN: (*pauses*) She says she wants to go home.

INSPECTOR: Tell her to just answer the questions.

CHIN MOO: *Gong kuey ngoi seung fon hui Joong-Gok!*

CHAN: *She says she wants to go back to China.*

CHIN MOO: *Huey mut-neh? Koi low, huey mut-neh? Mo ban fot-lah. Ngoi mu'hui. Ngoi fon huey Hong Sahn lah.*

Fade out on hearing; fade in on Gregory opposite on stage.

GREGORY: The other day when I took the women out for a walk, I noticed one of them with bound feet. They were so small—no more than the size of plums! She was hobbling down the side of the path, clutching onto tree branches to steady herself. So frail, so helpless. I offered her my arm—and, do you know, she was so touched, she wept. She actually wept. (*Pauses.*) Sometimes I give them a piece of candy, an orange or something sweet to cheer them. The least bit of kindness you show them makes them so happy. They are babes-in-arms, scared little girls, waiting to be rescued. When I see their frightened and inquisitive looks, when I hear their incessant weeping and nervous chatter, I know, deep in my soul, that the good Lord has chosen me to be the shepherd of this flock— the Angel of this Island.

Fade out.

47

Genny

Lim

Early morning. Ku Ling is asleep. Chin Moo is sitting on her bed fingering her red wedding tunic.

CHIN MOO: You were so handsome on our wedding day! I was so proud to be your wife. You told me I was as pretty as a plum blossom and you could hardly wait to pluck me off the branch. (*Laughs.*) Imagine me, dressed up in bright, fancy clothes and funny hats. Walking down gold-paved streets with my hand tucked in your elbow. (*Pausing sadly*) Why did you come back for me? Why didn't you marry an American girl and forget me? Don't you know I had buried you a long time ago? I can't even remember what I looked like. (*Touches her face.*) A dream is good only when you have someone to share it with.

She notices a tear in the garment and begins mending it. She sings "The Threading Song" to ward off evil spirits from entering the garment:

> *Gim-seen loon, ngoi m'lai ngien choon,*
> *Gim-seen nahng, ngoi m'lai ngien dahng,*
> *Choon-jeem, choo-thlen, m'choon ngoi thleem beng,*
> *Choon-ngoi ho, m'choon-ngoi chew . . .*

> Sew thread sew, protect us from harm,
> Sew thread sew, protect us from hate,
> Thread the needle, thread the thread,
> Don't bring us ill health,
> Bring us good fortune, not shame . . .

She hears the sound of a newborn baby. She puts down the garment and crosses to the door. Ku Ling awakens. Mei Lai enters proudly with her wrapped infant.

MEI LAI: (*bursting with pride*) Chin Moo, here is Yang Lee. (*She hands the child to Chin Moo.*)

CHIN MOO: (*picking him up and marvelling*) He feels so light, so fragile!

KU LING: (*cooing over baby*) Say hello to Auntie, little Yang, hm-m?

The Warden and interpreter Chan enter.

WARDEN: *Sai-guy! Ho sai-guy!* Mrs. Chin Bick Hop, Mrs. Moy Fook Sing and Chow Ku Ling! (*To Chan*) Tell them they're leaving on the next boat to San Francisco.

CHAN: *Lay day seung fow-lah. Jup ho sai-di yeh you bay jou-la!*

WARDEN: (*addressing Chan*) Will you please tell Mrs. Chin that under special consideration, she is being allowed to enter the U.S.

CHAN: *Chin si-nye, nay junhai ho choy. Jenfoo bay nay yup Gum San.*

The Warden and Chan leave.

KU LING: Chin Moo, Mei Lai, we're going to America! Can you believe it?

MEI LAI: Gold Mountain! (*Whirls baby around gently.*) Little Yang, little Yang, tomorrow you will see your Papa for the first time.

KU LING: (*noticing Chin Moo's disinterest*): Chin Moo, can I help you pack?

CHIN MOO: No. I'm not going to America.

Gregory enters with Chan.

GREGORY: Praise the Almighty! (*to Chin Moo*) *Yesu oy-nay.* (*To Mei Lai*) *Bee-bee chai.* Dear, dear, such a tiny miracle! We shall have to baptize you, now that you are—American. (*Gathering the women around her*) The Lord has answered our prayers for deliverance! (*Gesturing heavenward*) "Now these are thy servants and thy flock, whom thou has redeemed." (*With sudden brusqueness*) Now I need some information. Come, ladies. *Chaw-Chaw.* (*Gesturing them to sit*) Mrs. Chin? (*To Chan*) Ask Mei Lai where she will be living?

CHAN: *Lay joi Mei-Kuo ga day chi hai bien-doh?*

MEI LAI: (*apprehensively*) *Wa-sing-dun Gai.*

GREGORY: Tell her I need a number address.

CHAN: *Mehya hom ma?*

MEI LAI: *Ngaw m'ji doh.*

Gregory turns next to Ku Ling.

GREGORY: And what is your destination, Ku Ling?

CHAN: *Nay huey bien-doh?*

Ku Ling pulls a slip of paper from her pocket and hands it to Chan who hands it without looking to Gregory.

KU LING: *Li-doh.*

49

Genny

Lim

Gregory pauses, paling upon reading the note.

GREGORY: Ask her where she got this address.

CHAN: *Ligaw day ji bien gaw bay lay ga.*

KU LING: *Ngaw Ba-Ba bay ngaw. Kuey sic de-de yun mah?*

CHAN: She says her father gave it to her. She wants to know if you know these people.

GREGORY: (*touching Ku Ling protectively*) Miss Chan, will you tell Ku Ling this place is a house of prostitution.

Chan whispers the translation into Ku Ling's ear.

KU LING: (*shocked*) *M'hai, m'hai! Ngaw Ba-Ba ngaw do-jaw Gum San huey wun kuey day.*

GREGORY: I know, Ku Ling, believe me, I've seen this sort of thing happen time and time again. Thirteen, fourteen year old girls sold right under their noses. By their own families. If they think their daughters are being sold into wealth and luxury, they'd better open their eyes. Those filthy houses are rife with syphillis and tuber-culosis. Ku Ling won't last beyond thirty. (*Angrily*) The police will do nothing to stop it! Well, I'll have to fight it myself. Miss Chan, tell Ku Ling she need not fear anything, I will take her into the Church's custody.

CHAN: Miss Gregory, if I report this to the department she will be deported.

GREGORY: Then you will have to prove it, won't you? Anyway, you wouldn't want this poor girl deported on your account, would you, Miss Chan? (*No reply.*) That's what I thought. (*To Ku Ling*) Ku Ling, you are a very lucky girl. The Lord has shown you divine mercy. May the Lord save you and in His goodness raise you up!

CHAN: *Nay m'sai dahm sam. Kuey wui bong nay gow dim sai.*

GREGORY: Tell her from now on her name shall be Ruth. After the Moabite woman who left her own people to marry Boaz of Beth-lehem.

CHAN: *Nay-ga sun meng gew-jo* Ruth.

GREGORY: It's a good Christian name.

KU LING: (*adamant*) *M'hai. Ngaw hai Gu Ling.*

GREGORY: My dear, in time you will come to accept the ways of the Lord. You destiny is God's will, (*Emphatically*) Ruth.

KU LING: (*angrily*) *Ngaw Hai Gu Ling!*

Gregory ignores her and exits with Chan. Mei Lai crosses to Ku Ling and places a supportive hand on Ku Ling's shoulder.

Fade out.

SCENE 14

Men's dorm. Lee is putting the finishing touches on his poem, when Henderson enters with Chan.

HENDERSON: Moy Fook Sing?

LEE: I am.

HENDERSON: (*to Chan*) Tell him that he is being released.

CHAN: *Nay seung fow-lah.*

LEE: (*bursting with joy*) *Jun-hai, maw?* (*Suddenly worried.*) *Ngaw-ga tai-tai mah?*

CHAN: He's asking about his wife.

HENDERSON: Yes, yes, your wife, too. Get your things. Let's go. *Fie-di, fie-di.*

CHAN: *Hai law nay gay tai-tai. Sahm diem joong. Hoi bin.*

LEE: (*to Henderson*) Thank you.

FONG: *Ah Chan-si-nye, yow mo siu sie yah?*

CHAN: (*shaking her head*) *Mo-lah.*

Henderson and Chan exit. Lee busies himself packing his belongings, his carving knife and scrolls of his poetry. He notices Fong standing alone. He crosses to him and embraces him.

LEE: I'll see you in San Francisco, Fong.

FONG: (*hands Lee a small red envelope*) This is for the kid.

LEE: Thank you. It won't be long, huh, Fong?

FONG: Sure, sure.

They bow to each other and Lee exits. Alone, Fong prepares for the next group of recruits. He cleans his barber's tools and arranges them.

FONG: I'm not a scholar or a poet like Lee. I'm not a dreamer like Chin Gung. I'm not a hero like Lum, I'll probably never be a success. I just want a chance to make a few dollars so when I get old, I won't have to be buried in a pauper's grave. That's all I want. That's all I want.

Fadeout on Fong; fade-in on Chin Moo. The sound of a distant tolling temple bell.

CHIN MOO: I can hear the evening bell. It's the mountain temple ringing. The fishermen are rowing home. I hear them singing. I hear the sound of women beating clothes. The children gathered at the ferry, waiting to go home. I want to go down to the river and watch the fish leap and the heron flock along the sandbars. I'd soak my toes in the moss and smell the jasmine breeze.

Forty years have passed me by like a river. What does an old village woman like me know about talking electric boxes and motor cars? Can a woman who stays home and raises pigs be happy here?

Sound of foghorn. She crosses to the window.

It looks like rain. (*Sighs.*) How I long to see springtime in Toisan!

Fade out.

THE END

THE MUSIC LESSONS

❀

WAKAKO YAMAUCHI

"I was born in a desert on an autumn day," says Wakako Yama-uchi—hence the wide and isolated setting of her first two plays *And The Soul Shall Dance* and *The Music Lessons* is the landscape of her early childhood.[1] Together these two lyrical and passionate dramas paint a portrait of the first generation of Japanese immigrants to California in the early decades of this century.

Born Wakako Nakamura in the town of Westmoreland in California's Imperial Valley in 1924, Yamauchi turned early to writing and reading as an escape from the isolation of farm life. "When I was a little girl I wanted to be a writer. . . . in the country there's nobody to play with, there's nothing to do but read old newspapers and magazines. So you have this dream world you can live in. It became fun to make up stories . . . but they were all white stories I was dreaming." Acknowledging the irony of growing up in a marginal community of Japanese which nonetheless was strongly influenced by an omnipresent white America, Yamauchi reflects, "All our heroes were white—Errol Flynn, Shirley Temple, all the matinee idols. Shirley Temple embodied everything that was American to us. She was everything we weren't—white, free, wealthy."

It is this that emerges in her early work: a sense of a people pushed, abandoned, without a country, whose children live between worlds. The plays focus on the second period of Japanese immigration to this country which occurred between 1908 and 1924. Unlike European immigrants arriving on the opposite coast, the Japanese found themselves prohibited from owning land or intermarrying with whites and ineligible for naturalization and the rights of citizenship. Consequently they were locked out of the body politic, unable to vote to change the legislation which discriminated against them. According to Yuji Ichioka in his monumental study *The Issei*: "This state of powerlessness is a central theme in Japanese immigration history."[2] Unaccepted by their new country and unprotected by a Japanese government which readily sacrificed them on the altar of diplomatic advantage, they struggled for existence while their children grew up between two cultures, aspiring to American culture without the benefits of full acceptance into American society. Of the duality of her Japanese American background and her purpose as a writer Yamauchi is clear. "I'm an American writer. I'm not a white American but I'm writing American stories. People want to know what's the difference between me and a white American. If you say Asian American they want exotica. They don't [want to] read what happened to us. . . . they don't hear the fact that we never got to own land . . . or that we didn't get waited on. These are stories of people living in America."

Yamauchi's evolution as a Japanese American writer began with the abandonment of "the white stories I had been dreaming." She came to the conclusion that "you can't write a good story without really feeling it or living it or knowing every aspect of it." Much of this knowledge she attributes to her mother, who gave her an integrated identity, as a woman and as a person of Japanese ancestry. "My mother gave me a sense of a woman being a whole person, of being a special person. . . . she was very independent—she expressed her opinions. . . . She made a lot of decisions . . . even though my father was very stubborn and would do the opposite." Even before the outbreak of World War II and her subsequent internment in Poston, Arizona, Yamauchi was pointedly aware of her Japanese ancestry: "I never deceived myself to think that I was white. . . . my mother never let me. It wasn't so much what she said [directly]. . . . We'd go to a store and they wouldn't wait on us or they'd wait on everyone else before us. . . . She'd get so angry— she'd bang whatever she was holding on the counter and say '*Nihonjin dakara baka ni suru*' (Because we're Japanese they're making fools of us). . . . People talk about identity crisis. . . . my mother let me *know* I was Japanese."

That consciousness of cultural identity was not merely the response to racial discrimination, but a nostalgia, an immigrant yearning for a country and culture left behind. "My mother had this longing to return to Japan—always this longing to return. [According to her] . . . the food was better . . . the fruits were sweeter, the surgeons were the greatest. She told me ghost stories and tales of lovers' suicides. I think this is where the sense of tragedy in my writing comes from."

A second early influence on Yamauchi's life and writing came from Nisei writer Hisaye Yamamoto, the pioneering, widely published fiction writer and author of a collection of short stories *Seventeen Syllables* (Kitchen Table Press, 1988). They first met in Oceanside, California, after Yamauchi's mother convinced her father to abandon farm life and seek greater opportunity in the city. The Yamauchis worked in the canneries and opened a boardinghouse where their teenaged daughter met itinerant Japanese, many of whom would become inspiration for characters in her fiction and drama. In Oceanside, Yamauchi began to realize that the isolation she had experienced as a child was not exclusively a fact of rural life, but also a result of her interests and attitudes, which were not typical of other Nisei youth. "I always felt like I was on the outside looking in—and then I made friends with Sy." Encountering this kindred spirit was the beginning of a lifelong friendship which would span from Oceanside to Poston, where they were both interned, and endure through the 1970s when Yamamoto encouraged her to pursue writing seriously.

From the time they met in Oceanside, Yamauchi greatly admired Yamamoto who at seventeen was already a serious fiction writer and more important, one who wrote unselfconsciously and naturally from a Japanese American perspective. "I thought she was such a terrific writer—and that I could never write like that. One thing I noticed about her writing is that she was very honest—she always talked about the fact that she was Japanese—the food she ate, her relationship with her father and brothers and that really surprised me. I learned a great deal from her."

The war years represented a complete upheaval and transformation for Yamauchi. After being evacuated to Poston with her family at the age of seventeen, she obtained permission a year and a half later to leave camp for Chicago, where she worked in a candy factory and attended art school. She returned to Poston upon hearing that her father was dying, only to arrive and find that he was already dead. "We were the last contingent to leave camp so we hurriedly cremated him and left." Like many other Nisei coming of age during the war, Yamauchi's rite of passage into adulthood was marked not only by personal trauma, but also the destruction of community and family life and the dissolution of traditional Japanese social structure.

It was not until the later 1950s that she began to write. Married in 1948 to Chester Yamauchi, she took up writing when her daughter Joy began school. "When I started to write . . . I had no plans of making it a vocation. . . . I just wanted to write one story, one beautiful story." The result, "And the Soul Shall Dance," is regarded as a seminal work in Asian American literature and has been widely anthologized, in both play and short story version, in publications including *AIIIEEEEE* (Howard University Press, 1974) *West Coast Plays, 1982 (California Theatre Council), Worlds of Literature* (W.W. Norton, 1989), and *Between Worlds* (TCG, 1990). In 1959, however, when the story was written, there was no audience for Yamauchi's work. While she routinely collected rejection slips from national magazines and journals, she was able to see her work in print in Los Angeles' Japanese American vernacular press *The Rafu Shimpo*, whose editor, Henry Mori, she knew from camp. She negotiated an arrangement whereby in exchange for having her stories published she did illustrations for the newspaper. For unsurmisable reasons, Yamauchi never received any comment on her work, either from editors or from the community. "I got so tired of writing and nobody saying 'boo' so I decided I won't write anymore and then watch the letters come in saying, 'Where's Wakako Yamauchi?' Well nobody said anything! I even thought of writing myself a letter and that's when I decided that was it—I gave up."

Between 1961 and 1975 Yamauchi abandoned writing and pursued painting and might never have returned to writing if not for a phone call from Hisaye Yamamoto. "Hisaye said, 'There's some Asian American guys who are going to print an anthology—why don't you send something in?' I was so sick of being rejected. She advised me, as she knew everything I did. I didn't hear from them for a year and then Shawn Wong wrote." Wong, along with Jeffrey Paul Chan, Lawson Inada, and Frank Chin, was in the process of compiling the milestone anthology *AIIIEEEEE*, and he responded to her manuscript of a half-dozen stories with elation. "Her stories knocked me out. They were amazing glimpses of Japanese America before the war in the thirties and forties. When we were trying to find the authors who wrote in the generation that came before us we ran across some really bad books, fake books, Chinatown tour guides, and all kinds of really strange things. Wakako's work was a revelation."[3]

Subsequently Yamauchi accompanied Wong and Frank Chin to the East West Players in Los Angeles where she saw Momoko Iko's *When We Were Young* and met the theater's founding artistic director, Mako. Mako convinced her to adapt "And the Soul Shall Dance" for the theater in 1974. "He said, 'I don't care if it's long or short, all I want you to do is keep the mood of the short story'— that advice really freed me." Although she is considered a pioneering Asian American woman playwright, the path of Yamauchi's career is evidence of a cross-fertilization between Asian American women writers; the precedent of both Yamamoto's fiction and Iko's drama impelled her exploration of the two literary forms.

Like *And the Soul Shall Dance, The Music Lessons* was originally a short story, entitled "In Heaven and Earth." Adapted to play form in 1977, it evolved from ideas, situations, and characters that are autobiographical in origin. In turning to autobiography Yamauchi began to make connections between people in her life who intrigued her intellectually and personally and the social forces at play around them. Chizuko, the central figure in *The Music Lessons*, a widow who works the fields dressed in the clothing of her dead husband, was based on a woman Yamauchi knew as a child. "I always admired this woman, who seemed so fragile yet drove a truck and ran a farm and raised children alone." For a young wife and mother considering her own choices and decisions of whether to write, paint, or try new forms of expression, engaging this character caused her to reflect with renewed interest on the nearly forgotten women of her childhood.

Yamauchi subtly comments on the lack of choices for many Issei women and their enduring sense of sacrifice and obligation. In *The Music Lessons* Chizuko reflects in a rare moment of vulnerability,

> When I left Japan I never knew it would be like this. The babies came so fast . . . and me, by myself, no mother, no sister—no one—to help. I was so young . . . never dreamed it would be like this. Never thought my life would be so hard. I don't know what it is to be a . . . a woman anymore . . . to laugh . . . to be soft . . . to talk nice . . . I hear myself: "Don't do this; don't do that. Wear your sweater; study hard . . ." I try to say other things: "How smart you are; how pretty you look . . ." but my mouth won't let me. I keep thinking, life is hard. I shouldn't let them think it would be easy.

Yamauchi alludes to the suffering of those women who were unable to adjust to their arranged marriages when Chizuko, responding to her daughter's accusation that she never loved her dead husband, asks, "How could I love him—I didn't know him." This sense of people isolated from each other by physical distance, overwhelmed by the burden of their labor, and challenged by the disparate values of overlapping cultures, gives resonance to a play that otherwise might be dismissed as a simple love story.

Although Yamauchi's plays have been widely produced and critically acclaimed she has had to contend with a preconception among producers that no audience exists for her work. She was told by one white Hollywood producer that as much as he liked it, "you have no drawing card" (translation: white actor-star). A playwriting teacher who read the first draft of *And the Soul Shall Dance* told her, "You are never going to get this play produced—who cares about a bath house burning down." While Yamauchi has written in recent works such as *The Chairman's Wife* of events and figures of epic proportions, it is the small events of life—a bath house fire, an itinerant laborer with a passion for music—that continue to be her primary thematic concern. "When I write these stories they're really about very ordinary people. I think it's important because I'm an ordinary person. There's a lot of us doing ordinary things and yet there is courage in our lives."

Notes

1. Editor's interviews with Wakako Yamauchi, Gardena, California, 18 January 1983 and 28 February 1991.
2. Yuji Ichioka, *The Issei: The World of the First Generation Japanese Immigrants, 1885–1924* (New York: Free Press, 1988), 2.
3. Editor's interview with Shawn Wong, 21 August 1991.

THE MUSIC LESSONS

A Two-Act Play

WAKAKO YAMAUCHI

Time: September 1935
Place: Imperial Valley, California

CHARACTERS

KAORU KAWAGUCHI, thirty-three, Japanese male, itinerant
CHIZUKO SAKATA, thirty-eight, Issei widow farmer, mother
AKI SAKATA, fifteen, daughter of Chizuko
ICHIRO SAKATA, seventeen, son of Chizuko
TOMU SAKATA, sixteen, son of Chizuko
NAKAMURA, forty-five, male, Issei farmer
BILLY KANE, fifteen, white, friend of the children
WAITRESS, middle-aged, non-Asian

ACT ONE   Scene I

Time: September 1935
At rise: Center stage left is the interior of the Sakata kitchen. It is
spare, almost stark. There is a table with at least three chairs, some
crockery (water pitcher, glasses) on a cupboard. An upstage door
leads to the bedrooms. Upstage left is a screen door leading out-
side.
Stage right is a tool shed. There is a cot turned on its side, crates and
some tools. The interior of the shed is kept dark until it is used.
Nakamura, Issei farmer, dressed in farm clothes of the era, and
Kaoru Kawaguchi, Japanese itinerant, in a sport coat, hat, and
carrying a violin case and an old-fashioned suitcase enter from
stage left.

NAKAMURA: I don't see the truck. Maybe she's not home.

KAORU: You're sure she'll hire me?

NAKAMURA: Well, I'm not *sure*. You said you're looking for work
and I thought, well, maybe Chizuko. She runs this farm all by
herself and . . . Chizuko-san! One thing you ought to know about
farming; there's always work to be done; the problem is money.
There's not a lot of it around these days. (*he opens the door and*
peers in) I guess she went out. Depression's still here for us farmers,
you know.

KAORU: Yes, I know.

NAKAMURA: (*looking at his pocket watch*) Well, I gotta be going.
(*Kaoru picks up his violin case, continuing; stopping him from*
following) You ought to wait for her. She'll be back (soon) . . .

KAORU: (*quickly*) You do all your own work? I'd like to . . . you know, you don't have to pay me right (away) . . .

NAKAMURA: (ha-ha) I got two grown sons to help me. Now Chizuko, her boys are still young, and well, it's hard for her. It's hard for *me*; it's gotta be rough for her. You wait here. She'll be back soon. (*Kaoru puts down his violin and wipes his brow.*) Not used to the heat, eh? N'other thing: I'd hide the violin if I was you. (*he almost takes the case from Kaoru*) No good to look too . . . You gotta look like you can *work*. You know what I mean?

KAORU: I see.

NAKAMURA: Why don't you mosey around while you're waiting? See what people do on a farm. (ha-ha) Maybe you won't *want* to work here.

KAORU: Yes, I'll do that.

NAKAMURA: I live about a mile down this road. If Chizuko doesn't want you, come on down and I'll give you a lift back to town.

KAORU: Thank you. Thank you for being so kind to a stranger.

NAKAMURA: Japanese stick together, eh? (*he stops on his way out*) Oh, you tell her you picked grapes in Fresno and cut lettuce in Salinas. Tell her I sent you.

KAORU: Yes, I will. Thank you.

NAKAMURA: Good luck.

Nakamura exits left. Kaoru puts his suitcase in an inconspicuous place and still carrying his violin, he walks upstage center and exits behind the tool shed.
   The Sakata offspring: Ichiro, son, in cotton twills and plaid shirt, hair cut short; Tomu, son, similarly dressed, and Aki, daughter, hair clasped with one metal barrette at her neck, dressed in a cotton dress of the period, have just returned from shopping for staples. They enter from the left carrying the groceries.

AKI: It's no fun shopping: shoyu, rice, miso . . . Always the same old stuff.

ICHIRO: Stop complaining. Next time, don't go.

AKI: Boy, Ichiro, you're getting just like Mama. Wouldn't even give me a quarter. You could have loaned it to me. I would have paid you back.

ICHIRO: With what? Tomatoes?

AKI: I could do extra work for Mama.

ICHIRO: Who gets paid for extra work?

TOMU: Ma doesn't pay for work. Period.

ICHIRO: You get food in your belly, consider yourself paid.

Chizuko Sakata, Issei, gaunt and capable-looking, hair bunned back, wearing her dead husband's shirt, pants, heavy shoes and hat, enters from stage right. She does not see the suitcase. She carries a basket of peas.
   Aki comes downstage to the yard.

AKI: He wouldn't even give me a quarter, Mama.

CHIZUKO: What do you want a quarter for? (*They enter the kitchen.*)

AKI: I just wanted to get a small book, Mama.

ICHIRO: (*giving Chizuko the bill and change*) It's all there.

CHIZUKO: (*counting the change and putting it away in a jar*) Money has to last until spring.

AKI: But Mama, a quarter . . .

CHIZUKO: A quarter buys two pounds of meat.

TOMU: We ought to be able to spend for something else besides just keeping alive.

ICHIRO: Quit complaining, will you?

CHIZUKO: After harvest you can have treats.

AKI: I won't want it then.

TOMU: She only wanted a quarter, Ma.

ICHIRO: (*silencing the two*) Hey!

CHIZUKO: I told you we don't spend right now.

TOMU: Yeah, Ma.

AKI: It was different when Papa was here.

ICHIRO: Well, Pop's not here.

AKI: He always brought stuff for us. Remember that dog, Tomu?

TOMU: Oh, yeah, Maru.

ICHIRO: Well, it's different now. You might as well get used to it.

Kaoru enters from upstage center. He picks up his suitcase. Ichiro notices him in the yard and goes out.

KAORU: Oh, hello.

ICHIRO: Hello.

CHIZUKO: Who is it, Ichiro? (*she comes to the yard*)

KAORU: Oh. You are . . . Sakata-san?

CHIZUKO: Yes.

KAORU: Ah! I am Kawaguchi.

Kaoru extends a hand and Chizuko reluctantly takes it. It's not a Japanese custom to shake hands.

CHIZUKO: Kawaguchi-san?

KAORU: Kaoru. I was . . . a . . . with Nakamura-san a little while ago. He brought me here. He said you might be needing help and I . . .

Aki and Tomu come out. Visitors are few and they are very interested.

CHIZUKO: Nakamura-san brought you? (*she feels obligated to invite Kaoru in*) Sah, dozo . . .

Chizuko opens the door and everyone enters the house. Ichiro pulls out a chair for Kaoru.

KAORU: Yes, yes. I was looking for work and he thought you might be able to use me.

CHIZUKO: I don't know why he'd do that. He knows I don't have the money to hire. There's plenty of work here, but I just don't have the money right now.

KAORU: We can talk about that later . . . when the crop (is harvested) . . .

CHIZUKO: Well, we never know how it turns out. Sometimes it's good; sometimes, bad. A lot depends on weather, prices . . . things like that. Besides . . . (*She looks him over shamelessly.*) I need a man who can work like a horse.

KAORU: Ma'am, I know how to work. I come from peasant stock.

CHIZUKO: Then sometimes, when it rains, there's nothing to do.

KAORU: Pay me what you can.

CHIZUKO: (*dubiously*) You look like a city man.

63

Wakako

Yamauchi

KAORU: (*pressing*) If you put me up, I'll only need a little now and then—not right away—for cigarettes and things, you know.

CHIZUKO: Well . . .

KAORU: If you do well with the harvest, we can settle then. I promise you I won't be idle. When there's time I can . . . (*he brushes the dust from his violin case, and changes his mind*) Can I help your boys with their math work?

TOMU: Boy, I can sure use some help there.

AKI: Maybe you'll make a "C" this year.

KAORU: I can keep books for you. That's what I did in the city—bookkeeping.

CHIZUKO: (*starting to shell peas*) Looks like you're a man of talent—culture.

KAORU: (ha-ha) Well, I came to America as a boy. I finished high school here. You know, school boy—live-in. I lived with rich white folks and did the gardening and cleaning while I went to school. The lady I worked for was a musician. She taught me to play this. (*he laughs wryly*) She wanted me to be a musician.

CHIZUKO: Oh? What happened?

Aki gives Kaoru a glass of water. Kaoru gratefully drinks it.

KAORU: Thank you. Well, I don't know. As soon as I was able, I left them. I wanted to be on my own. But there's no chance for a Japanese violinist in America.

CHIZUKO: You worked in the city all the time?

KAORU: Most of the time, yes.

CHIZUKO: What did you do?

KAORU: This and that. Waited tables, cooked—worked as a fry cook. And bookkeeping. I did that the last few years.

CHIZUKO: Maybe better you stay at a nice clean job like that than work on a dirt farm like this. Why did you want to come out here?

KAORU: Oh, I didn't get fired. To be honest, I wanted to . . . start something new. I was tired of city life. I wanted a change.

CHIZUKO: I want a change too. But some of us . . . (*she glances at her children*) we're not free to do that. Change.

Kaoru sees the futility of going on. He just about gives up but gives it one last try.

KAORU: I understand your doubts about me. I have no references or recommendation, but I'm an honest man and I'll work hard for you. I give you my word.

Chizuko looks quickly at Ichiro. The children are excited.

CHIZUKO: All right. But no pay until after the harvest.

KAORU: You won't regret this, Ma'am.

From stage left, Billy Kane, white neighbor, pedals his bicycle into the yard. It's equipped with a raccoon tail, reflectors, stickers, etc.

BILLY: Tomu! Hey, Tomu!

TOMU: That'll be Billy.

KAORU: (*to Chizuko*) You have another son?

ICHIRO: It's Billy Kane. He lives down the road.

AKI: He comes over a lot. They're rich.

Tomu goes downstage to meet Billy.

TOMU: (*to Billy*) Hi.

ICHIRO: They're not that rich. His father works for the American Fruit Growers. On salary.

BILLY: (*astride his bicycle*) Guess what? We went to Yosemite last week.

The conversation is heard in the kitchen.

TOMU: Oh, yeah?

CHIZUKO: (*to Kaoru*) My boys spent summer here—flooding, plowing, getting ready for planting. It was hot. Hundred ten degrees.

ICHIRO: We bought the seed today. Cash.

BILLY: (*in the yard; to Tomu*) There was a stream just outside the tent. It was cold!

TOMU: That right? (*he gets on Billy's bicycle*)

BILLY: (*showing Tomu a postcard*) See this?

CHIZUKO: (*to Ichiro*) You and Tomu clean the tool shed. Aki, get blankets and sheets for Kawaguchi-san.

Aki exits through the upstage doorway and Ichiro goes outside to join Tomu and Billy.

BILLY: We cooked over a fire. You know, the fish Dad caught.

ICHIRO: Come on, let's get this done. (*to Billy*) You too.

CHIZUKO: (*to Kaoru*) Looks like an act of Providence. We start planting tomorrow. If we get through in a week, the boys can start school together this year. I don't want them to get behind.

Aki appears with a pillow, sheet, and blanket.

AKI: They're both in the same class.

CHIZUKO: (*impatiently*) They have to be so they can teach each other.

KAORU: How's that?

AKI: They take turns going to school and the one that goes, teaches the other what he missed.

CHIZUKO: Not all the time. Only when work piles up here. Some things just have to be done on time.

Chizuko waves Aki away. Aki joins the boys in the shed.

CHIZUKO: When did you say you came to America?

KAORU: Nineteen nineteen. I was sixteen.

The children are in the shed putting hoes, rakes, etc., out and making the bed.

CHIZUKO: I'll call you when supper's ready.

KAORU: (*taking this cue to leave*) Yes, thank you.

He follows the children's voices to the shed. Chizuko begins chopping vegetables. Aki returns to the kitchen.

AKI: (*peering over Chizuko's shoulder*) Oh, don't make that again, Mama.

Fade out

Fill-in to make time for costume changes before Act 1, Scene 2, *and also to indicate the passage of time.*

The stage is dark. Kaoru is in the shed changing. Country western music of the thirties plays from a radio (suggestion: "Now and Then") and the announcer makes a weather report.

ANNOUNCER: This is Bucky Burns with the extended forecast for Saturday through Monday. Fair weather except for some night and morning clouds. A slight warming trend with highs ranging from seventy-five to eighty degrees. Low in the upper sixties. Northwesterly winds at five to ten miles. Generally fair for the next three days. Now back to your old favorites.

Country music continues until costume changes are made.

Scene 2

Time: October—afternoon
At rise: In Kaoru's shed. Kaoru has just returned from town. He's dressed in his good clothes. It's his day off and on the edge of the bed is a paper bag containing a small book of poems, magazines, some candy, and a pretty chiffon scarf. Kaoru's door is closed. Nakamura enters from stage left. He carries a small bottle of wine in his back pocket.

NAKAMURA: Chizuko-san . . . (*he opens the kitchen door and peers in*) Chizuko-san!

KAORU: (*opening his shed door*) Hello!

NAKAMURA: Oh! Chizuko told me she hired you.

KAORU: Come in. Come in. (*Nakamura enters the shed.*) Been almost a month now. Today's my day off.

NAKAMURA: (*looks for a place to sit and picks up the paper bag*) Been to town already, eh? Been shopping?

KAORU: Just some things for the kids. They don't have much fun.

NAKAMURA: You're a good man, Kawa. (*he looks inside the bag*)

KAORU: No-no, nothing much.

NAKAMURA: (*bringing out a small book*) What's this?

KAORU: For the girl. She likes to read. (*Nakamura pulls out the scarf and looks questioningly at Kaoru. The scarf should convey the kind of woman Kaoru loved.*) Oh, that. Reminded me of someone I once knew. I'm thinking of sending it to her.

NAKAMURA: Oh, yeah? (*he drinks from his bottle*)

KAORU: Maybe it's foolish.

NAKAMURA: No-no. (*he offers Kaoru a sip*) Where's Chizuko-san?

KAORU: (*refusing the drink*) I don't know. I just got back from town.

NAKAMURA: (*looking around and lowering his voice*) That woman never lets up. Works like a man. Maybe better, eh?

KAORU: Maybe.

NAKAMURA: Says she found a good man, Kawa. Thanked me for sending you down. (*he laughs raucously*) Yeah. She thinks we're old friends.

KAORU: I'm working hard. I'm going to try to get her a good harvest so I can make some money too.

NAKAMURA: (*laughing hard*) You think all you got to do to make money is to work hard? If that's the way, I'd be a millionaire now.

KAORU: You don't have to be a millionaire to have a farm. I want to save some money and start my own place. (*Nakamura laughs again.*) Sure. I'll work here for a while and get the feel of it; save my money and . . .

NAKAMURA: "Save," horseshit! Only way to do is borrow money.

KAORU: Who's going to lend me money? I got no collateral.

NAKAMURA: Well, first you get some names together. Good names. You can use mine. Sponsors, you know? Then you go to a produce company—in Los Angeles—put on a good suit, talk big . . . how you going to make big money for them. Get in debt. Then you pay back after the harvest. (*the futility of it occurs to him*) Then you borrow again next year. Then you pay back. If you can. Same thing again next year. You never get the farm. The farm gets you. (*he drinks from the bottle*)

KAORU: You never get the farm?

NAKAMURA: 'S true. Orientals can't own land here. It's the law.

KAORU: The law? Then how is it that (you) . . .

NAKAMURA: Well, I lease. If you have a son old enough you can buy land under his name. He's American citizen, you see? That's if you have enough money.

KAORU: I'll apply for citizenship, then.

NAKAMURA: There's a law against that too. Orientals can't be citizens.

KAORU: We can't?

NAKAMURA: That's the law. Didn't you know?

Nakamura again offers Kaoru a drink. This time he accepts and drains the bottle. Nakamura looks at the empty bottle.

Hey, let's go to town.

KAORU: I just came from there.

NAKAMURA: Yeah, me too. Come on, we'll get some more wine. (*he moves to the door, lowering his voice*) You know, Chizuko doesn't like drinking. Her old man used to (ha-ha) drink a little. Like me. He drowned in a canal, you know. Fell off a cat-walk.

KAORU: (*putting on his coat*) Is that right?

NAKAMURA: Yeah, six . . . almost seven years ago.

KAORU: That long?

NAKAMURA: Yeah. She got lucky with tomatoes a couple of years ago and paid back all her old man's debts. People never expected to see their money again, but she did it. She paid them back. Now she never borrows—lives close to the belly—stingy, tight. That's the way she stays ahead. Not much ahead, but . . .

They exit talking.

KAORU: That so?

NAKAMURA: What's she planting this year?

KAORU: Squash, tomatoes . . .

NAKAMURA: Tomatoes again?

Fade out

Scene 3

Time: Shortly after
At rise: On stage right there is a set-up for a pool hall. There is a table, two chairs, and a beer sign on the wall.
Waitress, heavily made-up, non-Asian, sits on one of the chairs, her feet propped on the other. She files her nails. Faint sounds of country music come from a radio off-stage.
Nakamura and Kaoru enter talking.

NAKAMURA: And the day after he was buried, she's out there plowing the field. (*he addresses the waitress rudely*) Oi!

WAITRESS: Oi???

NAKAMURA: I couldn't believe it. The day after she buried him. (*to the waitress*) Wine!

WAITRESS: (*shining up to Kaoru*) What kind of wine?

NAKAMURA: (*oblivious*) Red wine. (*to Kaoru*) Can you believe it? A woman behind the ass of a horse the day after her man's funeral. It ain't right.

The waitress brings the wine to the table and Kaoru pays her in small change while Nakamura fumbles with his wallet (a pinch purse).

WAITRESS: *Arigato!*

Kaoru looks the waitress over. Nakamura is irritated and waves the woman away. Since they are speaking in Japanese, the waitress doesn't understand them except when they talk directly to her.

NAKAMURA: She'll give you a disease, Kawa. You don't want to fool around with that kind. (*Kaoru laughs.*) I mean it. They can get you in a lot of trouble.

KAORU: (*laughing*) I know, I know.

NAKAMURA: Japanese stick to Japanese. Better that way.

KAORU: Yeah.

NAKAMURA: So I tell her, "Chizuko-san, you got a right to cry. Take time out to cry." She says no. So I say, "I'll do your plowing. Stay home for a while." And you know what she said?

KAORU: What'd she say?

NAKAMURA: She says that's the way she cries . . . by working. (*he calls for the waitress*) Oi!

KAORU: I guess there're all kinds of ways.

NAKAMURA: She must be crying all the time, the way she works.

They both have a good laugh on Chizuko.

NAKAMURA: Too bad. She's getting all stringy and dried up. Heh, I remember when she was young—kinda pretty—but she's getting all . . . oh-oh . . .

The waitress pours again and Nakamura makes a feeble attempt to reach for his purse. Kaoru pays again.

WAITRESS: (*to Kaoru*) You're a real gentleman. Thank you. (*she winks at him and leaves*)

NAKAMURA: Bet you had plenty of them, eh? All kinds?

KAORU: (*laughing*) All kinds.

They're feeling loose and happy from the wine.

NAKAMURA: Yeah? Bet you been in heaps of trouble, eh?

KAORU: Oh-yeah. (*he pushes up his sleeve*) See this? Bullet went clean through this arm.

NAKAMURA: Ever get one in trouble?

KAORU: Hunh?

NAKAMURA: Ever get one pregnant?

KAORU: Yeah, I did.

NAKAMURA: Liked her a lot, eh?

KAORU: Yeah.

NAKAMURA: I never been that way. A woman's a woman to me. Never been that way. (*he feels sad*) What's it like, Kawa? Never been that way. Must be a good feeling.

KAORU: Sometimes.

NAKAMURA: Old bastard like me, been married, the same woman—picture bride—twenty years. Still don't know that feeling. (*he drinks*) Is it good? Kawa, what's it like?

KAORU: Sometimes it hurts like hell. Rather be shot, sometimes.

NAKAMURA: Why's it gotta hurt like that?

KAORU: I don't know. Sometimes they're married. Then everybody gets hurt.

NAKAMURA: Married! What kind of woman's that?

KAORU: That's the way it happened.

NAKAMURA: What's the matter you do like that?

KAORU: I don't know . . .

NAKAMURA: The baby. What happened to the baby.

KAORU: No baby. Aborted.

NAKAMURA: Waaah! You lucky to get away from that kind.

KAORU: Yeah, I know. (*he is still morose*)

NAKAMURA: No good, Kawa! You got twenty-thirty more years. Let a woman grab your balls and you good for nothing. 'Specially that kind.

KAORU: You're right.

NAKAMURA: Sure, I'm right. I'm right. Oi! (*he calls the waitress*)

71

*Wakako
Yamauchi*

KAORU: No-no. No more for me. Well, maybe I'll take one with me.

NAKAMURA: Get my friend a bottle.

WAITRESS: To go?

NAKAMURA: Sure, I'm right. Laugh about it; you got to move on.

KAORU: 'S what I'm trying to do.

NAKAMURA: (*reluctantly standing*) You think 'bout what I said.

WAITRESS: (*to Kaoru*) You're going already?

KAORU: Pretty soon.

WAITRESS: (*whispering*) I'll be off in a couple of minutes.

NAKAMURA: Kawa, you coming?

KAORU: (*his attention on the waitress*) Pretty soon.

NAKAMURA: Come on, come on.

KAORU: All right. (*but he doesn't stand*)

NAKAMURA: (*noticing what's happening*) Well, I'll pick you up later.

KAORU: That's fine.

Light fades on Kaoru and the waitress sitting together and whispering.

Fade out

Scene 4

Time: That evening
At rise: Interior of the Sakata kitchen. Dinner is just over; Ichiro and Tomu are seated at the table. Aki is clearing the dishes and Chizuko puts out text books. A place is still set for Kaoru.

TOMU: (*picking his teeth*) The food is getting better around here.

ICHIRO: What you call company dinner.

AKI: It was good.

TOMU: Too bad Kaoru-san couldn't eat with us.

CHIZUKO: (*worried*) Maybe something happened.

TOMU: Maybe he couldn't get a ride back.

ICHIRO: Maybe he's looking around town.

AKI: Not much to look at. Five blocks and you're out of it.

TOMU: Why don't we go pick him up?

ICHIRO: Aw, he'll find his way back.

TOMU: But it's getting late. Eight miles is a long . . .

ICHIRO: No one ever worried about me walking eight miles. He'll catch a ride.

CHIZUKO: Ichiro's right. He'll get a ride.

AKI: There're hardly any cars on the road at night, Mama.

CHIZUKO: He'll find his way back.

ICHIRO: Or maybe he won't come back.

TOMU: He'll come back.

CHIZUKO: He'll come back.

TOMU: Besides, where would he go? Ma didn't give him much money.

CHIZUKO: I gave him as much as I could. After the har(vest) . . .

AKI: Yeah, we know. After the harvest.

CHIZUKO: Well, we'll make it up to him later.

Billy drives into the yard on his bicycle. He bleeps his new horn. The boys look up from their books.

BILLY: Tomu . . .

ICHIRO: Your friend, Tomu.

AKI: (*to Ichiro*) I suppose he has something else to show us. (*Tomu goes downstage.*)

TOMU: (*to Billy*) Hi!

ICHIRO: The bicycle horn. Didn't you hear it?

Billy and Tomu can be heard in the kitchen. The yard remains dark.

BILLY: (*honking the horn again*) Look at this.

TOMU: Swell! Did you buy it?

BILLY: Sold twenty-four Wolverine salves for it.

TOMU: Salves?

BILLY: Yeah. You can get one too. Just sell the salves. My Dad bought all mine.

TOMU: No thanks. I might get stuck with them. What'd I do with twenty-four salves?

ICHIRO: (*leaning toward the window*) What'd you do with a bicycle horn? You ain't even got a bicycle.

BILLY: (*to Tomu*) You can give them away. My mom's going to give them to friends for Christmas. (*Tomu honks the horn several times.*)

CHIZUKO: (*leaning out the door*) Shhh!

TOMU: My mom'd hit the ceiling.

AKI: (*to Ichiro*) Maybe he'll get one one day. How do you know?

ICHIRO: Yeah, when he's fifty.

Billy and Tomu walk into the kitchen. Billy gives Chizuko a quick nod.

BILLY: Hi! Want to see what I got, Ich?

ICHIRO: Don't have time.

BILLY: Aki?

AKI: I'm busy.

BILLY: Busy, busy, busy. This family's always busy. What do you do for fun?

ICHIRO: Oh, we have fun. We . . . we seed, we weed, we irrigate, and in winter we light smudge pots.

BILLY: That's fun?

ICHIRO: Lots of fun. Two o'clock in the morning . . . cold as hell. And pretty soon we'll be doing brush covers.

Aki snickers. Chizuko shrinks in pain.

TOMU: Yeah, and all the other times we study, study, study. That's the kind of fun we have.

CHIZUKO: It'll be better this year.

BILLY: (*to Aki*) Aren't you going to ask me to sit down?

AKI: Sit down.

TOMU: Come on, Billy, let's go to my room.

But Billy sits down. Off stage we hear the sound of a car driving into the yard. Nakamura and Kaoru enter from left with a bottle. They sing and laugh. The family sits frozen and listens.

KAORU AND NAKAMURA: Oyu no naka ni mo / Korya hana ga saku go / Choyna, choyna . . .*

KAORU: Oh-oh.

NAKAMURA: You all right?

KAORU: Sure. Thanks a lot. Appreciate it.

NAKAMURA: 'S all right. We do it again sometime, eh?

AKI: (*at the window*) He drinks, Mama.

CHIZUKO: That's not your business, Aki.

Nakamura exits left and Kaoru goes into his shed, sees the paper bag with the presents, picks it up and with his bottle, crosses the yard and enters the kitchen. His laugh is still on his face.

KAORU: (*he steps back to look at the family*) Hello-hello. What a nice picture.

CHIZUKO: (*dispassionately*) Did you eat?

KAORU: Oh-yeah. Ate, drank, and (ha-ha) . . . Got a ride back with Nakamura-san. Very friendly, nice man. Spent most of the day with him.

CHIZUKO: With a family waiting supper for him.

KAORU: (ha-ha) Got some things here.

He spills the presents, candy, magazines, and book on the table— all but the scarf. If the scarf happens to fall partially out, Kaoru will put it back in the bag. He distributes the magazines to the boys.

ICHIRO: What for? What's this for?

KAORU: They're presents.

The children come alive. Billy is happy for them. The bag with the scarf falls to the floor. The children's talk overlap.

BILLY: How about that?

TOMU: Gee, thanks.

ICHIRO: Thanks a lot.

Kaoru gives the book of poems to Aki with exaggerated gallantry.

* Old Japanese drinking song

KAORU: And . . . for Aki-chan!

AKI: Oh! Thank you!

KAORU: Now would you get me a small glass, Aki-chan?

AKI: Oh, sure.

Chizuko gets the glass for Kaoru and plants it firmly in front of him.

KAORU: (*elaborately*) Thank you, Chizuko-san.

CHIZUKO: (*clearing away Kaoru's dishes*) You sure you don't want something to eat?

KAORU: No-no, nothing. (*he pours his wine and lifts the glass as though to make a toast. The family stares at him—Chizuko with disapproval. There is an uncomfortable silence*) Well, I'd better go.

AKI: (*holding her book to her breast*) Thank you, Kaoru-san.

KAORU: Goodnight.

ICHIRO AND TOMU: Yeah, thanks.

BILLY: Goodnight.

Kaoru leaves. The children look at their magazines.

TOMU: Look, Billy.

BILLY: Oh! Hey, can I borrow that?

TOMU: (*kidding*) No.

BILLY: Man-o-man. (*to Aki*) Let's see the book.

Aki flicks it briefly in front of Billy. Tomu catches a look.

TOMU: Sonets from the . . . What are sonets?

AKI: Sonnets. Poems, dopey.

ICHIRO: Poems?

BILLY: Oh-boy.

AKI: (*reading from the book*)
"What can I give thee back, O liberal
and princely giver, who has brought the gold
and purple of thine heart . . ."

TOMU: What's she talking about?

BILLY: Beats me.

AKI: ". . . unstained, untold,
　　　And laid them on the outside of the wall
　　　For such as I to take or leave withal
　　　In unexpected largesse? am I cold . . ."

ICHIRO: Largesse?

TOMU: Woo-woo!

AKI: (*continues to read as much of the poem as it takes for Kaoru to get to his shed and start playing the violin*)

　　　"Ungrateful that for these most manifold
　　　High gifts, I render nothing back at all?
　　　Not so; not cold—but very poor instead
　　　Ask God who knows. For frequent tears have run
　　　The colors from my life, and left so dead
　　　And pale a stuff, it were not fitly done
　　　To give the same as pillow to thy head
　　　Go farther! let it serve to trample on." *

From the shed comes beautiful violin music that breaks the stillness of the desert (Bach?). Everyone is still for a while. Then Aki closes her book and starts out the door.

BILLY: Hey, where you going?

ICHIRO: I think they're playing our song.

TOMU: (*teasing*) That's our song?

BILLY: Aki, is that *our* song?

ICHIRO: "When I'm calling you ooooo . . ."

AKI: I'm going to the toilet!

BILLY: Don't forget to request some potty music. (*Aki is already out the door.*) Just kidding, Aki. Aki . . . ? (*Aki stands at Kaoru's door and listens to the music.*) I think I'll go home now.

TOMU: Yeah? Well, okay. (*he's engrossed in his magazine*)

Billy leaves. Downstage is dark. There's a light in the kitchen and we see the boys reading and Chizuko standing by the window. In the shed, Kaoru plays the violin.
　　　There is a narrow cot, a few upturned crates, a bottle of wine, and a glass near his bedside. The room is neat.

BILLY: (*to Aki*) What're you doing out here?

* Elizabeth Barrett Browning, *Sonnets from the Portuguese*

AKI: (*moving downstage*) Shhh!

BILLY: I'm going home now.

AKI: (*listening to the music*) Okay.

Billy gets on his bicycle, bleeps his horn and exits to the left. Kaoru hears the horn and comes out. Billy is gone.

KAORU: Oh. Aren't you cold out here, Aki-chan?

AKI: The music is so beautiful.

KAORU: Come inside. I'll teach you to play this. (*he holds the door open for her*)

AKI: (*hesitantly entering*) Oh, I don't know if I can . . .

KAORU: Sure, you can. (*Kaoru tucks the violin under Aki's chin and shows her how to hold the bow and lets her draw her own sounds. The noise is terrible.*) Put your chin . . . that's right. Elbow in . . . unhunh. . . . Hold your fingers . . . now draw down. Up . . . down. . . .

In the kitchen Chizuko and the boys hear the sounds and sit there shocked. Then they start to laugh.

ICHIRO: Sounds like a cat with a belly-ache.

TOMU: Ooooo—eeeee . . . (*imitating*)

ICHIRO: That's what you call the horse's tail hitting the cat gut.

TOMU: Maybe something under the horse's tail, huh?

CHIZUKO: (*stifling her laughter*) Well, she's got to start somewhere.

ICHIRO: Yeah, but why here?

TOMU: Why not in Siberia?

CHIZUKO: You have to hand it to her. Walking right in and asking to learn.

TOMU: You think she walked in his room and asked him to teach her?

ICHIRO: What else?

TOMU: I don't think Aki would do that. (*The music stops.*)

ICHIRO: You just don't know that girl. She'll do anything.

Chizuko glances at Ichiro. In the shed Aki hands Kaoru the violin.

AKI: It sounds awful. Would you play something for me?

KAORU: All right. What would you like to hear, Aki-chan?

AKI: Oh, I don't know. Something romantic. (*she touches her book of poems*) Something . . . something that will remind you of me . . . no matter where you are.

Kaoru takes a moment to consider the implication. He plays "Two Guitars." In the house the boys return to their books. Chizuko goes to the window; she appears happy. She walks on the downstage side of the table and notices the paper bag. She picks it up. Light slowly fades in the shed and focuses on Chizuko as she tries to fold the bag. She looks inside and finds the scarf. Light fades as she holds the scarf and returns it to the bag.

Fade out

A C T T W O   Scene I

Time: The next day
At rise: The Sakata yard. Kaoru and Chizuko enter from upstage right (behind Kaoru's shed), carrying hoes.

CHIZUKO: We got lots of work done. Almost half the field.

KAORU: I could have moved faster, but . . .

CHIZUKO: You did good. There's a big difference between the work of a man and the work of boys.

KAORU: (*has a terrible hangover*) I'm not so good today. Don't feel so good.

CHIZUKO: Maybe too much wine last night.

Kaoru laughs weakly. Chizuko grows self-conscious and smooths her hair. She looks better these days.

CHIZUKO: (*continuing*) Well, we'll stop for today. You want something to eat?

KAORU: No-no. I'm not hungry.

Kaoru starts toward his shed. Chizuko follows him.

CHIZUKO: How about coffee?

KAORU: That sounds good. I could use that.

Kaoru lies down on his cot as Chizuko goes to the kitchen to heat the coffee. She lights the stove and looks into the paper bag that

Kaoru left the night before. She takes out the scarf, returns it to the bag and carries it to Kaoru.

CHIZUKO: Kaoru-san. Thank you for all the gifts last night. You did too much.

KAORU: No-no. It's nothing. Unless you don't want me to.

CHIZUKO: It's not that. I didn't give you much money and it's not right for you to spend it all on the children.

KAORU: Just cheap presents.

Chizuko tentatively takes a step into Kaoru's room.

CHIZUKO: You left this bag last night.

Puzzled, Kaoru looks into the bag. He sees the scarf he'd bought for someone else. He pushes the bag back to Chizuko.

KAORU: Oh. You can have it.

CHIZUKO: (*not accepting the bag*) Didn't you buy it for someone?

KAORU: No. No one. It's for you. (*he takes the scarf out and hands it to her*)

CHIZUKO: But it's too . . .

KAORU: It's yours.

CHIZUKO: Too nice for me.

KAORU: Not at all. Please keep it. Wear it. (*he hangs it on Chizuko's neck*)

CHIZUKO: (*embarrassed*) I'll have to find someplace to wear it to. Oh! Coffee! (*she rushes back to the kitchen*)

KAORU: Don't hurry.

Kaoru slowly leaves his quarters and sits on the bench outside as Chizuko enters the kitchen, hums a small tune, touches the soft fabric of the scarf, picks up the coffee pot (with a cloth) and a cup and returns to him in the yard. She pours the coffee.

This will make me like new. I can still get in a few hours of work.

CHIZUKO: We'll stop for today.

KAORU: There're three good hours of daylight left.

CHIZUKO: Please. Kaoru-san, I . . . (*she watches him drink*) Thank you for the scarf.

KAORU: Nnn.

CHIZUKO: You're so kind. My children, my boys . . . they do good in school now.

KAORU: That's good.

CHIZUKO: And Aki. . . you teaching Aki to play music. Thank you, Kaoru-san.

KAORU: You don't have to say anything.

CHIZUKO: She seemed so happy last night.

KAORU: Aki is, you know, very sensitive. She's a lonely little girl.

CHIZUKO: They miss their father.

KAORU: Yes, of course.

CHIZUKO: They miss him. (*her voice goes dead*) Funny. He never paid attention to them—to any of us. Well, I guess this work wasn't suited for him. He was always too late or too early for everything: planting, harvesting . . . And dying like that—so soon. Leaving us with . . . But the children miss him.

KAORU: (*reluctantly*) It must be lonely for you too.

CHIZUKO: When I left Japan I never knew it would be like this. The babies came so fast . . . and me, by myself, no mother, no sister—no one—to help. I was so young . . . never dreamed it would be like this. Never thought my life would be so hard. I don't know what it is to be a . . . a woman anymore . . . to laugh . . . to be soft . . . to talk nice . . . (*she can't look at Kaoru*)

KAORU: Well . . . (ha-ha)

CHIZUKO: I hear myself: "Don't do this; don't do that. Wear your sweater; study hard . . ." I try to say other things: "How smart you are; how pretty you look . . ." but my mouth won't let me. I keep thinking, life is hard. I shouldn't let them think it would be easy.

KAORU: That's true.

CHIZUKO: Well, they're used to me like I am. If I change now, they'd think I went crazy.

KAORU: The important thing is, you're here. It's no good without a mother, Chizuko-san. I know.

CHIZUKO: You . . .

KAORU: My grandfather brought me up. My father was always in the rice paddy. He was a bitter old man. Old and bitter on a rice paddy. Growing old in the mud. I didn't want to die like that too.

CHIZUKO: And you never married? (*Kaoru gets another cup of coffee. Chizuko rushes to pour for him.*)

KAORU: When you're young, you think youth will last forever. You throw it away foolishly. When you finally decide you want more—a family, maybe, it's too late. Family means roots, money, and you're like one of those tumbleweeds out there. Seeds all run out of your pockets and you have no roots. No one wants a tumbleweed.

CHIZUKO: But you're not a (tumbleweed) . . .

KAORU: There're lots of tumbleweeds out there. Some have wives in Japan; some even children. Some—well, like me—never got started. Before they know it, time passed them by and nothing can bring it back. (*he moves away from Chizuko*) The stories are always the same. You hear them all over—in bars, gambling dens . . . forgotten men laughing at their lost dreams.

CHIZUKO: I'm forgotten too. My dreams are lost too. And my stories are all the same—one year following another, all the same.

KAORU: You have lots to look forward to: fine sons, a nice daughter.

CHIZUKO: I wonder sometimes, if it will not be the same for them too.

KAORU: (*trying to change the mood*) Cheer up, Chizuko-san. One of these days it will be time to harvest. Say! Nakamura-san told me yesterday he thinks you . . . you're getting quite pretty.

CHIZUKO: (*covering her embarrassment*) Nakamura-san's an old goat.

KAORU: He's all right. I like him.

CHIZUKO: (*trying to get back to a certain topic*) I don't know how I managed all these years by myself. I don't know how I did it. It's been a hard seven years. I don't think I can do it again.

KAORU: (*laughing*) Sure, you can.

CHIZUKO: I've been thinking . . . ah, wondering how you would feel about . . . what you think about staying on . . . on this farm, I mean. With us. (*she waits; Kaoru is silent*) I mean, share the profits . . . a partnership.

KAORU: I have no money, Chizuko-san.

CHIZUKO: (*quickly*) Oh, you pay nothing. I mean a joint venture. More or less. This farm is too much for a woman alone and I . . .

KAORU: Well, to be honest, I planned to work on a piece of land for myself one day.

CHIZUKO: You don't have to. You can stay right here.

KAORU: (*drawing away*) Well . . .

CHIZUKO: You don't like it here? You mean you . . .

KAORU: (*quickly*) No-no. Don't think me ungrateful. I mean, right now, I don't have anything to offer.

CHIZUKO: You give only what you can. (*Kaoru is silent.*) We like you, Kaoru-san. All of us. As a family, well, the children are quarrelsome sometimes, but they're good kids. They're not mean . . . no trouble . . .

KAORU: They're fine. You should be proud.

CHIZUKO: I . . . I promise to do my best to make it nice for you. (*with some discomfort*) I know I'm not an easy woman to get along with—being so set in my ways.

KAORU: You're a fine person.

CHIZUKO: (*desperately*) I'm so tired. Sometimes I wish . . .

KAORU: Chizuko-san, this is not a day to be so solemn. Look, the sun is shining, birds are singing . . .

CHIZUKO: (*depressed at not getting through*) Yes.

KAORU: Don't worry. Everything's going to be all right. (*it's a line that's got him by many times before*) Another couple days and the weeding will be done. I think you'll have a great harvest.

CHIZUKO: If this weather holds.

KAORU: It will. Nakamura-san said it'll be a mild winter. His son heard it over the radio.

CHIZUKO: They have a radio?

KAORU: A crystal set. Maybe I can get one for Ichiro to assemble. Then you . . . we can get the weather reports.

CHIZUKO: Ichiro can do that?

KAORU: Sure, he can. He's smart.

CHIZUKO: (*she brightens*) After harvest, we can buy a small radio for everyone to enjoy. We can listen to it in the evenings.

KAORU: That would be nice.

CHIZUKO: Maybe we can get a bicycle for Tomu. A used one.

Aki enters from stage left. She wears school clothes and carries books. She comes bounding into the yard.

AKI: A used what? Are we buying something? Hi!

Chizuko hurriedly pulls the scarf from her neck and stuffs it into her pocket.

KAORU: Hello there, Aki-chan.

CHIZUKO: Where are your brothers, Aki?

AKI: They're coming.

CHIZUKO: You got home early today.

AKI: I took a short cut.

KAORU: (*laughing*) Your face is flushed.

AKI: I ran all the way.

CHIZUKO: Go change your clothes, Aki.

Kaoru heads toward his shed, unbuttoning his shirt, preparing to start back to town.

AKI: Where are you going, Kaoru-san?

KAORU: I thought since we stopped work for today, I'd go (into town) . . .

CHIZUKO: Maybe this is a good time to repair the barn. There's a big hole in the north wall.

AKI: That's been there before Papa died.

CHIZUKO: Change your clothes, Aki.

KAORU: Yes, I noticed it. I'd better fix it. Winter's coming and the wind will blow right through.

Chizuko pushes Aki toward the house. Aki sulkily goes in. Ichiro and Tomu enter from the left. Kaoru, with a tool box in his hand, sees them.

Hello, boys. How's school. Is the math any easier?

TOMU: A lot easier.

ICHIRO: (*overlapping*) Not bad, not bad.

TOMU: (*to Chizuko*) Did Aki get home?

CHIZUKO: She's inside. What's the matter with you, Ichiro? I told you always to walk together. You're the oldest and . . .

TOMU: She ran away from us, Ma.

Kaoru exits to the right. The boys and Chizuko enter the house.

ICHIRO: God, she's a big girl now. I can't watch her all the time.

CHIZUKO: I want you to walk together. I told you that. Anything can happen.

ICHIRO: Like what?

CHIZUKO: Anything. Snakes, scorpions . . .

ICHIRO: Snakes? Scorpions?

TOMU: How about spiders and lizards?

ICHIRO: (*overlapping*) Yeah, and man-eating ants.

AKI: (*off stage, reading*)
     "A heavy heart, Beloved, have I borne
     from year to year until I saw thy face

Tomu and Ichiro groan and exit through the upstage door. Aki continues reading as the light slowly fades on Chizuko taking the scarf from her pocket and looking at it.

AKI: And sorrow after sorrow took place
     of all those natural joys as lightly worn"

Fade out

Scene 2

Time: A month later
At rise: Kaoru, Ichiro, and Tomu sharpen tools downstage. The sun is setting, there is an orange glow that slowly turns dark as the scene progresses.

TOMU: (*to Kaoru*) Is this sharp enough?

KAORU: (*feeling the edge*) Just a little more.

ICHIRO: (*teasing*) That'll cut butter real good . . . in summer. (*he takes the hoe from Tomu*) Here, I'll do it.

Nakamura enters from stage left.

TOMU: (*imitating Nakamura*) Nakamura-san's here. Haro-haro.

NAKAMURA: Haro-haro. You can stop now. Sun's gone down, you know.

KAORU: (ha-ha) How are you?

NAKAMURA: You caught it from Chizuko-san, eh? I didn't know work was catching.

KAORU: Just honing tools for tomorrow.

NAKAMURA: Go easy. You'll be all worn out by harvest time.

Aki comes out of the house and walks downstage.

NAKAMURA: Oh, Aki-chan.

AKI: Hello, Oji-san.

KAORU: (*to Aki*) Go on and start. I'll be there soon.

AKI: Okay. (*she enters Kaoru's shed and prepares to practice*)

NAKAMURA: (*watching her pass him*) They grow up before you know it, eh?

KAORU: Sometimes *they* don't even know it.

NAKAMURA: Yeah. Before you know it. Next year my son—the oldest—be twenty. If it was the old country, I would think about . . . about giving him a parcel of land . . . (*he laughs dourly*) Well, maybe in a couple of years I can get together a down payment for . . . maybe ten acres. Put it in his name . . . (*Aki starts practicing. Nakamura is surprised.*) Ah! She can play the violin!

ICHIRO: No, she can't.

KAORU: Well, I've been trying to teach her.

NAKAMURA: Oh, yeah?

KAORU: She's not a good player, but she's smart. She . . .

ICHIRO: (*to Tomu*) Let's get out of here.

TOMU: Yeah, let's go to Billy's.

They exit left.

NAKAMURA: Chizuko's kids are all smart. Nice boys too. Nice family.

Chizuko appears in the yard with a basket of laundry. Nakamura sees her first.

Ah! Chizuko-san! Nice, eh? Nice evening. I'm enjoying the nice music.

CHIZUKO: She's just a beginner. Sometimes I wish I were deaf. (*Aki hits some sour notes.*)

NAKAMURA: You know, Chizuko-san, when I first saw him in town—no job, nothing—just a suitcase and a violin—I felt sorry for him, then (I thought of you) . . .

CHIZUKO: Nakamura-san, did you . . . How is your family.

NAKAMURA: Fine, fine.

Aki's playing grows progressively worse. She tries to get Kaoru's attention. Nakamura winces at the sour notes. He prepares to leave.

Well, I better . . . Eh! I almost forgot what I came for. Chizuko-san, I'm irrigating tomorrow. You want water too? Might as well order same time, eh?

CHIZUKO: Well . . .

NAKAMURA: No trouble for me.

CHIZUKO: Kaoru-san, what do you think?

KAORU: Maybe we ought to finish the thinning first.

CHIZUKO: Yes. We'll wait a few days. Thank you anyway.

KAORU: (*shaking his head over Aki's bad playing*) I'd better get in there.

Aki stops playing.

NAKAMURA: That's better.

KAORU: (*in the shed, softly*) You're going to drive visitors away with your playing.

AKI: Why, thank you sir.

CHIZUKO: (*to Nakamura*) That was nice of you to ask.

NAKAMURA: Oh. Yeah. It's all right.

CHIZUKO: Would you like a cup of tea?

NAKAMURA: Tea? No-no. No tea (heh-heh). (*There's an awkward silence.*) Aki-chan's growing up fast, eh?

CHIZUKO: No, not so.

NAKAMURA: They're like weeds. You don't give them water but they grow anyway.

CHIZUKO: That's true.

NAKAMURA: Pretty soon the yard be full of young men. Maybe my sons come too, eh? Chizuko-san, you chase them out with your broom, eh? (*he laughs heartily but Chizuko doesn't find it funny*) I better be going. Goodnight. You're sure about the water?

CHIZUKO: I'm sure. Goodnight.

Nakamura exits left.

NAKAMURA: Goodnight.

CHIZUKO: (*without looking at the shed*) Kaoru-san, you want . . . would you like some tea?

KAORU: (*calling out*) No tea, thank you.

Aki and Kaoru laugh softly. Light fades on Chizuko still holding her basket of laundry.

Fade out

Scene 3

Time: Winter night—a few months later
On Rise: In the Sakata kitchen, the lantern is dimly lit. Ichiro sits at the table reading. Tomu has already retired.
Aki practices in Kaoru's shed standing over a music sheet. There is a bottle of wine and a glass on an up-turned crate. Kaoru sits on the cot listening. The music can be heard in the kitchen. Chizuko, in a robe, sweeps the floor. She opens the door to sweep out the dust. The door closes; the music stops. Chizuko grows restless and steps to the window. She returns to the table to work out some figures. The music starts again.

ICHIRO: (*looking at Chizuko*) So long as she keeps playing, eh, Ma?

CHIZUKO: What do you mean?

ICHIRO: Want me to talk to her?

CHIZUKO: About what?

ICHIRO: Okay.

Ichiro shakes his head and exits through the upstage door. Light fades in the kitchen and turns up in the shed.

Kaoru sits on the cot and watches Aki. It's been a bad day for both of them.

KAORU: (*pointing to the music sheet*) See this symbol? That's a sharp. You know all the f's are sharped. I told you that.

AKI: I know. I forgot.

KAORU: Now. The last three measures again.

AKI: The last three?

KAORU: That's what I said.

AKI: (*muttering and finding her place*) The last three . . .

She starts playing and makes another error. Kaoru jumps to his feet.

KAORU: Those are all eighth notes. One half of a quarter. Quarters go: on, two, three, four. Eighths are: one and two and three and four and. (*he taps it out*) We went through this before. (*Aki starts over, making another error.*) Sharp! Sharp! (*he takes the violin from her*) Here! (*Aki starts to cry. Kaoru reconsiders.*) I'm sorry, Aki-chan. I guess I'm tired. Here. Lie down. (*Aki is sullen and hesitant.*) Go on. Lie down. Close your eyes. Now this is how it should sound.

He plays the exercise. He stops and taps her knees with the bow. He plays something beautiful, possibly "Two Guitars."

Think of yourself as the violin. Feel the music coming from deep inside. Listen to it. Does it tell you what you want to hear?

AKI: No.

KAORU: (*patiently*) You see, Aki-chan, this instrument is not so different from people. The songs that come from us depend on how we are touched. If you want sweet music, you must coax and stroke—coax and stroke.

AKI: I can't do it.

KAORU: Yes, you can. If you hear it . . . and feel it, then it's only a matter of time. I know you can do it. Tell me why you want to play this, Aki-chan.

AKI: (*warming up*) Because . . . oh, because when I hear your music, I feel another world out there . . . full of romance and mystery. I feel like I'm missing so much. I want to know what it's like, I want to be a part of it; I want in . . . but . . . the door won't open for me.

KAORU: It will open. You have to keep at it and keep at it and one day . . .

AKI: How long will it take?

KAORU: I don't know. That depends on you.

AKI: Five years?

KAORU: More than that.

AKI: Ten? Twenty?

KAORU: Maybe. Maybe more. Depends on how hard you want to work.

AKI: I don't want to work twenty years just to be a second-rate fiddler.

KAORU: (*suddenly depressed*) I see.

AKI: It's only for fun anyway, isn't it?

KAORU: That's right. Only for fun.

AKI: Then why do we have to be so . . . serious? Why do we have to be so strict?

KAORU: That's right. Why? What does it matter?

AKI: I love the book you gave me.

KAORU: (*putting the violin away*) That's good.

AKI: (*taking the book from her pocket*) Listen Kaoru-san:
    "The face of all the world is changed, I think
    Since first I heard the footsteps of thy soul
    Move still, oh, still, beside me, as they (stole) . . ."
Do you like it?

KAORU: We'll practice again next week.

Kaoru does not turn. Aki waits. He does not face her. She finally leaves the shed.

Fade out

Scene 4

Time: Shortly after
At rise: Interior of the Sakata kitchen. Chizuko sits at the table deep in thought.
Aki, after waiting in the dark, contemplating what had transpired in the previous scene, finally enters the kitchen. She is careful to close the door quietly. She discovers her mother.

AKI: Oh. You're still up.

CHIZUKO: (*casually*) That was a long lesson.

AKI: (*trying to get away*) Un-hunh.

CHIZUKO: I didn't hear you play much tonight.

AKI: We talked. I guess he knows I'll never make a good player so he just talked to me tonight. About music. That's just as important.

CHIZUKO: For playing the violin?

AKI: We do have to talk, you know.

CHIZUKO: About what?

AKI: Things.

Aki starts for the bedroom.

CHIZUKO: What kind of things?

AKI: Music, composers, what kind of music they write . . . why . . . where they come from. We talk about other things too. Books, writers. He's been to high school, you know. Why do you ask?

CHIZUKO: I . . . I don't like you staying up so late. (*she starts to fold clothes*) You have a hard time in the morning . . . getting up. You know that.

AKI: Tomorrow's Saturday!

CHIZUKO: Shhh!

AKI: Then why do I have to go to bed so early?

CHIZUKO: The boys have to go to bed early because they work on Saturday. It's not fair to them.

AKI: *They* don't care!

CHIZUKO: Kaoru-san works in the morning too.

AKI: I know that.

CHIZUKO: Then you shouldn't keep him up so late.

AKI: I'm not keeping him up!

CHIZUKO: Shhh!

AKI: Well, if he wanted me to leave, he'd tell me.

CHIZUKO: He's too polite to tell you.

AKI: It's not that late anyway. God, he's a grown man. He can stay up as long as he wants and still work in the morning. That's all you think about: work, work, work!

CHIZUKO: (*warning*) Aki . . .

AKI: Well, it's true. You're always telling me what to do and how to do it. You're always trying to tell everyone what to do around here.

CHIZUKO: I'm not trying to tell everyone . . .

AKI: You're going to drive Kaoru-san away from here—bossing him like you do.

CHIZUKO: Take care how you talk to me.

AKI: Nobody likes that. Especially a man like Kaoru-san.

CHIZUKO: Enough. I'm not trying to tell everyone what to do.

AKI: Yes, you are! You're trying to control everything. It's a free country. If we want to talk, what's wrong with that?

CHIZUKO: You can talk in the kitchen.

AKI: We *can't* talk in the kitchen.

CHIZUKO: (*looking innocent*) Oh? Why?

AKI: Ma, you *know* why. Ichiro and Tomu sitting around all the time and making all those cracks . . . and you sitting there listening and making those faces . . . like telling me what I should say and when I should say it—when I should shut up and . . .

CHIZUKO: You don't want me to listen? You saying things you don't want me to hear?

AKI: No! But I try to talk about . . . about . . . *things*, and there's Ichiro and you sitting there. I know you're thinking: "How stupid!" (*she stands up for herself*) Yes! I don't want you to hear what I say!

CHIZUKO: You think you're the only one with feelings? You don't think anyone else has feelings they want to talk about?

AKI: Well, let them talk about it then. I don't care. (*she again starts toward the bedroom door*)

CHIZUKO: You don't care!

AKI: No! I don't care who talks to who!

CHIZUKO: That's what I mean. You don't care about anyone but yourself. You don't care *how* anyone else feels.

AKI: You mean *you?* (*she turns back*)

CHIZUKO: I mean other people! How do you think it looks: you all the time in a man's room?

AKI: I don't care how it looks.

CHIZUKO: (*lowering her voice*) I'm not saying you're doing anything wrong. I'm saying (that) . . .

AKI: You're saying *you* don't like it. No one else cares. You're saying . . .

CHIZUKO: Aki-chan. It's not like that. You don't understand. Kaoru-san is a grown man.

AKI: I just told you that.

CHIZUKO: Kaoru-san's twice your age.

AKI: He is not!

CHIZUKO: If you want a friend to talk to, find someone your age who can understand you.

AKI: Who? Name me one.

CHIZUKO: There're lots of boys—*and* girls. Friend doesn't have to be a man. Nakamura-san has two sons.

AKI: Hunh!

CHIZUKO: There's Billy.

AKI: He's a baby!

CHIZUKO: He's your age.

AKI: You think he understands me? Ma, you don't even know what I'm talking about, do you?

CHIZUKO: Kaoru-san is (old) . . .

AKI: I don't care!

CHIZUKO: I know you don't care . . . right now. I'm just saying you shouldn't let your emotions run away with you.

AKI: Emotions? What do you know about emotions?

CHIZUKO: How can you say that?

AKI: I'm not going to live like you. I'm not going to live all tied up in knots like you: afraid of what people say, afraid of spending money, afraid of laughing, afraid (of) . . .

CHIZUKO: Do you understand my problems?

AKI: Afraid you're going to love someone. Afraid you're (going) . . .

CHIZUKO: I have lots to worry about. I got to see you have enough to eat, give you an education, see you're dressed decent—so people won't say, "Those kids don't have a father." See you're not left with debts, like what happened to me. See you don't make a mess (of) . . .

AKI: I know you work hard. I'm grateful. But I can't . . . you can't tell me how to feel, how to live . . .

CHIZUKO: Aki, I don't want you to get hurt.

AKI: It's *my* life!

CHIZUKO: Your life is my life. We're one.

AKI: No! We're not! We're not the same!

CHIZUKO: I mean, when you hurt, I hurt.

AKI: That's not true. I hurt when I see how you live—dead! Nothing to look forward to. You think that's good. You want me to live like that. Well, I won't! I want more.

CHIZUKO: You will have more. Things are not the same as they were for me. You're young—you have lots to look forward to. I just don't (want) . . .

AKI: God, you never give up.

CHIZUKO: Someone more your age . . .

AKI: (*it dawns on her*) You're jealous!

CHIZUKO: Jealous?

AKI: Yes, because he . . .

CHIZUKO: What're you talking about?

AKI: Yes, because he pays attention (to me) . . .

CHIZUKO: That's ridiculous! He likes all of us. He told me!

AKI: It's more!

CHIZUKO: (*screaming*) No! No more!

Ichiro enters from the bedroom door. Both women stop talking.

ICHIRO: (*commanding*) Go to bed, Aki!

Aki exits through the bedroom door. Ichiro stands looking at Chizuko who avoids his eyes.

We hear Kaoru's violin ("Two Guitars") and we know he also does not sleep.

Fade out

Scene 5

Time: Spring—Evening
At rise: Interior of Kaoru's quarters. A bottle of wine and a small glass sit on an up-turned crate. The rest of the stage is dark.
Aki is practicing. Kaoru lies on the cot after a hard day's work. He appears to be listening, keeping time with his foot.
Aki's playing is improved but not much. She stops momentarily.

KAORU: Go on. Continue. (*Aki resumes. Kaoru looks at the ceiling and tries to keep awake.*) Getting old. (*he falls asleep*)

Aki watches Kaoru and her playing grows slower and finally stops. She quietly sits on the floor, opens the violin case, and starts to put the violin away. She holds it a moment.

AKI: (*stroking the violin*)
"My cricket chirps against thy mandolin
Hush, call no echo up in further proof
Of desolation! There's a voice within
That weeps . . . as thou must sing . . . alone, aloof"

KAORU: You know so little about life. What do you learn from those words? (*Kaoru sits up. He reaches over and pours a drink.*) Love is beautiful?

AKI: Of course.

KAORU: (*teasing*) Tell me about it, Aki-chan. What do you know about it?

AKI: Love is . . . Oh, you wake up in the morning knowing good things are going to happen. It's making . . . making people like me—nobodies—feel special. You *know* there's a heart beating inside—pumping, singing—and you *know* this is what people are born to feel. Everyone. It's sublime; its eternal and forever (and) . . .

KAORU: (Ho-ho) So that's what it is: beating and singing and eternal and forever.

AKI: Don't laugh at me.

KAORU: Let me tell you something, Aki. Love doesn't always sing. Sometimes it pulls you to the bottom. It drags everything along with it. Then all sense of right or wrong goes too.

AKI: I don't believe you.

KAORU: You don't know. It turns sour and pretty soon you start enjoying the sick smell of it.

AKI: That's not love. Love isn't like that.

KAORU: I loved someone once. (*he drinks wine*) Her name was Yoko. She didn't want me to leave. She begged me to stay.

AKI: (*angry and jealous*) Well, why'd you leave then? Why didn't you stay with her?

KAORU: She wouldn't marry me.

AKI: Well, why not? If she loved you, why wouldn't she marry you?

KAORU: She had a husband. A family.

AKI: That's awful!

KAORU: Things like that happen sometimes.

AKI: That's no excuse!

KAORU: Sometimes you meet someone you can love at the wrong time. Too late. She was already married.

AKI: (*jealous and hurt*) You shouldn't have let that happen!

KAORU: I didn't try to make it happen. It just did, that's all. It's something you wouldn't understand. Maybe one day it will happen to you. Maybe you'll understand then. (*he drinks*)

AKI: Never! I wouldn't let it!

KAORU: What does it matter? It's past. Gone. (*he drinks*) I've never been long with a woman. Even my mother left me. Every time I saw a pretty lady, I thought maybe she was my mother. I thought she was waiting for me somewhere. Somehow I wouldn't believe she was dead.

AKI: Was she?

KAORU: Who knows? Maybe she did die. Maybe she ran away with another man. No one talked about it.

AKI: (*sympathetically*) Oh . . . Kaoru-san.

KAORU: I never stayed long in one place. Always wandering away; always running. With Yoko was the longest. She was . . . warm, sweet . . . she was evil. (*he buries his face in his hands*) Too much wine. I'm a little drunk. (*he sits on the cot*)

Aki watches him for a moment, then sits on the cot and slowly, tentatively puts her arm around him. Kaoru shrugs her off.

Don't. (*Aki persists.*) Don't do that . . .

Aki will not let him go. His vision blurs, he sees Aki's innocent longing and responds to her embrace. They kiss and hold for a long moment before Kaoru puts her down on his cot. The embrace becomes sensual.

Chizuko who has been sitting in the kitchen gets up and walks to the shed. She listens for sounds of music and not hearing any, she flings open the door.

CHIZUKO: What's this? What are you doing?

Kaoru and Aki jump apart.

KAORU: Chizuko-san . . .

CHIZUKO: (*overlapping to Aki*) Get in the house. (*she pushes Aki out of the shed*)

AKI: Mama . . . (*she starts to cry*)

KAORU: Chizuko-san, please let me explain. Please . . .

CHIZUKO: "Please-please-please." Don't beg now! Pack your things and get out! (*she pulls shirts and things off the pegs and throws them on the bed*)

KAORU: Chizuko-san!

AKI: (*overlapping*) Mama! Don't!

Chizuko finds the violin case on the floor and picks it up. Kaoru holds her to prevent her from throwing it.

KAORU: Chizu(ko-san)

CHIZUKO: Don't touch me! Don't call my name!

KAORU: Calm down; please calm down.

CHIZUKO: You thought you could fool me. You . . . you violated my trust. You violated my daughter!

KAORU: Vio . . . ? I did nothing. Believe me, I did nothing.

AKI: Ma! Nothing! We did nothing!

CHIZUKO: Get in the house!

AKI: It's not his fault!

CHIZUKO: I'll fix you. I'll get the police!

KAORU: Be reasonable. Let's talk this over.

CHIZUKO: I said out! Tonight! Now! (*she pulls Aki downstage*)

AKI: (*balking*) Mama! Don't do this to us!

CHIZUKO: "Us"? What is "us"?

KAORU: Believe me. I meant no harm . . .

CHIZUKO: What did you do to *me*?

AKI: I'm sorry, Mama. It was my fault. All of it. *I* did it. *I* started it. It was me, Mama. Blame *me* . . .

CHIZUKO: I know his kind, Aki. He preys on women with his talk . . . his gifts. (*she tries to touch Aki but Aki draws away*) That's what I tried to tell you. How many women do you think he's lured with his . . . his sweet talk. Little country girls like you . . .

KAORU: I've made no pretenses. From the beginning, I told you . . .

Chizuko stops him before he says the terrible words that would prove how foolish she had been to dream.

CHIZUKO: I trusted you, I trusted you.

KAORU: I'm sorry. I didn't betray that trust. Tonight I . . . I had too much to drink. I know that's no ex(cuse) . . .

CHIZUKO: Get out. Get out!

KAORU: I have no money.

CHIZUKO: I'll give you money! (*she starts toward the house dragging Aki with her*)

AKI: Don't! Don't, Mama, I love him!

CHIZUKO: (*the word "love" stops her*) Don't say that. Don't say that word! You're confusing it with something else.

AKI: I do. I love him.

CHIZUKO: Do you really believe this . . . this old man loves you? (*Aki looks at Kaoru. He avoids her eyes.*) He doesn't know the meaning of the word. I know his kind. Where do you think he goes on his days off? To women! He goes to women, Aki.

AKI: I don't care. I love him.

CHIZUKO: (*contemptuously*) Where is your pride, Aki?

AKI: If you send him away, I'll go with him.

CHIZUKO: You don't know what you're saying, Aki.

AKI: I will. I'll go with him.

She runs to Kaoru's side and holds his arm. Kaoru reacts, drawing away from her.

CHIZUKO: (*pulling Aki away*) You know what you're asking for? From town to town . . . no roots . . . no home . . . nothing. Maybe one day, he'll get tired of you . . . throw you out . . . leave you in some dirty hotel for another fool woman. Think, Aki. And you'll come crawling (home) . . .

AKI: I'll never come home! I'll never come back to you! You're not a mother. You're a witch!

Kaoru goes back to his quarters and starts packing.

CHIZUKO: Witch? Who you calling witch? Someone who sacrificed a life for you?

AKI: You didn't sacrifice for me.

CHIZUKO: No? No? You think I like this life? You think I like grubbing in dirt and manure (and) . . .

AKI: That's the only way you know to live. You don't want to change your life.

CHIZUKO: You believe that? You believe this is all I want? That I lived with a man I hardly knew, didn't understand, didn't respect because (I) . . .

AKI: You didn't love him! You didn't love him, did you?

CHIZUKO: How could I love him—I didn't know him. All the time I was keeping our heads above water . . . singlehanded! Yes! While he was still alive, until the merciful day he drowned! Growing old before I was ready—dying before I ever lived . . .

AKI: Then you've never loved. Then you don't know anything about love.

CHIZUKO: I do! *You* don't know! What do you know about my feelings?

AKI: I know about them and I don't want to stick around and become the kind of woman *you* are.

CHIZUKO: (*in a towering rage*) (Annngh!) Go then. Go! Go! You'll find out. And when things get rough, remember tonight!

AKI: I'll never forget.

CHIZUKO: You think you know all the answers. You think every-thing's so simple. You haven't even tasted pain yet. You'll find out.

AKI: So I'll find out! (*she walks to the kitchen door*)

CHIZUKO: Aki...

AKI: Leave me alone!

Aki slams the door behind her. Chizuko is stunned. She sits on a bench until Ichiro comes out (in the next scene).

Fade out

Scene 6

Time: Immediately after
At rise: Awakened by the sound of angry voices, Ichiro, in pajamas, enters from the bedroom (upstage door). He peers through the screen door.

ICHIRO: You all right, Ma?

CHIZUKO: (*getting up and entering the kitchen*) Everything went wrong. Get the money jar.

ICHIRO: What?

CHIZUKO: Kaoru-san's leaving.

ICHIRO: What happened?

CHIZUKO: I don't know. I don't know what happened. Sudden-ly...everything happened and...and he's leaving us. Aki too.

ICHIRO: Aki? Goddamn kid.

Tomu enters from the upstage door. He wears p.j.'s and rubs his sleepy eyes.

CHIZUKO: I don't know what happened. Suddenly...Ichiro, what went wrong? She's going with him. How can things turn so bad?

TOMU: What turned bad? What happened to Aki? Where's she going?

ICHIRO: She's going with him. That stupid brat!

TOMU: Why?

ICHIRO: Never mind why.

TOMU: What's going on?

CHIZUKO: Get the money, Ichiro. I have to give them money.

TOMU: Don't let her go, Ma.

CHIZUKO: She wants to leave. We have to let her go.

TOMU: You can stop her, Ma. Stop her!

CHIZUKO: I can't. I can't anymore.

ICHIRO: Never mind, Ma. Give them some money and let them go. (*he gets the money jar*)

TOMU: Ma, stop her. Stop her! (*he starts toward the upstage door*)

ICHIRO: Tomu! Get back here, dammit!

CHIZUKO: Don't get mad. Let's not fight any more.

ICHIRO: (*counting the money*) I knew what was going on. I should have knocked some sense . . .

CHIZUKO: No. If . . . no. I was thinking of myself all the time . . . the farm. It was easier with a man helping. I was thinking . . . I'm getting old . . . tired . . .

TOMU: Why can't they both stay then?

CHIZUKO: That's not possible.

ICHIRO: Shut up, Tomu.

CHIZUKO: We can't stay here anymore. It will be too hard for us.

ICHIRO: Don't worry, Ma. We can make it. I'll quit school and . . .

CHIZUKO: No. It's no good. We have to move.

TOMU: Ma . . .

CHIZUKO: You can't quit school.

ICHIRO: Where will we go? The crop . . .

CHIZUKO: After the harvest. I was thinking . . . maybe San Pedro.

ICHIRO: Where?

CHIZUKO: Terminal Island. I hear there're lots of Japanese there. And the canneries. You boys can get part-time work. After school. That way you don't miss school so much . . . like you've been doing.

TOMU: We didn't miss this year.

CHIZUKO: We sell everything. Maybe just keep the truck and the beds . . . some furniture. Rent an apartment . . . How much should we give them?

ICHIRO: Just enough to get out of town.

CHIZUKO: Aki will need too. Poor Aki . . .

ICHIRO: Don't waste any sympathy, Ma. She asked for it. She's no good.

CHIZUKO: She's a good girl, Ichiro. She's not to blame.

TOMU: She's a good girl.

ICHIRO: She's a selfish brat. (*he finishes counting the money*) This should be enough (*Chizuko adds the rest of the bills.*) That doesn't leave us much.

CHIZUKO: That's all right. We can get credit at the store. Ishi-san will give us credit.

Aki comes out of the bedroom with her clothes in a pillow case.

ICHIRO: You spoiled everything for everybody.

Ichiro follows Aki downstage hoping to say a few more things but he sees Kaoru waiting with his violin case and bag and he stops. He slams the money on the bench.

Here. Give him that.

Aki gives Kaoru the money; Kaoru looks at it and slips it in his pocket. Aki takes his arm preparing to leave with him.

KAORU: (*gently detaining her*) I can't take you with me; you can't come with me, Aki-chan. You know that, don't you?

AKI: But I have to! I can't stay here.

KAORU: You understand why, don't you?

AKI: But what will I do here all by myself? You got to take me. Please take me with you . . .

KAORU: (*gently*) I can't.

AKI: Please take me . . . take me with you . . . (*she tries to embrace him but he will not permit it*) I'm going to die, Kaoru-san.

KAORU: (*firmly*) No, you won't.

AKI: Take me . . .

KAORU: Now go inside and apologize to your mother. Try to explain . . .

AKI: She won't understand; she won't take me back. Please, Kaoru-san . . . please . . .

KAORU: She *will* take you back. In time you'll both forget.

AKI: I'll remember all my life. (*she tries to embrace him again*)

KAORU: (*stopping her*) You must stop this.

AKI: Please . . .

KAORU: Stop it!

AKI: (*after a moment*) What will you do? Where will you go?

KAORU: I don't know. First to the bus depot. This time of year there'll be harvesting all along California. Grapes . . . peaches . . . Like she said: another town, another job.

AKI: Another woman?

KAORU: Another? You're not a woman yet. When you grow up to be a real woman, I'll be an old man. You'll be all right. Now be a good girl and say goodbye.

Aki embraces him and he permits it without responding. She releases him. He prepares to leave.

AKI: Will you write me?

KAORU: (*without turning*) You know I can't do that.

Kaoru exits left. Aki stands dejected and watches him go.

Tomu comes from the house. He reaches in his pajama pocket and gives Aki some money.

TOMU: Take this with you, Aki.

AKI: I'm not going.

TOMU: You're not going? (*We hear the sound of a truck approaching from a distance.*) Ma! Did you hear that? She's not going! (*he runs in the house pulling Aki with him*)

ICHIRO: He won't take you, eh? You should have figured that out yourself.

Chizuko hushes him.

The family is quiet. Kaoru hails the truck.

KAORU: (*off stage*) Hey . . . stop. Stop . . . (*The truck stops.*) Can you give me a lift to town?

TRUCK DRIVER: (*off stage*) Yeah. Hop in.

Aki walks to the screen door as the truck starts up again. She stands there until she can no longer hear it. Then she moves toward the bedroom door.

CHIZUKO: It's better this way, Aki, better.

Light fades slowly out.

Fade out

THE END

GOLD WATCH

❀

MOMOKO IKO

Momoko Iko's *Gold Watch* examines the tensions within a Japanese American family and community submerged in the panic and hysteria preceding their internment during World War II. The setting is the Pacific Northwest where local resentment for the hard-won success of Japanese truck farmers ran high. Iko was born in 1940 in Wapato, Washington where as a two-year-old child she was evacuated with her family of eight. The Ikos were evacuated to the Portland Assembly Center and later to Heart Mountain, Wyoming, one of ten internment camps administered by the Department of Justice. Like 120,000 other people of Japanese ancestry, two-thirds of whom were American-born citizens, the Iko family were incarcerated without trial, their constitutional rights ignored, victims of Executive Order 9066, which allowed for their wholesale removal from the western United States on the basis of "military necessity."

Of her three years at Heart Mountain, Iko has scant recollection, only those memories reinforced by stories family members have told her. Her older brother enlisted when government permission was granted and joined the U.S. Army Military Intelligence Service, serving in the Pacific. Some thirty-three thousand Nisei served in the U.S. armed forces, joining the Military Intelligence Service and serving in the 442nd Regimental Combat Team. They distinguished themselves militarily as their families and loved ones at home remained behind barbed wire.[1]

Despite the absence of direct personal memory of internment, the camp experience surfaces as a major thematic motif in Iko's work, directly in *Gold Watch* and indirectly in other works including *Flowers and Household Gods, Boutique Living and Disposable Icons, Second City Flat, When We Were Young,* and *Old Man.* "I have unconscious memories, I remember atmospheres, you could just feel there was always trouble around . . . and a lot of people. I know I absorbed a lot of the camps. . . . it comes out in dreams, in a sensibility, in senses. . . . I know when I write that's when it comes out."[2]

Upon release from Heart Mountain, Iko's family followed a circuit familiar to many Japanese Americans in the postwar period, traveling to Seabury Farms, New Jersey, to work as migrant farm labor and eventually settling in Chicago. Her mother did piecework sewing and her father did factory work; despite economic hardship the Iko apartment became a gathering place for displaced Japanese Americans seeking to resettle following the war. The internment camps effectively relocated the Japanese American population. Before the war 88.5 percent of all Japanese Americans lived on the West Coast; that number fell to 55 percent by 1947 as Japanese Americans moved to the interior and the East Coast.[3] Department of Justice policy was to give the internee twenty-five dollars and a one-way bus ticket in order to resume their lives.[4] This period of transition and resettlement was an interesting time for Iko, a child of five at the time of her release. "As I was growing up, our house was like a center for young Nisei . . . because after the war our home was one of the few where the family was together. . . . There were always people coming in and out. . . . I know a lot of stories come out of that period."

Iko began writing in college while at Northern Illinois University and later as she completed her degree in English at the University of Illinois, Champagne/Urbana. "I started to write when I started to have arguments in class and I wanted to make clear my point of view." Her writing began as personal essay and later took the form of fiction when she began to experiment with the short story and novel forms. Though she was a theatergoer, it was not until she saw Lorraine Hansberry's *A Raisin in the Sun* that she recognized the political potential of the theater. "My sister took me and we were stunned . . . it was the first time theater had any real meaning to me. . . . I realized that her [Hansberry's] sensibility was more similar to mine than anything I had ever seen." In *A Raisin in the Sun* Iko recognized parallel characters and situations from Japanese American life. "There's a young African nationalist, the boyfriend of the girl—I understood him because I could see it. I saw him in young Nisei men. Some became hoodlums—they were bright, they could have gone to college but because they still remembered the war they . . . turned out totally different."

Iko did not, however, turn immediately to writing for the theater despite the literary possibilities she had glimpsed. Writing a play in English, reflecting an Asian American experience, interpreted by Asian actors, was novel to her. "I still didn't write plays . . . until I saw this notice about the East West Players [playwriting contest]. That was the catalyst—I saw there was a theater that was looking for my plays."

Adapted from a portion of an unpublished novel, *Gold Watch*'s central characters are loosely based on Iko's father and mother. Hailing from Hiroshima prefecture, Iko's father was from a fishing family and her mother of the merchant class. "He came over more for the adventure . . . he wanted to get out from the kind of tyranny that existed [in Japan]. He felt that his life [in America] was a freer life. . . . My mother considered Japan a confining experience. She loved visiting but she was glad she never lived there, she found the role she was assigned to too confining." Like the character Masu, Iko's father possessed a rebellious nature and poetic soul. "It was not a useful spirit in an economic climate like America," says Iko of a man who farmed, cut lumber, and worked canneries, fishing boats, and factories. The character of Kimiko less directly resembles Iko's mother who was extremely independent. "She went places she wanted to go with her friends, she flew in an airplane before my father did, she went to movies by herself." Iko invested the character of Kimiko with her mother's strength. "The spirit of that person is in Kimiko. She handled the world—the bankers, the grocer, the people they owed money to—she handled them."

Iko is insistent that the characters of *Gold Watch* are neither prototypical nor symbolic. "These are specific people within a specific situation." Yet the response from the Japanese American community contradicts this assertion. "Many people [after seeing the play] come back to me and say that I described their fathers. One guy even asked, "How did you know my father so well?" The character Masu becomes emblematic of the first-generation Japanese male, his frustration is that of a man embodying a collision of cultures. In *Gold Watch* he explodes at his wife, "This isn't Japan. This is America! I know. I know! What do you want, *obahan*? You want me to go around with a wooden bowl? Would that make me more American? Tanaka's a friend. What friend makes you feel like a beggar? What friend? Your son is ashamed of me. You make him ashamed of me, and me, I make him hate me. I would rather have that!" In investigating the particular dynamics between a man with a fiercely independent spirit in conflict with social forces that conspire to restrain him, Iko strikes a sensitive chord within the Japanese American community: exposing the tension between individualism and the dynamics of the group. In doing so she challenges the myth of Japanese American complacency in the face of the evacuation order, dramatizing the range of responses to that edict.

Gold Watch is inhabited by characters representative of the highly complex social stratification of the prewar Japanese immigrant community. Ironically, despite their disenfranchisement as a group and their shifting economic status, many of the immigrant Issei retained their class chauvinism. The friendship between Masu and Tanaka, a man who lacks education, underscores this irony. "Tanaka has probably never understood why Masu considers him a friend. They represent an old and new world. Tanaka is the kind of person who would have been servile to Masu in Japan. In [their American] reality, he's a successful businessman and Masu's a poor farmer." Tanaka's eagerness to befriend Masu collides not only with Masu's immense masculine pride, but also with the principles that compelled him to leave Japan in the first place. Iko explains, "In that sense he [Masu] is a new world man. Not an American, but he moves forward. He's not interested in the past and he is certainly not interested in a past which he feels people in his community have fabricated in order to ease their present lives rather than facing the realities of it. They construct artifices—samurais in their background when there aren't any."

Gold Watch also sheds light on the position of the Kibei in the prewar period. As American-born children of Japanese immigrants who were educated in Japan, the Kibei had stronger Japanese language skills and a greater understanding of Japanese society than did their Nisei counterparts. Their attitudes and allegiances varied: some Kibei living in America volunteered for military service; others caught in Japan at the outbreak of the war were treated with suspicion because of their American nationality; still others rejected the country of their birth, repatriating to Japan for a host of personal, moral, and political reasons. In the relationship between Hiroshi and Tadao, Iko points to the need for certain young Nisei and Kibei men to find an alternative to an America which limited their opportunities and rejected their race. "Tanaka's son may have been attracted not to Japan's fate in the history of the world, but to [the image] of a very sure, confident young man, confident of where he is going. You can talk about black nationalists in the same sense—they were looking back to Africa for a model in the same way Hiroshi and Tadao were looking back to Japan."

In making reference to the internment experience throughout her work, Iko has exorcised what playwright Phillip Gotanda has called "the psychic scar of Japanese America."[4] For Iko, this devastating experience, shared by 90 percent of Japanese Americans living during the war period, has created psychic aftershocks that reverberate to this day. "I think even the way that the Yonsei (fourth generation) act comes from their people being put in camp—and they don't even know about the camps. You don't have to know about something to have it affect you—[it's their parent's] values, what they warn you against, what they want you to do, what they try to give you, what they encourage in you, what they accept in you. I find it extraordinary that young Japanese American kids are encouraged so strongly towards certain things, very material, very practical—there's an enormous amount of energy invested in those things, to want that kind of life. . . . and I think the source of that is the camps. Even though the [cause for] fear doesn't exist any more, [the fear is] being passed on." Predating the redress and reparation movement, *Gold Watch* is an early call to break the silence and end the shame surrounding incarceration. Through the unfolding of this domestic drama, an unconscious lapse of memory is bridged and the silence of shame is ended.

Notes

1. Bill Hosukawa, *Nisei: The Quiet Americans* (New York: William Morrow and Co., 1969), 417–18.
2. Editor's interviews with Momoko Iko, Los Angeles, 18 January 1983 and 2 March 1991.
3. Roger Daniels, *Concentration Camps USA* (New York: Holt, Rinehart, 1972), 166.
4. Galen M. Fisher, "Resettling the Evacuees," *Far Eastern Survey* 14 (26 September 1945), 267.
5. Editor's interview with Phillip Gotanda, San Francisco, 1981.

GOLD WATCH

MOMOKO IKO

Time and Place: The play takes place in the Pacific Northwest on the Murakami truck farm and in the Japanese Christian community's church. The time is the fall of 1941 to the late spring of 1942.

CHARACTERS

MASARU (MASU) MURAKAMI, a man in his forties, lean, hard-muscled, wiry. His face is weathered and dark tanned, his hands, roughened. He is a farmer who uses his body when he talks and is given to mimicry, expansive gestures. MASU wears long-sleeved shirts (worn Pendletons) over undershirts, work boots, khakis, and a beat-up porkpie hat.

KIMIKO MURAKAMI, a woman in her early thirties, with a body that moves as lithely as a girl's, but quietly. She is pale, and in contrast to Murakami, her face looks older. She is invariably gracious but proud. KIMIKO wears cotton housedresses with cardigans, aprons, and slippers, and at Christmas, a homemade, unfrilly party dress with midheel party shoes.

TADAO MURAKAMI, boy of fourteen, skinny, well coordinated. His movements are quiet and unobtrusive but there is an underlying intensity or concentration. TADAO has overalls and work shoes for farm; shirts with sweater vest, cord pants, and winter jacket. He has a good Sunday suit, which he wears in Christmas scene.

CHIEKO MURAKAMI, a four-year-old, full of play and affection, direct in her expressions of feeling. CHIEKO wears cord bib pants, blouses, cardigan, and a frilly homemade velvet dress at Christmas with Mary Jane shoes.

TANAKA, also in his forties, owns the only Japanese tradestore in the area. He tends to scurry along, duck his head before speaking, and is formal in manners. With MASU, he is more direct—a naturally courteous man. TANAKA always wears conservative but contemporary suits and hats.

SETSUKO TANAKA, Tanaka's wife, a blooming woman who likes to gossip and visit. Basically, she is a blunt but decent human being. She dresses nicely for any occasion, midheels, gloves, hats, and winter coat.

HIROSHI TANAKA, a slim, erect young man of nineteen who through a rigid posture masks his youthful idealism and pain. He wears a conservative suit or Japanese school uniform and cap of the times.

REVEREND SUGANO, a well-meaning man of the church. Dress accordingly.

JAPANESE COMMUNITY PEOPLE, mostly farmers and wives. Most

are in their thirties to forties; some younger, some older. Dress accordingly.

THREE NIGHTRAIDERS, three white men dressed as farmers or country people. Dress accordingly.

ACT ONE

Time: Dawn, Labor Day weekend, 1941

The interior of the Murakami two-room house: one room serves as a kitchen, dining and living area: wooden table and four unmatched chairs, pot-bellied stove and stack of kindling and Japanese newspapers beside; small laundry tub sink with one faucet jutting from wall; a wooden icebox next to sink; upturned vegetable crates—papered and flour sack curtained—lined with jars of peaches, pears, cherries, corn, eggplant, tomatoes, mushrooms, etc; dishes, pots, pans, glasses, cups, rice bowls are organized on all available flat surfaces and shelves above sink; under the sink are a wooden vat of Tsukemono (pickled vegetables) and bottles of homemade sake. In living area is an overstuffed chair and hassock, rough hand-crafted table and bookcase, kerosene lamps, a faded carpet at door and curtainless windows. The second room is divided into two bedrooms by a heavy curtain strung across the middle and short curtains separating bedrooms from living area. In the parents' section: a brass double bed covered by a handmade Japanese futon; nice dresser of wood inlay on top of which is a Japanese lacquer box for gloves, hankies, jewelry (Kimiko's special things), brush, comb, and mirror. The children's section: cots and orange crate shelves personalized by Tadao and Chieko. Chieko has a girlish homemade quilt on her bed.

On Rise: Kimiko gets out of metal frame bed, goes into the kitchen and dishes out rice, misoshiru (soup), puts some tsukemono on plate, goes back to bedroom to wake up Masu.

KIMIKO: *(getting dressed, pinning back hair)* Okinasai, Masu. Okinasai, neh. *(casually)* The bank man, maybe he will give us more time to pay back the loan . . .

MASU: "Pay back croptime" . . . "pay back croptime!" The crops are in. Everybody gets paid back.

KIMIKO: But, Masu, there will be nothing left over. Chieko needs shoes for school. If she has to wear Tadao's old work shoes again . . . you know what a fuss she made last year. I promised.

MASU: How much did you make from the people who drive by?

KIMIKO: Eighty dollars.

MASU: You have enough!

KIMIKO: Until next year?

MASU: Pay everyone back! Pay for everything you buy today. Next week, we start again. "Pay back croptime." "Pay back croptime."

KIMIKO: Tadao needs a new pair of pants for school—corduroy—from store. He needs money for school and

MASU: (*shoving it aside*) Aaah! I've got work to do.

Masu jumps out of bed, goes into the kitchen, grabs an egg, cracks it over his rice and eats breakfast. Kimiko is trying to decide whether to approach him again. In the time she decides and enters kitchen area, Masu leaves. Lights fade and rise on front porch—dinnertime—same day. Masu entering house, turns and seek Kimiko, Chieko, and Tanaka returning from shopping.

MASU: Hoh! Tane, you're just in time for some sake before supper.

CHIEKO: (*running up*) Papa, see all the good stuff we bought . . .

KIMIKO: (*cutting in*) Atokara . . .

Kimiko skirts direct confrontation with Masu, carrying in some purchases, shooing Chieko into the house. Tanaka comes onto steps carrying groceries and a visible bolt of cloth.

MASU: (*putting down melons*) Sonnofabitch! What have you got there?

He eyes the bolt of cloth elaborately.

TANAKA: (*embarrassed, trying to change the subject*) Melons! This late?

MASU: Found them . . . clearing the field. Still good.

His good humor at seeing Tanaka disappears as he continues to eye the cloth.

What's new in town?

TANAKA: It gets chillier every year. Let's go inside. (*opening door for Masu*) I didn't mean to bother your dinner. How are they? We could sell some at the store?

The two men enter house.

MASU: Kimi! Get Tanaka sake!

Kimiko gets the sake cups and pitcher and gets the bottle from the corner. Masu goes to the sink to wash up. Tanaka gives Kimiko the cloth. Kimiko, a quick look at Masu, takes the cloth into the bedroom. She returns, fills porcelain pitcher with sake and heats it in a pan of hot water on stove top. Masu, washing, takes large handfuls of water from the tap and splashes his face and arms. He makes smacking sounds with his hands against his face and body.

CHIEKO: Papa, look at my new shoes—Mary Janes!

Kimiko tries to shut up Chieko with gestures. Masu grabs a towel hanging from a nail, and goes into the bedroom to change his shirt. Tanaka and Kimiko exchange glances as Masu enters bedroom.

KIMIKO: *Sa!* Sit down, Tanaka-san. Make yourself comfortable.

Kimiko takes pitcher of sake from pan and pours some sake into the cup beside Tanaka. She leaves the pitcher by his cup. Masu comes out from the bedroom in zori slippers and a fresh change. He sits down across from Tanaka, slapping his thighs as he does. He takes the pitcher and pours himself a drink, raises his cup, "kampai" and drinks. Then he pours another cup and settles into his seat, ready for a chat. He offers Tanaka another cupful.

TANAKA: (*refusing by putting his hand in front of the sake cup*) No, no more—just one to warm up . . . have to get back for dinner too.

MASU: (*laughing*) Tanaka-san, you come here, you ask how are the crops . . . you have one sake and now you are leaving. For a visit, it's too short. If it is business, it hasn't been stated.

TANAKA: You know, Setsuko. I must get going.

MASU: Besides that, you forgot your bundle. Your large parcel. Kimi, get Tanaka-san his parcel.

KIMIKO: (*preparing dinner, stiffens*) Masu, I paid for it.

MASU: (*knowing she's lying*) Kimi, get Tanaka-san his parcel.

TANAKA: Tanaka-san, Tanaka-san, we are not strangers, Masu.

KIMIKO: Masu, think about the children.

MASU: Kimi . . .

Masu ignores her and goes to get the cloth.

KIMIKO: Masu, please . . .

TANAKA: Masu, listen, don't be stupid. This has got nothing to do with pride. Do you hear—nothing.

Masu hands him the bolt. Tanaka won't take it.

KIMIKO: (*disgusted and angry*) Your pride, your pride. Is that all there is?

Masu goes to door, exits onto porch and slams the bolt across the porch rail and walks away. Tanaka exits to porch. He sighs like a man who has witnessed this scene too often to expect any different and yet is always expecting a change to occur. Kimiko comes onto porch and takes the cloth in with her. Masu watches her.

MASU: Why does she have to do it like this?

TANAKA: You're too stubborn, a stupid mule.

MASU: Sometimes I want to put a blanket over my shoulders and move on again.

Tanaka offers Masu a cigarette. Masu takes one, hunkers down, they light up.

TANAKA: What else could she do?

MASU: Was I asking you?

TANAKA: Don't talk so loud within my hearing!

Tanaka joins him and the two continue to smoke. Tanaka gets out his case and offers Masu another. He refuses. Tanaka looks for an opening.

If you were just a little bit more sensible, Masu. You know you have credit with me.

MASU: Still? Is that so? I still do?

TANAKA: Masu . . .

MASU: (*jumping up*) To pay you off, all I need is a rainbow, stretching from waaay over there . . . to right here. And I will need that rainbow five years running.

TANAKA: You exaggerate. It's not your fault the crops brought in so little, but it's not Kimiko's either—not the children's. Why should they suffer?

MASU: You are "sensible," Tane.

TANAKA: (*bitterness creeping into his voice*) Listen, *bozu-san*, in Japan, we would not be friends, true? But this is America, Masu. You don't owe me. Take the cloth.

MASU: (*uncomfortable . . . rises, slaps his thighs.*) All right! Next year, you will have the best vegetables in the valley. Come warm up before you go.

TANAKA: No, the wife.

They walk to porch.

MASU: (*indicating missing bolt of cloth*) Kimi is a practical woman.

TANAKA: Then listen to her sometimes.

MASU: (*laughing*) I can't. Life is sad enough.

The men say goodbye. Tanaka exits. Masu lingers on the porch and enters house. Kimiko looks up sharply at Masu's entry.

KIMIKO: Chieko . . . dinnertime!

MASU: Tadao. Tadao!

KIMIKO: He's not home yet. He said he was going to play foo-to-bal-lu.

MASU: Foo-to-bal-lu? What is that?

Chieko enters with book and goes to Masu, climbs on his lap, wanting him to read to her. He attacks the book warily, trying to read but he can't—the book is in English. Tadao enters, carrying school books.

MASU: You're late for dinner!

TADAO: Sorry.

Tadao takes his seat at the table, relaxed.

MASU: Playing footobalu?

TADAO: (*looking swiftly at Kimiko*) Huh, yeah.

Kimiko keeps dishing out food.

MASU: What is foo-to-bal-lu?

CHIEKO: (*unmindful of others*) Papa, read to me after dinner? Okey-dokey?

MASU: Your brother will read to you. (*to Tadao*) What is foo-to-bal-lu?

TADAO: (*full of himself but apprehensive*) Well there's eleven guys on each side, and. It's a game where you . . .

MASU: (*gesturing*) With a footo and a balu?

TADAO: (*laughing but upset*) Yeah, Papa, with a foot and a ball.

Masu uncertain now. Fact? Jest? Putdown? He does not know what football is, so he shrugs it off and grunts. He begins eating. He wolfs down rice. Chieko begins to copy him and gets gentle reprimand from Kimiko. Kimiko clears the table. Chieko renews her attempt to get her father to read to her. His embarrassment is getting him angry. He sends her away. She sits on the chair and tries to read the book. Tadao helps to clear table.

TADAO: (*to Kimi*) The shoes cost more than you gave me.

Kimi indicating Tadao should ask father. Tadao refuses. Kimi goes to bedroom and gets her purse. She returns. Masu is reading Japanese papers and drinking sake.

TADAO: He won't let me work off the shoes, Mama.

KIMIKO: Talk to Papa.

TADAO: He won't understand.

KIMIKO: You do it. Take this blank check.

She presses blank check and bank note on Tadao and leaves. Tadao is angry but he goes to the table and sits down, clears his throat. Masu looks up.

TADAO: (*placing in front of Masu the note, then check*) You have to sign these. Fertilizer and stuff and this . . .

Masu responds with grunts, expressions, then takes the check, looks at it.

MASU: For what?

TADAO: I need some money for school stuff.

MASU: (*cutting in*) How much?

TADAO: It won't be much, Papa.

MASU: *So-ca*? How much?

TADAO: I put some money down on some football shoes.

MASU: (*tired of hearing about football*) Foo-to-bal-lu shoes?

TADAO: All the guys have them.

MASU: (*getting angry*) You need special shoes for a game? For this foot-to-bal-lu? Make your own!

TADAO: You can't do that . . . I never got the bike . . .

MASU: (*waves it off abruptly*) We have food . . . we have a house . . . we have clothes because of Tanaka . . . but no money.

Chieko comes up to Masu, disgusted.

CHIEKO: I can't read this!

TADAO: (*low but determined*) I want those shoes, Papa.

Masu hears but doesn't respond. He indicates to Tadao to read the book, takes the note and signs it, but leaves the check unsigned on table. Tadao notices this, and in anger goes to bedroom. Chieko takes book and follows, pushing it on Tadao. Kimiko enters and sets up table to cut material from homemade patterns made out of newspaper. Masu moves to soft chair.

TADAO: (*from behind the curtain reading "The Boy Who Drew Cats"*) That night, he goes to this haunted house, on a dare . . . and even though he tries to be brave, he's scared.

CHIEKO: *She's* scared. When Mama reads me the story, the little boy is a little girl like me.

TADAO: Who's reading this story, anyway?

CHIEKO: You are, maddy-cat!

TADAO: All right. He tries to sleep but he can't sleep, thinking about the evil rat. He finds a corner, and he gets his blanket and mat, and tries to go to sleep again.

KIMIKO: (*cutting material around pattern she's made*) I can make you a shirt. You could use a new shirt for *Kenjinkai* and *Senryu*.

Masu does not respond.

KIMIKO: (*trying a new approach*) It's left-over material, you know. Put a curtain on the window. That will be nice. Then you could move the cloth aside and look at the sky.

MASU: (*turning to newspaper*) I can see the sky without a curtain. The emperor and his warlords are at it again.

KIMIKO: Don't tell me. I don't want to hear about such horrible things.

MASU: Why not? Don't you have a samurai up your family tree somewhere?

KIMIKO: Don't talk so vulgar.

MASU: Look around here: farmers, fishermen, peasants. That's what we were! That's what we are! Still we crawl around, sniff at holes. Hoh, Samurai! *Doko desuka! Bushido* was never ours! Son-ofabitchcocksaccas.

KIMIKO: Masu!

MASU: All right, all right. Shimizu had trouble in town?

KIMIKO: Haruko-san was so afraid. Said the men were drunk.

MASU: Shimizu is always a samurai when he's drunk.

KIMIKO: (*taking up some mending*) Tadao wants those football shoes so much, Masu.

MASU: You don't let up, do you?

KIMIKO: Beginning spring I will be out there all day with you. We'll have more money. A good year is due. I can do it.

MASU: That's no good, you keep losing babies on me that way.

Kimiko falls silent and becomes very still. Masu, rising, tries to placate her.

You're not as strong as you look. Come on, let's go to bed.

KIMIKO: (*continues darning the sock*) You go. I have things to finish up.

MASU: Leave it. Let's go to bed.

KIMIKO: (*flaring up*) This isn't Japan! This is America! When are you going to understand that!

MASU: (*mimicking*) This isn't Japan. This is America! I know. I know! What do you want, *obahan*? You want me to go around with a wooden bowl? Would that make me more American? Tanaka's a friend. What friend makes you feel like a beggar? What friend? Your son is ashamed of me. You make him ashamed of me, and me, I make him hate me. I would rather have that!

KIMIKO: (*rising abruptly, upsetting her darning*) Let's go to bed. Come on, let's go!

Masu waves her away. Kimiko goes to the sink and begins sorting the dishes to be washed. She is still angry. Tadao enters. He has on a light jacket. He's going out.

KIMIKO: (*sharp, transferring anger to son*) Where are you going?

TADAO: Out.

KIMIKO: (*frightened re: Shimizu*) It's too late . . . go study.

TADAO: (*exiting through door*) I finished.

Kimiko looking to Masu to stop Tadao.

MASU: This is America.

KIMIKO: Let's go to bed.

Kimiko goes into bedroom, Masu following. Tadao, on porch, takes out a cigarette from a hiding place, lights it and continues to exit offstage. Lights fade to black and rise on:

Pearl Harbor Interim—Roosevelt's declaration of war re: the attack on Pearl Harbor.

Lights fade up on the Murakami home. Kimiko is busy trying to get ready for party. Chieko enters with Masu dragging in an evergreen.

CHIEKO: (*excited*) Papa got three trees, but this is the best one, huh, Papa?

TADAO: (*entering from bedroom, dressed in white shirt, tie*) What's the others for?

MASU: For our cheap friends.

Tadao helps set up the tree in the stand. Masu is happy.

CHIEKO: (*pestering*) Now, Mama, now. Let's decorate now. Please, pop the popcorn.

KIMIKO: Later, after the party.

CHIEKO: Aw, Mama, please.

Kimiko relents and begins popping corn, shaking pan so as not to burn the corn.

CHIEKO: You take so long!

KIMIKO: (*indicating popcorn and cranberry strings already made*) So impatient. Start putting those on the tree.

CHIEKO: Help me, Taddie! Don't be a maddy cat.

Tadao and Chieko begin decorating tree but Tadao is also too slow for Chieko; she runs back to Kimiko, urging her to be faster.

KIMIKO: Stop that, pes-ky child, and don't eat "popu cornu," string it. (*as Masu grabs her, being playful*) Masu, you're going to change your clothes, neh?

MASU: No! Don't I look good enough?

KIMIKO: (*as Masu lifts her off ground*) Stop it, stop it, Masu. What will the children think?

MASU: They will think their mama and papa did have a reason to get married, hey, Kimi?

He releases her, but is still playful. For the first time, some of her softness and gayness shows.

CHIEKO: (*to Tadao who is decorating the tree*) You okey-dokey, Taddie?

TADAO: Just string the popcorn.

Chieko sits and strings popcorn and cranberries, every so often sneaking popcorn into her mouth. Masu and Kimiko help decorate.

KIMIKO: Why did you get so many trees? What are they for?

MASU: (*expansive, mimicking*) One's for Tane. He likes the whole idea, but he needs an excuse. The other's for Jiro Yamada, that *kechinbo.* I saw him on the way to the pass, and I offered him a ride. I thought he might want to get a tree too. He gets on his high tone. "I'm Buddhist. I don't observe 'Cu-rissu-chan' holidays!" he says. That man, Kimi, didn't even know he was Buddhist until he came to this country. "I'm surprised, shocked at you, Murakami-san!" he says, "you, who almost became a Buddhist monk." "Ya-mada-san," I say, "only a real Buddhist could appreciate 'Cu-ri-ma-su' as I do." Kimi, what do you think? I take a tree to him, present it with a short lecture about Buddhist acceptance, and give him the hand of Buddha!

KIMIKO: (*laughing*) Oh Masu, no. You can't do that. That would be terrible.

MASU: Why not? The sonofabitchcocksacca.

CHIEKO: Papa, Taddie says to put up the star.

MASU: *Atokara.*

CHIEKO: (*shoving tin star into his hand*) Aw, papa.

KIMIKO: (*helping him onto chair*) Come on, *jichan,* put up the star.

Masu, still expansive, clowning, gets on a chair, puts up the star, and gets down.

MASU: (*surveying tree and getting sake and cup*) Bi-u-ti-ful!

He starts to go outside, gestures to Tadao to go join him.

Tadao!

CHIEKO: Where are you going?

Tadao indicates it's none of her business. Masu indicates they are going outside.

Don't forget to tell Santa Claus I want a Shirley Temple doll, Papa.

MASU: *So-ca?*

Kimiko shushes Chieko and she continues to decorate tree with Chieko while Masu and Tadao exit to porch.

MASU: About Mama's present.

TADAO: Can I have some, Papa?

MASU: Sure, sure.

He fills his own cup and gives it to Tadao. He laughs nervously. He is not quite sure how to handle this situation.

MASU: Women with women—men with men. About Mama's present, sa, Tane will bring the "gasu." *Atokara*, you go and turn on the fire and . . .

TADAO: (*breaking in*) Okay, Papa, can we talk?

MASU: (sitting) Sure.

TADAO: Papa, I've been thinking . . .

TANAKA: (*off stage*) Masu! Hop-pi Cu-ris-su-ma-su!

MASU: (*standing to greet Tanaka*) Hoh, Tane . . . Hop-pi Cu-ris-su-ma-su! (*to Tadao*) Later.

Tanaka, Setsuko, and Hiroshi enter. They are carrying presents and food. Ad lib greetings, bowing, etc.

MASU: (*giving Tanaka a cup of sake*) This Hiroshi? Big . . . nineteen?

TADAO: Hi Hiro, how you been?

Hiroshi, stiff, nods brusquely.

MASU: (*alerting family*) Mama! Chieko! (*to Tanakas*) Come in, come in!

All entering. Setsuko and Kimiko exchange greetings. Setsuko puts down food wrapped in furoshiki and pulls out Christmas-wrapped gifts from a bag.

CHIEKO: Oh goodie, presents.

KIMIKO: Hush!

SETSUKO: Nothing really, but children should have some presents.

KIMIKO: Always so very kind.

CHIEKO: (*shaking one gift*) What's in here?

KIMIKO: Never mind—put them under the tree.

Everyone being good hosts or good guests. Hiroshi takes sake offered him by Masu but moves away from group.

MASU: (*to Tanaka*) Four years, sa, a long time . . . a boy can change in four years.

SETSUKO: Not Hiroshi. What do you think we sent him back for? Not just to be high tone. Good thing, too. Stay around here, just become another dirt farmer (*cutting herself off*) Anyway, no monkey business for him over there. American children: No respect, no self-control, flighty . . . head in the clouds. Kimiko-san, you understand, neh?

KIMIKO: (*all graciousness*) Maybe too much radio, *neh*. Hiroshi's turned into a handsome young man. Everything all right now?

SETSUKO: Fine. I told those FBI, I'm American born. Before you close us down, go close that dimestore across the street too. Germans own it. They closed us for a week anyway. I don't care.

KIMIKO: You were very bold.

SETSUKO: (*with a who-needs-them attitude*) Some wholesalers won't sell to us anymore. Hiroshi is a good son and once we find him a sensible wife . . .

Kimi demurs and begins setting out dishes of food.

SETSUKO: (*helping Kimiko*) You still using these old cups? Why don't you write home and have them send you some new ones.

KIMIKO: They're special to me. They were my mother's. I thought this Christmas should be extra special.

SETSUKO: (*not so much snide as tactless*) Don't look special to me. Are you still working on the embroidery? If you need more thread, we have it. We can't sell it anyway now.

KIMIKO: (*distaste covered*) No . . . I don't need it, but thank you, *neh*.

TANAKA: (*shuffling Hana cards*) Masu, what do you think? Will Japan advance this far? Pearl Harbor is Pearl Harbor . . . they make it very hard on us.

TANAKA: (*re: Hiroshi*) He says the bombing was in retaliation for the embargoes.

HIROSHI: (*an observer of this holiday scene*) Last year scrap steel . . . before that, oil. Japan is slowly being starved to death. The United States is jealous of Japan. I told the dumb FBI . . .

TANAKA: (*cutting in*) Idiot! It took all my talking to make them understand he's a stupid, hot-headed boy.

MASU: What did he say?

TANAKA: Nothing! Just acting arrogant with them, that's all.

Hiroshi is visibly annoyed.

MASU: (*tasting dishes, showing great relish, kidding with women*) Not bad, not bad.

SETSUKO: What do you mean, not bad!

MASU: I don't see what I want.

SETSUKO: And what is that?

MASU: (*improvises lewd, sexual remark in Japanese*)

SETSUKO: (*in Japanese*) Oh, you bad boy!

TANAKA: (*trying to get Hana game started*) Come on, sit down. Hiroshi!

HIROSHI: (*coming to table*) It had to be the embargoes. Japan was slowly being starved to death.

MASU: (*lacking solemnness*) Sa! Certain death to possible starvation?

HIROSHI: The Imperial Way cannot be defeated. It is the only way! Still, I wasn't prepared for Pearl Harbor. I believe Pearl Harbor was Japan's way of letting America know that she must be respected. What are these white countries screaming about anyway? We, I mean, Japan, does in Asia only what white people do all over the world. Asia belongs to yellow people. The bitter struggle is with China. Who will lead the yellow people of Asia?

TANAKA: (*dealing out cards*) Shut up, you young fool. War is no game!

MASU: (*looking at his cards*) Asia belongs to yellow people, or yellow rulers?

HIROSHI: Japan's rulers think only of their people.

MASU: That is what the ruling class always say. Who starts?

HIROSHI: Are you questioning the sincerity of the Japanese government?

MASU: Questioning? No, all governments lie.

SETSUKO: Masu, you're Japanese, don't forget.

TANAKA: (*beginning play*) I'll start.

HIROSHI: How can you be so blinded. Look what they do to us—arrest us with no reason. I'm an American citizen but . . .

MASU: (*cutting in*) To think, Tane, you sent him over there to be educated—curious the process of education.

TANAKA: (*shrugs off, and slaps down card*)

SETSUKO: He went to one of the best common schools in Tokyo.

MASU: I'm sure he did.

SETSUKO: They produce more leaders . . .

MASU: (*cutting in*) I'm sure they do. (*to Hiroshi*) One minute you are for Japan and, then, you are an outraged American.

HIROSHI: You, Murakami-san, you don't get angry?

MASU: I'm always angry—that's why it never shows.

TANAKA: (*to Hiroshi*) Your turn. Play!

HIROSHI: (*catching card*) Philosophical thoughts are useless at a time like this.

MASU: (*slapping down and catching card*) And war is useful? Yes, I suppose it is useful. Forget what your teachers have taught you—what do you feel?

HIROSHI: (*struggling with real feelings*) I'm disillusioned with this country . . . I feel we have no future here.

MASU: You may be right.

HIROSHI: (*finding rote words*) Manchuria is important to Japan. We are entitled to our territorial integrity. China must not swallow us up.

MASU: (*beginning to take Hiroshi seriously*) Territorial integrity . . . who taught you such clever words?

HIROSHI: Murakami-san, you question integrity for yellow people?

MASU: No, but what has integrity to do with the rape of China?

HIROSHI: (*used to rote answers*) The Chinese will smother us to death. They are worthless swine anyway.

MASU: (*no longer any hint of joking*) Then we must be worthless swine, too. They have been our teachers for centuries.

HIROSHI: (*outraged and puzzled*) The Chinese?

MASU: Yes, the Chinese. You have no doubts about the Imperial Way?

HIROSHI: (*indicating parents*) Of course not. I wanted to stay on but they forced me to come back here. But I'll get back.

TANAKA: (*cutting in*) *Bakatare.* Don't talk idiot-talk!

Hiroshi leaves table.

TANAKA: (*angry*) All the time talking about things we can't control. Setsuko, come play!

TADAO: (*approaching Hiroshi*) What's Japan like?

HIROSHI: The Imperial Way, how can I explain it? You know what is happening? Them—they don't understand.

Setsuko is too busy to play. Tanaka throws his cards in, disgusted. Masu pours him another sake.

MASU: Drink up.

HIROSHI: (*indicating Masu and Tanaka*) They are simple men, behind the times. Japan was fated to rule Asia.

TADAO: Yeah, sure, but if a guy went to Tokyo, what would it be like for him? What do you do at school?

HIROSHI: We have drills and economics, history. I am fluent in Japanese now. You grow up to be a man fast.

TADAO: That sounds okay! Do they teach you how to fly? I'm interested in airplanes—the Messerschmitt, the Zero, the Grumman Wildcat, the Spitfire—I got drawings of them all—I can recognize them too.

TANAKA: What do you think, Masu, could he be right? Why do the FBI pick on me? I love this country.

MASU: Who knows? The sonofabitchcocksaccas are full of themselves. *Kuso de ippai.*

TANAKA: These are serious times.

MASU: I won't deny that, Tane.

MASU: (*turning to Hiroshi*) Such confidence in the Imperial Way. You would join the Imperial Army?

HIROSHI: Of course. If they'd have me.

TANAKA: (*cutting in*) *Nani? Bakamono neh? Nan ya yutterun no?*

MASU: If he wants to, he will . . .

TANAKA: Stupid wild talk! He will not go back!

MASU: How will you stop him?

TANAKA: I am his father! (*under*) Don't encourage him.

MASU: (*tiring of the subject*) Come on, we have business. Tadao, give Hiroshi more sake. Anyone so certain he is a man needs more sake.

Masu indicates to Kimi he's going out for a smoke. In house, the party continues with ad lib conversations, re airplanes, food, etc. Masu and Tanaka move to off stage truck and return with Kimi's present as lights rise on bath house. Tanaka and Masu struggle to set gas heater under tub, placing tanks of gas and air. They stop, survey their work. Tanaka lights a cigarette.

TANAKA: Turn that handle there.

MASU: Is this all there is to it? I could make one myself.

TANAKA: Quit complaining.

Masu lights a match, warily tries to light the burner. The flames flare up and make him rear back. Tanaka offers Masu a cigarette.

MASU: (*accepts and lights it off the burner*) You think she will be happy with a present like this?

TANAKA: What a question! Of course. No pumping. No lugging pails.

MASU: I don't know. If I were a woman . . .

TANAKA: (*cutting in*) Take my word.

MASU: Still, not very pretty. A fine piece of silk for a dress. She might like that better.

TANAKA: What does she need silk for?

MASU: True, this costs more in the long run. Having to buy gas and air. Think of that! Buying air!

TANAKA: Take my word, it will make her very happy.

MASU: Hah, you're right. If you say so, you're right. You two understand each other much better than I do. You should have married her.

TANAKA: Don't talk stupid!

MASU: She would be much happier.

TANAKA: I have a wife.

MASU: (*teasing*) We will trade. How about that? Would you like that?

TANAKA: Maybe it was a foolish expense at a time like this.

MASU: *Hoh*? What do you mean?

TANAKA: Only that the future is uncertain. When the FBI questioned me, I told them I trusted Uncle Sam but they didn't believe me.

MASU: That was a bad night?

TANAKA: They were so well-prepared . . . picked us up that very Sunday. I never thanked you for looking after Setsuko.

MASU: Forget it.

TANAKA: They said Hiroshi came back from Japan to spy. I explain and explain: I personally love America but still want my son to have a good Japanese education. They let us go but they didn't believe me. I hear in the cities, they keep you in jail.

MASU: (*back to burner*) So ca? Think of it . . . fast hot water. Not so solemn, Tane, it's cu-ri-su-ma-su. Don't let them stop you from living. *Hoh*, I have a present for you.

TANAKA: So?

Masu goes offstage, Tanaka following as lights fade in bath house, rise on house, Kimiko and Setsuko moving toward door.

KIMIKO: Oh and, again, thank you for the *han-pan*, the *mochi-gashi*, the smoked salmon. All such delicacies. Masu will enjoy them so much.

SETSUKO: Nothing, it means so little to us, but . . .

KIMIKO: (*finishing train of thought*) The children will be so happy.

SETSUKO: (*re: popcorn balls*) What are these called again?

KIMIKO: "Pop-pu-cor-nu-ball-tsu." Chieko wanted to make them. And thank you again for . . .

SETSUKO: (*cutting in*) So pretty and cheap to make. Oh it's nothing, nothing.

Masu and Tanaka enter. Masu has tree in hand.

MASU: Such a formal man you are, Tane. Do you know something, you only laugh when you are embarrassed or apologizing for something.

The boys come out. The women are on the porch.

No time to get you drunk.

Masu stands up tree and presents it to Tanaka, formally.

Hop-pi Curisumasu, Tane!

TANAKA: (*visibly touched*) Yes . . . Hop-pi Curisumasu to you. Make sure to come for New Year. The best Japanese food anywhere.

Tanaka hands the tree to Hiroshi.

KIMIKO: *Domo arigato gozaimasu. O-tsukai sama desu.*

Goodbyes again. Tanakas exit. Family goes into house.

CHIEKO: They're gone, they're gone—goody!

KIMIKO: Chiecha, mustn't say such things.

CHIEKO: Come on Taddie, let's eat the *mochi*!

KIMIKO: Not tonight . . .

MASU: (*surveying tree*) Let her. A fine tree, a fine tree!

CHIEKO: (*at tree, picking up a big present*) Taddie, do you think this is big enough for a Shirley Temple doll?

KIMIKO: Santa Claus hasn't come yet.

MASU: Tadao, what do you think? Should we take a Cu-ri-su-ma-su bath?

TADAO: Yeah, come on, Mom, let's take a bath.

KIMIKO: Tomorrow, neh?

MASU: You and me, Chie-po. We'll take a bath then.

Masu and Chieko prepare for bath. Kimiko is cleaning up.

KIMIKO: It will take all night. You should have told me sooner. There is no water, nothing.

TADAO: Papa and me will do the work.

KIMIKO: All right! It will be a cold bath! It will take all night to heat the water.

TADAO: No, it won't. I'll do it.

Tadao exits. Masu begins to dance, showing Chieko as they move. Chieko tries but becomes impatient and wants to be swung instead.

CHIEKO: No, no, on your shoulders Papa . . . on your shoulders . . .

Masu grimaces, acts like a weary old man and swings Chieko on his shoulders and does a slow bon odori. She does not like it.

No, no, run—run, Papa!

Masu gives her a mock disgusted look and she laughs. Masu switches dance to horse, back to dance.

Faster . . . faster . . .

Kimiko enters anywhere in this sequence. She is dressed in a yukata, has a towel hanging from her neck, and carries a bar of soap. She begins to follow in the dance. Tadeo comes back in zori and pants, carrying Masu's change. They slip winter jackets over their shoulders as they exit to bath. Lights fade and rise on bath house.

Actors are nude and in place in an old wooden Japanese-style tub with an aluminum corrugated roof siding. Kimiko slowly sinks in, Tadao climbing in, until they are in tub. Masu standing in bath, holding Chieko who is resisting.

CHIEKO: It's too hot, papa!

TADAO: Japanese baths are supposed to be too hot, dummy.

CHIEKO: Dummy you too.

MASU: (*putting Chieko on edge and slipping in tub himself*) Enough!

KIMIKO: What a fine present, Masu. A hot bath makes everything better, neh?

TADAO: Mama is a good faker.

MASU: You knew?

TADAO: She always knows. When did you find out?

KIMIKO: (*playful and teasing*) I didn't know for certain. Just like when Tanaka-san and Papa smoke . . .

Kimiko showing the way Masu smokes.

Men always think we women are fooled! But . . . that's our secret, *neh* Chiechan? Besides, when the two of you conspire, everyone knows!

CHIEKO: Papa, it's too hot!

KIMIKO: This is wonderful . . . wonderful.

TADAO: Japanese always take hot baths, right Papa?

MASU: (*grunts in agreement, to Tadao*)

He grabs Chieko and dumps her quickly in and out of tub's hot water, she screaming.

You are Japanese, Chieko.

Lights fade down and up—short time passing. Everyone languid. Masu drinking sake.

MASU: Time to scrub!

Chieko protests as Masu lifts her out of tub and soaps her down with Japanese hitchime. She wants to get back into tub now and Masu follows her. He then sinks deeper into water and putting towel on his head, stretches out and starts singing a Japanese tune. He begins to flirt with Kimiko. She responds to him. He scoots deeper into the water and pinches her. She jumps and yelps.

KIMIKO: Masu, the children!

MASU: It's Cu-risu-masu . . . Kimi . . . for your own Je-su-us Cu-ri-su-to sake, let them see us happy.

Lights fade slowly and rise slowly as family gets out of tub, dresses, and comes back to house.

KIMIKO: *Sa*, time to go to sleep, Chiechan.

CHIEKO: I don't want to go to sleep.

KIMIKO: Chiechan . . .

CHIEKO: I don't want to. Why does Taddie get to stay up?

TADAO: Go on, po-head.

CHIEKO: Papa, I don't want to . . .

KIMIKO: (*cut in*) Now be good or Santa Claus won't bring you anything.

MASU: Don't say that. So, po-po, you don't want to go to sleep?

CHIEKO: (*delaying bedtime*) Sing my song, Papa, I'll help you.

MASU: Will you go to sleep then?

CHIEKO: Maybe . . .

Masu sings the song, "Chie, Chie, po, po, Chie, po po, suzume no gakko, sensei wa," etc. getting faster toward the end.

MASU: Now, will you go to sleep?

CHIEKO: (*taking Masu's hand*) You come with me.

MASU: You're a big girl. Mama will sleep with you.

CHIEKO: I don't want her. I want you.

MASU: Chie.

CHIEKO: I hate you, Papa.

KIMIKO: Chiechan. Mustn't say such things.

CHIEKO: Taddie said so. I can too. Taddie says you're a dirty Jap.

Masu looks at Tadao. Tadao glares at Chieko and exits. Chieko does not understand what she has said and is surprised at how serious everyone has gotten. She knows she did something bad. Masu takes her in his arms again.

MASU: Chie-po, wasn't it nice today?

CHIEKO: (*agrees*)

MASU: Don't you wish this nice day could go on and on into tomorrow and tomorrow night?

CHIEKO: (*agrees*)

MASU: Then you have to do your part. You have to sleep. Will you?

CHIEKO: Yes, Papa. (*Chieko gets up to go, returns to Masu.*) Papa, good night.

MASU: Good night, Chie-po.

Chieko goes with Kimiko to bed. Masu gets sake, grabs jacket and goes out. He opens door to find Tadao sitting on porch. He stands, considering his son.

TADAO: She's lying, Papa.

MASU: Is that so? You didn't say that? Sure you didn't.

Masu takes a drink. Offers some to Tadao. Tadao refuses.

The years go by so fast. I don't feel any different, but you . . . sometimes, I forget, you are not a boy anymore. I enjoyed myself this morning—when we filled the tub. You did most of the work.

TADAO: Mama got a bang out of it.

MASU: (*continuing his train of thought*) And I realized that the reason I was enjoying myself so much was that we haven't been like that for a long time. Years, I guess. That's strange, Tadao, to think, years.

TADAO: Papa . . . do you ever think about going back to Japan?

MASU: No . . . why?

TADAO: Nothing, doesn't matter.

MASU: Tell me.

TADAO: I hate it here.

MASU: Hiroshi has impressed you.

TADAO: You think you know so much, Papa.

MASU: I wasn't making light of what you said. It's getting worse at school?

TADAO: It's rough in town, at school, everywhere, but that's not it, Papa. Hiroshi just makes sense to me. We weren't . . . you weren't poor in Japan, were you?

MASU: *Sa* . . .

TADAO: Mama says you come from a good family . . . that you were going to be a priest . . . a Buddhist monk. Why did you come here?

MASU: You have grown up . . . right here, in this house and I didn't even notice it. I was the black sheep of my family. Everyone who comes here is the black sheep of their family . . . their class . . . their country. They were not wanted where they were. Strange, the only people who are not black sheep are black people.

TADAO: (*annoyed his father is getting off point*) Papa!

MASU: It's true. Before I married your mama, I worked on a ship. I worked with some black men, and they told me. Their fathers didn't want to come here. Slave traders brought them.

TADAO: Papa! I'm not interested in niggers! Not now!

MASU: (*dealing with a new word*) "Ni-gas?"

TADAO: Black men.

MASU: *So ca* . . . is that it?

TADAO: What?

MASU: On the boat, sometimes, I hear white men say "nigas," but I didn't understand. You say it, now, I understand!

TADAO: (*frustrated*) Papa, sometimes you act like—like you came from Mars—like you don't know anything!

MASU: (*cutting in*) I know well enough! I know enough. How do you know, Tadao? There are no black men around here. We are all "ni-gas." Everyone here! Tanaka-san and men like him came here because men like my father, my brothers, said: "You don't want to starve? Go somewhere else then, but don't bother us! So Tanaka came here and he stopped starving but he can't forget—he can't forget he was a "ni-ga" in Japan and he wants to forget. He wants to forget very bad. So he does to other men what my father and brothers did to him. He thinks that will stop making him a "ni-ga," but that won't do it!

TADAO: If we go back to Japan, it'll be better. Papa, you never think about other people's feelings. If you loved Mama . . .

MASU: (*cutting in*) I don't know, Tadao. Your mama is a good mother, not much of a wife—but a good mother. She's had a lot to bear. Sometimes she is so good, so fine, but most of the time it is hard to find the woman in her. You smoke? (*Tadao indicates no.*) Neither do I. You are right, Tadao. In Japan, I would have been a different man. I might not have married. And you . . . you wouldn't be here to worry about such things. I'd be a good man, but no husband at all. Here the problems are different.

Masu moves around, debating with himself.

(*decided*) I wanted to be a monk. When I was fourteen, I entered under a master. When I was seventeen, I decided I didn't want to be a monk, and I was sent to Hawaii to stay with an uncle. My uncle was like my father so, when I could, I came here. I worked as a lumberjack. Then I worked the fishing boats . . . up the Columbia River. The salmon jump. They jump high! They leap like the soft arch of a rainbow. They glisten but their color does not disturb the eye. At the lower reaches of the river, where the spawning salmon begin their struggle upstream, they are lovely and full of wonder. They are not weary yet, not desperate to be born again. Their time is still immense and boundless . . .

TADAO: It's different now. It's not just the white trash. It's every-body.

MASU: (*pulling out his watch*) You like this watch? One day, I'll give it to you. You like it?

135

Momoko

Iko

TADAO: Yeah. Was it your father's?

MASU: (*laughing*) No, I bought it in a pawnshop, off the wharf in Seattle. It's pure gold . . . see, pure gold. When you were six, Mama took you back to Japan, you remember?

TADAO: Sort of. I think I liked it there.

MASU: Because it was different.

TADAO: Why stay where you're not wanted.

MASU: Do you know why I stayed here? I was freer. I could see what it was like to be a lumberjack, a fisherman, and anything else that came my way. Try it out and forget it. Put a blanket on my shoulder and go where I wanted. This land was wide and boundless once. Every act still had no name, and every piece of land and sky was not spoken for. It's different for you. You were born here, and so, when other people tell you that you don't belong, it must hurt. That didn't hurt me. I knew I didn't come from this land. I knew what I came from. It can't be helped. We were born, Tadao, to different times, so our lives are different, must be different, if we are to survive.

TADAO: I want to go back, Papa, I hate it here.

MASU: It will be hard in Japan.

TADAO: (*cutting in*) Hiro's going back! He says the war will be over in six months. He says we belong there!

MASU: (*considering the possibility*) Mama has relatives in Japan. You can be my present to my father. I could talk to Tane . . . he likes to see me in debt to him.

TADAO: Papa, let's try it. If it doesn't work, we'll come back here.

MASU: It's too bad you had to grow up so fast, Tadao. You're still very young.

TADAO: I understand a lot of stuff you don't.

MASU: So, Hiroshi says the war will end in six months . . . he sounds like the American generals, doesn't he? I must be getting old, Tadao. I want you to understand me. It's late. One more drink apiece.

Drinks, offers Tadao one, which Tadao accepts.

TADAO: You're going to talk to Mr. Tanaka then?

MASU: What? Yes . . . I will. But think this over, Tadao. Some decisions you can't go back on.

TADAO: I don't care about that. We belong there. When we all go back . . .

MASU: (*cutting in*) What? You, maybe you. Not me!

TADAO: But you said . . .

MASU: You wanted this man-to-man, now you have it. You, maybe Mama and Chie, you can go back, but not me. I can't go back! I can't go back.

Masu exits to packing house. Tadao goes into house. Lights fade and rise. Masu sits at kitchen table, his sumie brush and stone at hand and he writes in Japanese.

MASU: I am sorry about football shoes. Take this watch instead. In Japan, if you go, it will be more useful.

MASU: (*looking over his notes, says in Japanese the same thing*)

Masu places the watch and message under the tree, and exits. Tadao enters, has some handcrafted gifts. He notices the watch, checks back toward the bedroom, takes the watch and note, tries to read the Japanese by the tree light, moves to chair, tries to read the note as lights fade to black.

End of Act One.

During intermission, more war news and forties music.

ACT TWO

Time: Late spring, 1942
At entrance to church basement where there is a table/lectern in front and American flag. Chairs are set up for meeting. Setsuko Tanaka and Reverend Sugano wait for Masu.

SETSUKO: They put sugar in Shimizu's tractor—why does he have to go around saying: *Yat-ta-do! Yat-ta-do!*

Masu enters

REVEREND SUGANO: Stupid, plain stupid, talking out of turn.

SETSUKO: And they broke in Kagawa's tool shed.

TANAKA: *Chikisho!*

REVEREND SUGANO: Now, Tanaka-san, keep your head.

MASU: What did they say?

TANAKA: We have six days.

MASU: Six days . . . how? How are vegetables to be ripe, picked, crated, and sold in six days?

TANAKA: Other communities had two days . . .

MASU: Answer the question! Did you negotiate? I thought it was agreed; if we planted, we would harvest.

TANAKA: Masu, I tried. Some things can't be helped.

MASU: Don't say it, Tane!

TANAKA: It's been hard for all of us . . . you know that!

REVEREND SUGANO: It's not Tanaka-san's fault. The rules keep changing every day. No one is sure from day to day.

MASU: I heard that, General George Armstrong Custer! Military necessity! First it was evacuate, go inland. Then, no one can leave without army permission. We would be allowed to stay, work our farms, be protected from the scavengers. They're toying with our lives, Tane.

TANAKA: The reverend is right. We must go along.

REVEREND SUGANO: That's why we wanted to talk to you before the meeting. People listen to you.

MASU: (*ignoring Sugano*) Go along?

REVEREND SUGANO: Murakami-san, things are confused. Everything is terrible. These are bad times. His own son still wants to leave home, go back to Japan, join the Imperial Army. It is worse for you and the other farmers, but there must be someone to keep a level mind.

TANAKA: I'll store your equipment with my merchandise. The government has storage depots.

MASU: Store goods? Who will ever buy them? Mice? Listen to me, Tane . . . listen to one who is not sane, so level-minded. In insane times, listen to me.

REVEREND SUGANO: Murakami-san, this is not a year's crop.

MASU: I know that!

REVEREND SUGANO: The more mature the grain, the lower the head hangs.

MASU: (*under*) *Kusokue*

TANAKA: Masu, go along.

MASU: (*to Tanaka*) So you are listening to him again.

MASU: (*to Reverend Sugano*) Proverbs are the answers of dead men!

Masu leaves.

TANAKA: Masu, reconsider!

Lights fade and rise on church basement—before dusk—same day. People of community begin to enter the church meeting hall. The theater itself can be considered the hall, with the actors at strategic points in the audience. Crowd enters from different entrances in groups and scatters. Enter group A: M.1, M.2, M.3, W.1 (wife of M.3) and W.2.

MAN 1: Did you hear about Kagawa?

MAN 2: Worse than the Shimizus?

MAN 1: He went into that bar after the sign went up, and they beat him up.

MAN 2: He and Shimizu were always pushy. The nail that sticks its head up, gets pounded down.

Man 4 enters to join group A

MAN 4: That *yat-ta-do* fool. Shimizu deserved what he got!

MAN 1: Shame . . . how can anyone say that?

MAN 4: He should have watched his tongue.

MAN 3: The seed store wouldn't refund our money.

MAN 2: I don't believe that. They have been good to me.

WOMAN 1: If Kagawa-san had a wife, everything would be different.

Group B: W.3, W.4 enter

WOMAN 2: Well, what do you think? They say we'll have to leave.

WOMAN 3: No . . . no!

WOMAN 2: I hear in California . . .

WOMAN 3: (*cutting in*) Rumors . . . just rumors . . .

MAN 4: (*to woman 2*) I said so. Your husband should have sold early like me. It's your own fault.

Man 4 moves to another part of hall.

WOMAN 4: My children blame Japan. They say Japan makes trouble for us.

Group C: Mr. and Mrs. Shimizu enter. Mrs. goes toward women, Mr. toward men.

MRS. SHIMIZU: (*crying*) Burning down our shed, putting sugar in our tractor. Why are there such terrible men? What did we do?

WOMAN 2: Now, now, don't blame yourself . . . God will punish them.

MRS. SHIMIZU: But what will we do?

Enter Kagawa, reassures Mrs. Shimizu and goes with her to Mr. Shimizu. Leaves her with Mr. Shimizu and Setsuko and goes to side of hall.

REVEREND SUGANO: (*at table*) Please, please, sit down . . . please.

Some community members seat themselves, others stand, or lean against posts.

Members of this community and church. We face trying days ahead, and we must look to our inner resources to help guide us now. Let us have a silent prayer. (*ad libbing prayer*) Now, I have to tell you, we will have to leave here and go into camps.

A confusion of reactions. Hiroshi enters.

SHIMIZU: They're going to take us to the mountains and shoot us.

SETSUKO: Don't be silly.

Goes off to join group D: M.5, M.6 and W.5 (wife of M.6), M.7.

MAN 5: They say they built camps out where no one can see them.

MAN 6: That's what I heard.

WOMAN 4: (*to no one in particular*) They're going to put us in camps?

MAN 7: What are the Buddhists going to do?

WOMAN 5: Jiro Yamada went to Utah. I told you we should have gone inland when we had a chance.

MAN 6: Leave me alone.

Group remix: Setsuko, M.7, W.5, W.2, M.5.

SETSUKO: Don't cry.

WOMAN 5: They're going to shoot us!

SETSUKO: No, no, rumors! Irresponsible rumors!

MAN 5: They put some city people in buses with red flags and curtains pulled down so nobody could see inside. Tell me what that means!

SETSUKO: To protect us. So the *hakujins* can't see us and get mad.

WIFE 5: Oh, no! Right after Pearl Harbor, they take away my brother in Seattle. His wife ask and ask, but they don't tell her nothing.

REVEREND SUGANO: Please, please, as long as we cooperate, we have nothing to worry about. Let Tanaka-san explain to us the way we will get ready.

Sugano sits down

TANAKA: (*going to table/lectern*) Yes, now, if we all stay calm, everything will be all right.

MAN 7: What are they doing at the temple?

MAN 1: It must be bad. Tanaka-san is not smiling.

TANAKA: The official name of the order is: Civilian Exclusion Order 9066

KAGAWA: Get on with it!

Agreement by others.

TANAKA: What it says is that we must all register and report in at Portland Assembly Center six days from now. There we will learn exactly where we are to go.

A confusion of reactions by community members. Some are loud, some are heard only by people close by.

MAN 6: What? Six days.

WOMAN 4: This is terrible . . . terrible.

WOMAN 3: They can't mean that.

MAN 1: They don't mean it . . . they don't mean it.

MAN 7: (*to no one in particular*) What do the Buddhists say?

MAN 3: What about our crops?

WOMAN 2: What does it mean?

TANAKA: Please . . . please . . . now, let us have some order.

MAN 7: Yes, let him talk.

KAGAWA: What about the crops? Didn't they say we could harvest . . .

TANAKA: (*cutting in*) No, no. What the government man said was that in his personal opinion, we could harvest what we planted. He did not promise . . .

MAN 3: (*cutting in*) But he said so. He's an important army man, isn't he?

MRS. SHIMIZU: I told you not to seed.

MR. SHIMIZU: They're going to take us away in buses too and kill us.

MRS. SHIMIZU: (*starting to cry*) Don't say that . . .

WOMAN 1: Please, don't cry.

MAN 7: (*very loud*) What are the Buddhists going to do?

REVEREND SUGANO: (*scurrying up to podium*) They are going to cooperate the same as us. We had a meeting.

KAGAWA: Does that mean we let the crops rot in the ground?

TANAKA: The government man made it very clear. He said if he were in our position, he would . . .

MASU: (*cutting in*) He was never in our position. He never will be!

REVEREND SUGANO: Murakami-san, you speak out of turn.

MASU: And you, Preacher, you are not even useful in the pulpit.

WOMAN 5: What did Murakami-san say?

WOMAN 3: It's disgraceful . . . he has no shame. Why is he yelling? He never could farm—he has nothing to lose.

MR. SHIMIZU: So?

MAN 3: He's never been a good farmer, you know that.

MR. SHIMIZU: He's no farmer but he's telling the truth now.

MASU: They lied to us.

TANAKA: You know there are few established procedures. You know when he said . . .

KAGAWA: (*cutting in*) By all means, of course, you can harvest your crops . . .

TANAKA: (*cutting in*) Please, let me finish . . .

MASU: (*cutting in*) Round-eyed words, Tanaka! They mean nothing!

TANAKA: (*ignoring Masu*) The curfew comes soon. We must get clear in our minds how to proceed in the next few days. If we understand what we are to do, there will be no trouble. First of all, we must get together all important papers: birth certificates, passports, entrance registration . . .

MASU: (*cutting in*) First of all, crate what we can and sell what we can . . .

TANAKA: (*cutting in*) No! It's more important now to get ourselves ready! Pick out what you love best; I have been told, we can take only what we can carry. We will need blankets and . . .

MASU: (*cutting in*) We will stay and tend our crops and we will harvest them.

MRS. SHIMIZU: Yes. Yes. They promised us.

TANAKA: No! No promises were made.

MASU: Only self-righteous threats.

REVEREND SUGANO: (*placating*) Murakami-san, we can talk later.

MASU: About what, Preacher!

WOMAN 1: He's only saying the truth.

WOMAN 4: It's shameless.

TANAKA: No, Murakami-san. If we do not follow the army's orders, they will show us no mercy.

KAGAWA: (*to Masu*) What will you do?

MASU: I will tend my crops and pick them. If they keep me from the fields, I will sit on my front porch and wait until they come get me.

MR. SHIMIZU: That's no answer. What is the Japanese Consul doing to protect us?

TANAKA: (*pleading*) Masu, this is an emergency. Your pride is of no concern here.

MASU: Untended fields are an emergency. Unpicked cucumbers and asparagus and radishes and tomatoes and melons are an emergency. We seeded, cut out the irrigation ditches, weeded; we worked hard in good faith. And now, they say: One week. I say: Go to the bottom of hell.

REVEREND SUGANO: You are talking about material, worldly things. We are talking about our lives.

MASU: (*to community*) So am I! You know the Shimizus. Like the rest of us farmers, both of them get up before dawn and work until there is no light. We take time and patience making caps out of wax paper, and we go out and place these wax paper caps over every melon plant. Do we do that to become rich? Why grow melons? Why work stubborn land? Because that careful labor is the only way to make melons grow, and that is our lives. Now a government puts out a price book . . .

MAN 5: (*cutting*) Two dollars an acre for unharvested crops—the dogs!

MASU: (*continuing*) And vultures circle . . .

MAN 6: (*cutting in*) Some *hakujin* had the nerve to offer me twenty dollars for my tractor. Twenty dollars!

MAN 2: I got almost book price for my tractor.

MASU: They barter our lives cheap and, Tanaka, you want us to agree to that?

MAN 3: I told you they weren't going to let us stay.

TANAKA: (*fighting back*) There are old people to consider. There are children. Our families, our safety, our reputations—these are what are important. Not your stupid pride.

MASU: (*to community*) Dogs, let loose, destroyed Shimizu's equipment, burned down his shed. This order is more of the same. If we say no, they will have to stop playing with our lives.

REVEREND SUGANO: His way will lead only to disaster.

MASU: And your way, Preacher, will destroy a people.

TANAKA: Masu, you have a responsibility to the rest of us.

MASU: So do you! Don't sacrifice us to your fears!

HIROSHI: Murakami-san, leave these old women, come back to Japan with me.

TANAKA: Arrogant men who put their own honor above all else have no place here. There are larger loyalties.

MASU: *Bakayaro!* Do you understand me so little?

TANAKA: (*to community*) Bah . . . well, I am certain about my loyalties. I am loyal to the land that fed us. I am loyal to the land that put a roof over my head for the first time in my life. I am loyal to . . .

HIROSHI: (*cutting in*) Tell us, old woman!

MASU: Hiroshi, quiet!

TANAKA: (*angered*) I am loyal to the land that let me live. We are not going to sacrifice ourselves for your filthy honor.

MASU: But you sacrifice us to those who want to destroy us.

TANAKA: If you don't like the smell of the stables, hold your nose or get out!

MASU: Stables don't offend me. They are occupied by honest animals.

TANAKA: Arrogance like yours must be destroyed!

MASU: (*exiting*) Dead men, ever and always, dead men.

HIROSHI: Murakami-san, wait!

Masu gestures, shove it. Lights fade to black and rise on Murakami house—early evening—same day.

MASU: (*on porch, yelling at Tadao and Chieko who are outside*) Tadao, go check the water. Take Chiechan with you!

Masu enters the house. He slams his hat on the table. Kimiko, flustered, worried, harried, trying to set up table for food.

MASU: A land of cocksaccas! They talk about freedom but they hate and fear it.

KIMIKO: Nightriders shot up Shimizu's place.

MASU: I heard at the meeting.

KIMIKO: And the packing shed burned down and they put sugar and sand in all the machines.

MASU: I said I heard!

KIMIKO: (*fearing the worst*) Masu, what happened at the meeting?

MASU: They will be good Japanese peasants and listen to their leaders. A minister who could not serve the needs of a flea . . .

KIMIKO: (*cutting in*) What about the crops? Will we be able to harvest them? The tractor, the pickup?

MASU: (*continuing*) . . . and a merchant who sells us death.

KIMIKO: (*cutting in sharply*) Masu! What was decided!

MASU: Six days from now we will meet at the church and go to Portland. At Portland, they will let us know where the sheep are to be taken. We will be shipped at night so we do not disturb the sleep of the "decent" people. That doesn't frighten you, Kimi? No! Of course not. You can have your minister hold your hand! (*Kimiko does not take bait.*) Kimi, this time, it will take more than quick wits to save us.

KIMIKO: Masu, some things cannot be helped . . .

MASU: (*upsetting the table*) That's all everyone says!

Kimiko scurries to gather up the dishes, which infuriates Masu. He grabs her, she struggles; he holds onto her until he is calmer.

Storms, yes. Storms cannot be helped . . . and weather and seas and stubborn land. Have you ever been at sea during a storm?

KIMIKO: (*indicating no*)

MASU: (*continuing*) The thunder fills up the entire sky, no small portion of it. The fright is awesome. The waves pound high and threaten to grab you up and plunge you back into its depths. And on land, out there, in the fields, the lightning streaks from horizon to horizon and the rain pounds down. There is so much energy, you cannot believe in it. But it is there, demanding that you remember what you left: the earth, the sea. That I understand. To that I can say, *shikataganai*. But men, not men. They don't impress me the same way. Cocksaccas, sonofabitchcocksaccas.

KIMIKO: (*anxious, cutting in*) The house, the crops, the equipment? I know we don't have much but if we go into the camps . . . if we go without anything at all . . . afterwards, what will happen, afterwards.

MASU: Afterwards? Afterwards. Do you know why I left the temple. Because even Buddha described my perfect state as one when everything vital and necessary in me is gone. Gone, in one wave of a hand.

KIMIKO: Six days . . . they can't mean we must be ready so soon.

MASU: Why not? An emergency is an emergency and in an emergency, life can be ignored.

KIMIKO: What can we take with us?

MASU: We're not going.

KIMIKO: Talk sense! Masu, talk sense!

TADAO: (*entering from porch where he's stood listening*) Didn't you hear? We're not going. We're going back to Japan. Aren't we, Papa? Aren't we?

Masu grabs his hat, tips over his chair in a rush to get away from Tadao and exits. Tadao looks to his mother for an answer. Kimiko picks up the scattered dishes. Lights fade to black and rise on dimly lit kitchen area—very late that night. Masu is stumbling about in the dark, trying to get a bottle of sake opened. He is drunk. Kimiko, hearing the clatter, enters and tries to get him to come to bed. He is cut up and obviously got the worst of a fight.

KIMIKO: No more, Masu, no more, please.

MASU: Go back to bed, Kimi. Leave me alone.

She tries to grab the bottle and he rears away.

You sonabitch woman, get away from me.

KIMIKO: Tadao! (*Tadao enters*)

MASU: Leave him out of this!

They struggle. Masu has a knife that he was using to open the sake bottle. He is unaware of this but it is the knife that activates Tadao. He barges in and flings the two apart. Masu falls to the floor, bottle in hand, knife in hand. Kimiko tries to help him but she is brushed aside.

MASU: (*to Tadao*) You have always stood with her against me. Maybe she needs it.

He crawls on all fours to the table and gets up and plops down on a chair, trying to open the bottle again.

Any woman who lets two children die for every one she manages to keep alive needs something.

TADAO: Shut up, Papa! Shut up!

KIMIKO: (*low, intense*) And why did they die? Tell him. Tell him why. Because you could not afford a doctor. Because you could not afford not having me in the fields. Tell him! Tell Tadao!

TADAO: Shut up, Mama! Please shut up!

KIMIKO: You should have become a monk. It would have been better for both of us

MASU: (*sometimes angry, sometimes ironic*) Always a pack! Always someone to support you! Isn't that right, *kusobaba*! Turning Tadao against me, probably turning Chieko right now.

Drops the knife, falls on all fours looking for it, crawling around the floor again.

After being with you, Tanaka sneaks around me like a sniffing cat. (*He sniffs at Kimiko's dress.*) Tanaka, a friend? What friend makes you feel like a beggar?

KIMIKO: (*quiet and deadly*) You men run the world. That's the price you pay.

MASU: You, Tanaka, *bakayaro* Cu-ri-su-chan minister, this country, made for each other! (*mimicking*) I hate war, don't talk about it and it will go away, and your Je-sus Cu-risto will save you.

TADAO: We're not going back to Japan, are we, Papa?

Masu, now turning toward Tadao.

MASU: (*again switching ironic/angry*) No! We're not going back to Japan. No, we're not going back to Japan. So go comfort your mother. Go on! What are you waiting for?

Tadao crosses to Kimiko. Masu tries to get on chair, manages or doesn't.

That's right. That's right. I went into one of those No Ja-pu! bars. I knew. I knew, before I went, there was nothing there I wanted. But my son, my cocksacca son, dying to get in. Mad and dying. When they say no, he wants to run away to Japan. (*mimicking*) "Oh, Papa . . . why stay where you're not wanted."

Wringing his hands, implying his son is a woman, Masu gets out of the chair, knife falls to the floor, and makes a lurch at his son to say "dir-le Jap."

Does he fight back? Oh, no . . . he's ashamed and his father is a dir-le Jap!

TADAO: (*moving away*) That's right. That's right. You talk so big. But you can't do anything. Nothing but get drunk. Get drunk and nothing else. If it wasn't for you, if it wasn't for you

He sees the knife, picks it up, and he points it at his father, which infuriates Masu.

MASU: Put that down. Put that knife down!

TADAO: Stay away from me, Papa, I'll kill you. I'll do it, I will . . .

MASU: (*calm*) He would . . . he's your son. (*Moving in on Tadao.*) Sonofabitchcocksacca.

Chieko enters, rubbing her eyes, not sure of what's happening but whimpering.

TADAO: (*dropping knife*) Stop crying. I'm sick of it.

MASU: (*gentle, turning toward daughter*) Chieko . . .

TADAO: (*getting gold watch and tossing it on table*) I'm not going to need this.

Tadao exits as lights fade to black and rise on Murakami home— day before departure. The room is bare of everyday clutter. The moving out process—visible with clothes and articles in piles, a few packed boxes here and there. Soft armchair sits amidst the emptiness. Next to it, a packed orange crate. Tadao enters house. Kimiko is packing.

KIMIKO: Did Chieko cry?

TADAO: One of the ladies gave her some candy and there's lots of kids at the church. She calmed down and started playing with them. I told her we'd be there tomorrow.

KIMIKO: Good. (*They start packing.*) I wish you would tell Papa you are sorry. We all said things we are ashamed of, didn't we?

TADAO: (*not responding*)

KIMIKO: (*indicating handmade end table*) Papa's left the watch over there ever since that night. You could have taken it back and nothing would have been said.

TADAO: Why are you sticking up for him now?

KIMIKO: (*exasperation*) Tadao! Why do you have to be so stubborn, like your father?

TADAO: I'm nothing like him.

KIMIKO: Don't say such things! You only bring bad things on yourself. It will be hard enough! You know that. You know how Papa says if we don't all hold together now, we might as well be dead. Well, he is right in that. He has been running around, trying to get everything done. He's trying to make up. You must do your part.

TADAO: I'm helping you.

KIMIKO: Papa left the watch for you for three days and you did not even touch it.

TADAO: I don't want it, Mama. Can't you understand? I don't want it.

Kimiko, worn out, tired, ready to cry.

Don't Mama . . .

KIMIKO: Papa and I made up . . . patched things over.

TADAO: You should have left him long ago.

KIMIKO: And gone where? Tell me?

TADAO: Anywhere! We would have been all right.

KIMIKO: That is not true, Tadao, that is just not true. You don't have to say you are sorry. If you work with him, he will know. He is doing all this because he feels so bad.

TADAO: He's doing all this because he's a big number one zero nothing!

KIMIKO: I will not listen!

She begins to pack furiously, slamming things around, pounding clothes into boxes, shooting angry looks at her son. As she packs, she suddenly comes across a faded, delicately colored kimono and fancy Japanese slippers, high, very small. She looks at the shoes, makes a gesture of comparison, her feet now, the shoes. Slowly, she slips back through time and although she is talking to Tadao, she is talking to herself, remembering. There are many abrupt swings of mood as she lives out her past—young, shy, playful, angry, thrilled, pleased with herself, totally open. Eventually, she returns to present and focuses on "now."

KIMIKO: When your Papa came back from America, his uncle and my older sister decided he should marry. He was over thirty, so he accepted the idea. I never liked my sister. I know I shouldn't say that, but I never did. She was so proper and so bossy . . . and pretty. So pretty. She was always trying to run my life! And she thought my idea of going to college was silly and improper, but I was smarter than her. I graduated common school and passed all the examinations. Then I found out they were going to marry me off to him, I was so angry! I thought my sister had talked everyone into it, Mama, Papa, my relatives, for spite. So I couldn't go to college. Then I met your papa. He was nothing like his uncle, my sister's husband. He was generous, and he loved to make people laugh and be happy. They called him the great *yan-cha*: lazy, good-for-nothing, but loved. Maybe a little crazy, too. In Japan, men are very arrogant. They don't think twice telling a woman she is ugly. Can't cook. Can't dance. Can't serve properly. Can't keep up a proper home . . . whatever. But your Papa, not once, not even to the others, did he talk badly of me. I was told to leave the room so they could discuss the marriage arrangements. His uncle, Mama told me afterward, said: Well, she is very clumsy for her age. And Masu, your Papa, said: But I think she might smile in bed. Do you? he asked my sister. Oh, he made her squirm. Well, Kimi-chan, Mama said, it was not the proper thing for him to say, but she liked him, said he would be just right for me. After the wedding, at the party, my sister was here, there, fluttering about, scolding me . . . don't touch your hair so! Sit straight! Be graceful! And I made this face to your father, and he understood. He said to her, right out loud, in front of everyone: "Get away from here—you're not my wife!" Such consternation! My sister was outraged. Then Masu expected me to come back with him. Me, with you in me. My sister didn't like that. But I think the sea air did me good. You were the healthiest of my babies. Tadao, Papa forgave you. When are you going to forgive him?

TADAO: (*not answering*)

KIMIKO: (*back to now*) If you don't do it now . . . one day it will be too late . . . and you will never have the right to ask your son to forgive you.

TADAO: I won't need to.

KIMIKO: That's what your father thought.

Lights fade to black and rise on front porch—almost dawn. Masu, talking to himself, inventorying the farm.

MASU: Hidalgo will see the crops through harvest: split the profit. Pickup: Goodrich. The bank will hold the tractor. Sell it for me. Who knows. Still need the pickup. He can collect it at the church. Damn! have to go tell him. Maybe we can take it to Portland. He can get it there . . . no . . . maybe . . .

He hears noises off in the packing shed and goes to investigate.

Cocksacca! . . . get away from there!

One nightraider runs upstage, Masu in pursuit, two raiders behind him, crates being thrown, two of the men get some kind of grip on him—one trying to find opening to hit him with butt of rifle. Tadao and Kimiko, hearing commotion, enter to porch. Tadao charges from porch, gets man with rifle. Man throws Tadao off, finds his opening, smashes Masu in the head. Tadao scrambling to feet, grabs shotgun. Man lets go in a panic to leave. Masu lying still. Tadao falls to packing shed ground and begins shooting at fleeing men.

TADAO: (*shooting*) Sonofabitchcocksuckers! Sonofabitchcocksaccas!

Kimiko is trying to pull Masu to house. She gives up, tears cloth from robe and tries to wipe away blood.

KIMIKO: Is this better, Masu? Tadao, hurry, please hurry. *Okinasai*, Masu. *Okinasai*.

Tadao joins mother at body. She is still in midst of emergency; he is spent out.

TADAO: He's not going to wake up. He's dead.

KIMIKO: Help me, help me carry him to the house. Clean off the blood.

TADAO: Why? He's dead.

KIMIKO: Go get Tanaka-san!

TADAO: He's dead, Mama—that's the truth.

He falls down on his knees and begins scrambling over the body, searching the pockets for the gold watch. Kimiko is shocked. She cannot believe what she is seeing.

KIMIKO: Have some respect!

TADAO: (*gold watch in hand*) It's mine. He gave it to me, remember.

KIMIKO: Lucky, Masu, always lucky.

TADAO: (*grabbing body of Masu*) Him?! Lucky?! Get up, you sonofabitchcocksacca! You goddamned sonofabitch Jap cocksucker, get up!

KIMIKO: (*soft to Masu*) Truth? What is this true to? To you? Is this what is true in you? Didn't you know that dreams are for night and the quiet after love? Didn't you know? *Okinasai* Masu, *neh*? On a clean bed . . . on clean sheets . . .

KIMIKO: (*suddenly attacking Tadao*) Stupid boy! Do you think he would want Chieko to see him like this . . . Or you or me . . . what is this true to?

She rises and goes to edge of packing shed to maintain composure. Tadao takes the watch, talking softly to his father, wanting to tell him he does love and respect him.

TADAO: It's too late, Papa. It's just too late now.

Picks up shotgun and strides away.

KIMIKO: (*calling him back*) Tadao!

No response. She returns to body of Masu.

Okinasai, Masu. Wake up. It's morning time.

THE END

T E A

❀

VELINA HASU HOUSTON

Velina Hasu Houston's *Tea*, which she calls "a poem to my mother," is the final play of a trilogy based on her family. The trilogy begins with *Asa Ga Kimashita (Morning Has Broken)*, which details her Japanese mother's decision to marry an African American–Native American Indian G.I. and leave her ancestral home. It is followed by *American Dreams* which finds the young couple confronted by hostility and intolerance upon meeting their African American relations stateside. *Tea* concludes the series, reaching beyond immediate autobiography to encompass a community of Japanese women, one of whom is based on Houston's widowed mother.

In her playwright's notes for *Tea* Houston writes:

> My passion for these Japanese international brides is both personal and political. An Amerasian born of America's first war with Asia, I am the daughter of one such Japanese woman and an American soldier who was half Native American Indian and half African American. My creative explorations of my family history, though born of artistic and personal passion, are nevertheless historical because they document history—the Japanese "war bride" and the Japanese American experience—that otherwise might have been lost to the mainstream, history that Japan has side-stepped and about which America never knew or never cared.[1]

A prolific writer and one of the most widely produced Asian American playwrights, Houston's work has evolved from autobiography to plays that address a wide range of issues. The decision to become a single parent in *The Legend of Bobby Chicago*, the racism of adoption in *Necessities*, and *Christmas Cake*, a comedy about a Japanese man sent to bridegroom school, are themes from a sampling of her recent work. The common thread in all her writing is an ongoing exploration of the politics of culture, race, and gender, particularly as they affect interracial relations in America. Houston is particularly interested in what she terms, "the Afro-Asian diaspora," asserting that this "whole element of our culture is often ignored in the dramatic literature."[2] She criticizes the fact that the discussion of race in America is generally limited to the black/white confrontation. Her plays examine a set of social dynamics, cultural nuances, and racial problems which reflect aspects of America's troubled plurality, a reality which is rarely treated in literature, or on the stage.

Born in Tokyo, Japan, in 1957, Houston immigrated at the age of two with her Japanese mother and American G.I. father. They settled in Fort Riley, Kansas, one of several army bases where the U.S. Army segregated nearly one hundred thousand "war brides"—Japanese, French, German, Italian, English, and, later, Korean and Thai women—married to active-duty American servicemen between 1946 and 1960. Houston grew up in a strange and insular America: "The town had an international population but to walk into it you would never know—it was as if the communities were hidden unto themselves." Within the walls of their home the Houstons lived as if in Japan. "In my house Japanese culture reigned. Father adhered to this and we ate Japanese food every day. My mother was adamant about keeping that. These women, in a sense, are more Japanese than Nisei."[3] Because of the distance from centers of Japanese American culture like Los Angeles or San Francisco, the world of Houston's childhood was uniquely Japanese and yet, "I never saw Asian men—in the whole town there was only one Nisei married to a German woman." Outside of the home she faced prejudice from both whites and, ironically, African Americans, whom she later came to realize were expressing their own frustration with oppressive circumstances. She found understanding and friendship within the community of Amerasians, families and children of mixed Asian ancestry like her.

Houston prefers the term *Amerasian* to identify her multiracial, multicultural heritage. "My mother called us American Japanese or Afro-Japanese, which I still use a lot. But the term Amerasian was important to me because more than being multiracial, I'm multicultural and binational. My difficulty is deciding whether I'm more Japanese or more American and how I feel about that and usually I feel much more Japanese than American. Because of that the term *Amerasian* was appealing to me because it meant an amalgam of the American and the Asian which was indivisible. . . . Someone's always saying she's Japanese and Native American Indian, and African American . . . like a recipe . . . and you're always feeling like you're made up of two or three pieces, that you're a fragmented human being. But I'm a whole being. The term *Amerasian* is a reflection of my biological and cultural truth."

Because her father died when she was eleven, Houston and her sister were raised by her mother, and, because of the failure of relatives to accept her parents' interracial marriage, her mother managed without the assistance of an extended family. "I laughed when I saw the film *Steel Magnolias* because I had written an essay entitled 'Steel Chrysanthemums' years before and that's how I think of my mother. . . . She's a very gentle soul, this provincial woman from Japan cut from the prewar Kansai woman mold, and yet she survived. . . . Most people think she's so malleable and quiet and unobtrusive, but the reality is that my mother is very strong and there's a steel core inside."

In *Tea* Houston focuses on Himiko, a Japanese woman unlike her mother, a woman who could not adapt to her new life in America. Four Japanese women are brought together following Himiko's suicide, a death that forces them to reflect on what they have endured to live in America and what their relationship is to each other.

Houston utilizes the ritual of taking tea, but she is quick to explain, "This is not tea in the Japanese ceremonial sense, but the ritual of everyday life." The women of *Tea* come from widely different class and cultural backgrounds within Japan and have married equally diverse American men; the ritual of drinking tea becomes a device that draws them together, forcing them to examine their common experiences and the essence of what being Japanese means. Houston illustrates the women's differences through the very manner in which they take tea. Atsuko, who holds herself superior to the other women because of her class background and because she is the only one who has married a racially pure (albeit American) Japanese, prefers premium tea, "lukewarm in a fancy Japanese cup." Teruko, who married a white Texan, comes from a humble background; her preference is for plain, "peasant" tea, "I like it cool, any cup will do." Chizuye, the most assimilated of the group and the widow of a Mexican American prefers American instant coffee, "I choose my drink like I chose my husband; strong, dark, and with a lot of sugar." It is Setsuko, the widow of a black American who, in dealing with the most prejudice from both Americans and Japanese, preserves the delicate balance in the ritual, just as she served as the link in life to Himiko, the suicide victim. Setsuko was the only woman who took tea with Himiko while she was alive; the other women shunned her because of her erratic behavior, the causes of which they chose to ignore. Houston utilizes cross-gender and crossgenerational casting to provide insight into Himiko's tormented life, as the Japanese women transform into their husbands and also their teenage daughters. It is through them that we see a life of abuse, most vividly depicted when the "husbands" are on a hunting trip:

> TERUKO: I remember the time your wife ran out of your house wearing a slip. She said you'd had a fight and you told her you wanted to kiss and make up. (a beat as the others relive this, too) And you kissed her, all right—and bit off part of her lip. They had to sew it back on.
>
> HIMIKO: What can I say. There's nobody like her. Never has been. (a beat) Never will be. She's the only fuckin' prize I ever won. (The others eye him like a jury and Himiko laughs)
>
> SETSUKO: What did you expect, Hamilton? You'd bring her home and she'd sprout blue eyes and whistle "Dixie"?
>
> HIMIKO: (anger simmering just under the surface and finally busting loose) Hey, what do you want me to do? Huh? She crawls under my fist like an orphan beggin' for love and my knuckles come down like a magnet. Like a fucking magnet man. I got eight younger brothers and sisters and I lived in a trailer the size of a pencil box, working three jobs while you guys was jabbin' broads in the alley. Fuckin-ay man, give me some room to breathe in.

Thus Himiko is transformed from a tragic, mentally unstable victim to a woman who attempted to control what was within her power by killing her husband and later herself.

It is the authenticity of the world Houston creates and the intimacy established with the audience of witnesses that is the primary power of *Tea*. As an inside member of this world, she was able to do research for the piece from a privileged position. She originally began her investigation as an oral history project, interviewing some fifty women who reluctantly consented to speak with her and then only because she was a member of their community. These interviews, lasting up to ten hours in length, were wracked with emotion as the women revealed their long-concealed stories. Ultimately she determined that the subject would be best served in dramatic form and she decided to abandon the content of the interviews, preserving the emotional intensity, and turning instead to her own knowledge of women she had grown up with, including her mother.

It was her mother who first motivated Houston to write: "I remember when I was six years old she would sit me down to write what she called 'haiku' but what was probably just gibberish . . . but it did start me writing poetry." Houston went on to win several Young Kansas writers' awards for her poetry and wrote her first play at the age of thirteen. Her affinity for the genre was immediate: "Writing in that form possessed me—it felt so natural. I felt I had found home." Houston continued playwriting as a journalism/mass communications and theater major at Kansas State University and achieved a Masters Degree of Fine Arts in playwriting in 1981 at the University of California at Los Angeles. Her first professional production of *Asa Ga Kimashita* was at the East West Players in Los Angeles in 1984.

Although she has received both productions and staged readings at multicultural and ethnic theaters like the East West Players, the Negro Ensemble Company, the Seattle Group Theater, and the Asian American Theater Company, Houston points to difficulties she has experienced working in the ethnic theater as a consequence of something she calls "color against color oppression." She has been disturbed by "a type of racism that often goes unexamined by the Euro-American mainstream and also by people of color." In her experience as a binational, multiracial playwright she has encountered ethnic theaters that hesitate to embrace her work because of her refusal to choose a single aspect of her heritage over another. "Too often I have heard the artistic director of an Asian American or an African American theater tell me that one of my plays is either 'too Japanese' or 'not Japanese enough' or 'not African American enough' for their theater. . . . In the theater, the oppression of multiracial people who defy traditional racial categories personally and in their work is an oppression of exclusion." Ironically Houston has found inclusion on the stages of theaters headed by Euro-American artistic directors. Jack O'Brien of the Old Globe Theater, Lynne Meadow of Manhattan Theater Club, Olympia Dukakis of the now defunct Whole Theater, and Dennis Carroll of Kumu Kahua are among the visionary individuals who have produced her work, opening doors to future productions by playwrights of color.

While recent projects have led her to an ever-widening number of themes and characters she continues to be intrigued and inspired by her mother's legacy. "My favorite type of character to write about is the Shin-Issei Japanese woman, any native-born Japanese woman who comes to America and grows through the process of trying to survive here. It is the native Japanese woman in America who fascinates me; culturally I feel very close to her. I relate to her struggle—their cultural struggle is my cultural struggle."

Notes

1. Velina Houston, playwrights' notes for *Tea* from the program for the Manhattan Theater Club, 6 October 1987.
2. Editor's interview with Velina Houston, Los Angeles, 1 March 1991.
3. Jon Matsumoto, "Surviving Junction City," *Los Angeles Japanese Daily News*, 13 March 1991.

TEA

VELINA HASU HOUSTON

This play is dedicated to

the Japanese women of Kansas

especially my mother, Setsuko, and Kazue Logan.

With thanks to Patti Yasutake

and Julianne Boyd.

The playwright gratefully acknowledges Manhattan Theatre Club, its artistic director, Lynne Meadow, and its managing director, Barry Grove, for supporting the development of *Tea* and giving the play its professional premiere. Her gratitude also is extended to the late Jonathan Alper, producer, and to Tom Szentgyorgyi, the theater's former literary associate, who discovered the play in the American traffic of scripts.

Time and Place: 1968. The home of Himiko
Hamilton in Junction City, Kansas, and an obscure
netherworld where time moves at will.

CHARACTERS

SETSUKO BANKS   HIMIKO HAMILTON   CHIZUYE JUAREZ
TERUKO MACKENZIE   ATSUKO YAMAMOTO

SETTING: The stark set includes both a representation of the netherworld (in which time is elastic and the spirit can journey) and a
representation of the home of Himiko. The home is a combination
of 1960s Americana and things Japanese, including a raised area
that abstractly comprises a Japanese tatami room bordered by lino-
leum. In the room are a pile of zabuton (flat Japanese sitting cush-
ions), an antique, round-hooded trunk overflowing with Japanese
cloth materials, kimono, and so forth, and an oval, red lacquer tea
table. The reality is distressed.

This play is to be performed without an intermission. Average
running time is between eighty and ninety minutes.

DRAMATIST'S NOTES: This play is based on the virtually undocu-
mented historical fact of communities of Japanese "war brides"
who have lived in Kansas over the last twenty to forty years. More
than 100,000 native Japanese women married American servicemen during the American Occupation of Japan. These families
returned to the United States between the years of 1946 and 1960.
Depending on the time of their return, any American servicemen
married to "Oriental" women were required under that army's
resettlement policies to be stationed at remote forts, such as Fort
Riley, Kansas. Hence, in an area of Kansas known mostly for German and Irish American Protestants and agriculture, there came to
exist dispersed communities of Japanese women and their multiracial, multicultural children. This background and my family history catalyzed this play, in addition to extensive interviews with
fifty Japanese women residing in Kansas who were international
brides.

PRELUDE   Invitation to Tea

*In the darkness, an unaccented, female American voice belts out
"The Star Spangled Banner." A traditional Japanese melody—perhaps "Sakura"—cuts into the song's end as lights fade in slowly to*

half to suggest a netherworld. Himiko kneels downstage center. She is a pale, delicately boned woman wearing a feminine but mysterious dress over which is a kimono of distorted colors. The dress is long and muted in tone; its skirt, short in front, trails the floor in back and the outer hems are ragged. In its little-girlishness and antiquity, the dress suggests a different era. A white petticoat hangs underneath it, its shredded edges peeking out. Quiet, traditional Japanese music haunts the background. Crumpled like paper, Himiko rises gradually, relating to a presence that we cannot see. She is beautiful, but beaten, and exudes an aura of sultry mystery. There is no lunacy in this woman, rather the sense of one who has been pushed to the edge, tried desperately to hold on, and failed. She is, indeed, resolute. Himiko reaches out to the presence and speaks in a voice that carries the weight of the world, moving from a hoarse whisper to a more audible tone.

HIMIKO: Billy. Can't you see it's me? Himiko Hamilton. You gave me your name and, this day, I give it back. You have forsaken my spirit and it is left shaking in the cold mist left behind by your restless breath. As you walk. Fast. And always away. Leaving me to wander between two worlds forever. (*a quiet smile appears*) But listen, Billy, listen. I have learned your Christian prayer: "Now I lay me down to sleep. I pray your Lord my soul to keep. And if I die before I wake. I pray your Lord my soul to take."

Himiko's attention is suddenly drawn to another presence which absolutely delights her; she moves toward it slightly.

HIMIKO: Mieko-chan? This is your mother. Come close. Let me smell the confusion of your Amerasian skin. For you are the only gift I ever had. Beautiful half-Japanese girl, fill the holes in my kimono sleeves with your soft laughter. Lead me to peace.

Himiko removes a pistol from her kimono sleeve, bows as she offers it to time and space, and places it before her. She kneels and looks again toward her vision of Mieko.

HIMIKO: Mieko, my child. (*She looks in the opposite direction.*) Billy, my beloved husband. (*She looks down stage center, her voice louder, but not too loud*) Mother? Can you hear me? Wait for me, Mother. I am coming to have tea with thee.

Himiko lifts the pistol and aims it toward her throat. Blackout as a gunshot followed by a deafening atomiclike explosion fills the theater, leaving behind trails of smoke. Half light up as, from various dark corners, Teruko, Atsuko, Chiz and Setsuko enter one by one and take staggered positions. Spotlights simultaneously fade in on the women who bow as they speak their first lines. The style of the bows reflects their personalities.

SETSUKO: Shall we have tea at three?

TERUKO: Please come over for tea.

ATSUKO: Join me for tea, just the two of us.

CHIZ: Tea. *O-cha.* That's our word for it.

SETSUKO: I drink it hot in a pretty Japanese cup.

TERUKO: I like it cool. Any cup will do.

ATSUKO: Lukewarm in a fancy Japanese cup.

CHIZ: Very hot. In a simple cup.

TERUKO: Tea is not quiet.

ATSUKO: But turbulent.

SETSUKO: Tremblings.

CHIZ: So fine you can't see them.

SETSUKO: So dense it seems to be standing still.

TERUKO: We Japanese women drink a lot of it.

ATSUKO: Become it.

SETSUKO: Swallow the tempest.

CHIZ: And nobody knows.

ATSUKO: The storm inside.

TERUKO: Ever.

SETSUKO: We remain . . .

TERUKO: Peaceful.

CHIZ: Contained.

ATSUKO: The eye of the hurricane.

SETSUKO: But if you can taste the tea.

TERUKO: If it can roll over your tongue in one swallow.

ATSUKO: Then the rest will come to you.

CHIZ: When the tea leaves are left behind in the bottom of a cup. (*Himiko reenters carrying Rayban sunglasses and a long, blonde wig; she comes upstage center.*)

HIMIKO: When we are long gone and forgotten. (*puts on the sunglasses and holds out her arms in welcome to the audience as the other women exit.*) Come, . . . it is time for tea.

(*Himiko pulls on the wig, crossfade to the tatami room.*)

SCENE ONE   The Art of Tea

Atsuko and Teruko drift to the tatami room where piles of books and a wild-looking wig are on the floor. They take off their shoes outside of the room and enter. Atsuko has brought her own booties and puts them on. She removes her sweater, and studies the room with mixed feelings of revulsion and attraction, as if she has vicariously imagined this room's experiences. She sniffs the air with displeasure, and covers her nose and mouth with a handkerchief. They set up the Japanese-style table and place four zabuton as Himiko observes from the darkness. Whenever Himiko speaks to the audience, it is as if she is on trial and offering a matter-of-fact defense.

ATSUKO: Ugh. How were you able to have tea here with this stench! (*studies the floor*) Maybe we should keep our shoes on.

TERUKO: It didn't smell here before, Atsuko-san!

ATSUKO: Yes, it did. You said it did.

TERUKO: I said it smelled like liquor and burnt candles.

ATSUKO: Well, you know that's from bringing home men and making sex.

TERUKO: (*insistently protective*) Before her husband died, Himiko lived a quiet life.

Atsuko picks up the wild wig as if to negate Teruko's statement. Teruko starts to exit to the kitchen.

I'm going to find the teapot and cups.

Atsuko hurriedly drops the wig and looks around the room as if she has seen or suspects ghosts.

ATSUKO: Don't leave me alone!

TERUKO: We must begin. (*Teruko exits to kitchen.*)

HIMIKO: (*to audience*) Yes, we must begin . . . Tea for the soul; tea to cleanse the spirit.

Atsuko examines the room carefully as if afraid of getting dirty and begins to put things away. She puts on her glasses.

ATSUKO: Himiko was so wild after her husband died. Maybe she was like that in Japan, too. I don't know how she passed the screening tests for army brides. They took so long and the Yankee officers asked so many stupid questions.

HIMIKO: (*addresses Atsuko as if echoing a reminder, encircling her as she speaks*) "Are you a Communist? Why do you want to marry this man instead of one of your own native Japanese? Do you think moving to America will afford you personal financial gain? Are you suffering from insanity? Are you an imbecile or idiot?" (*a beat*) "Are you now—or have you ever been—a prostitute?"

ATSUKO: The nerve of that Amerikan Army! Did the army ask you if you were a prostitute?

Teruko returns with a teapot, cups, lacquer coasters, and two cloths—one wet and one dry—all on a lacquer tray. She handles them delicately.

TERUKO: Yes. I told them we weren't all bad girls just because we fell in love with Amerikans. (*looks around the room as if drinking in Himiko's life*) Poor Himiko.

ATSUKO: Where is Setsuko Banks? I thought she was the one most friendly with Himiko. (*looks around the room eerily*) I heard the tatami was covered with blood. It's funny, isn't it, how one moment someone is full of life and the next, they are ashes.

TERUKO: Atsuko-san, ne, if you're that uncomfortable, go home. Setsuko and Chiz (*pronounced like "cheese"*) and I can take care of this.

ATSUKO: As head of our Buddhist chapter, how would it look to headquarters if I didn't do everything I could to help a member? (*feigning an innocent smile, she peers over her glasses*) Besides, I wanted to see the inside of this house.

TERUKO: Well, Setsuko-san went home to pick up o-sushi.

ATSUKO: And "Chiz" is always late. Her nickname sounds so stupid. Like food. She even wears pants now and grows her hair long like a hippy. (*removes a crocheted green-and-purple poodle toilet paper cover from the trunk and shakes her head at its oddity*) She's just as silly as Himiko was.

Atsuko takes out her own tea cup, admires it, and places it on the table. Teruko wipes Himiko's tea cups, first with a wet cloth and then a dry one. She carefully arranges the cups with coasters and teapot on the table. Atsuko moves Himiko's tea cups away from her own.

TERUKO: (*removes a folded newspaper article from her wallet; reads from it with officiousness*) Listen. I cut this out. "Death Notices. September 9, 1968. Himiko Hamilton, thirty-nine, widow of Chief Warrant Officer William Hamilton, passed away in her home from a self-inflicted gunshot wound. She was preceded in death by her husband and, recently, her daughter, Mieko, eighteen. A Japanese war bride, Mrs. Hamilton was a resident of Junction City for twenty years. She leaves no survivors."

HIMIKO: (*to audience with quiet dignity*) But, still, I ask you to listen. Please. (*a beat*) I am suspended between two worlds. There is no harmony here (*indicates the women in tatami room*) nor here (*indicates her soul*).

TERUKO: Well, she *did* leave survivors.

ATSUKO: Who?

TERUKO: Us.

ATSUKO: Not me! Just because I'm Japanese doesn't mean I have anything to do with her life. Dead is dead, Teruko-san, so what difference does it make? Who knows, ne. Maybe next it will be me. Do you think the Japanese women in this town are going to pray for my soul just because I happen to come from Japan?

TERUKO: (*shocked at Atsuko's callousness*) Atsuko-san. We must respect the dead.

ATSUKO: Only because they no longer have to fear the darkness. The rest of us must wait, without any idea of when our time will come to an end.

TERUKO: (*as if she feels Himiko's presence*) No, sometimes even the dead must wait. In limbo.

ATSUKO: (*a smile*) Well, Himiko should wait forever after what she did to her husband.

TERUKO: But you know what he was doing to her.

ATSUKO: Nobody really knows.

HIMIKO: Nobody would listen.

ATSUKO: Maybe she wasn't a good wife.

HIMIKO: I was the *best* wife.

TERUKO: He never let her out of the house and hardly let her have guests. Remember during the big snow storm? The phone lines were down and—

HIMIKO: —I didn't have any tea or rice left. Billy had gone to Oklahoma to visit his family. He said, "Don't leave the house" and took my daughter, Mieko, with him. So there I was, starving to death, standing behind—

TERUKO: (*overlapping with Himiko's last two words*) —Standing behind the frosty glass. She looked like she was made of wax.

HIMIKO: (*smiles at herself*) I asked him once. I said, "Why did you marry me?" And he said he wanted a good maid, for free.

ATSUKO: Maybe she wanted too much.

HIMIKO: I never asked for anything. Except soy sauce and good rice. And dreams . . . for Mieko.

Himiko glows with love for her child, turns around, and seems to see her as a tot, and beckons to her.

HIMIKO: Mieko-chan! My little girl! (*Himiko exits as if chasing "Mieko."*)

ATSUKO: Teruko, I saw your daughter last week. She looks Japanese. (*a compliment*) That's nice. Too bad she isn't friends with my girl. My girl's always with Setsuko-san's daughter. Have you seen her? Looks Indonesian, not Japanese at all. Shame, ne.

TERUKO: But Setsuko's daughter is the only one who cooks Japanese food. My daughter likes hamburger sandwich and yellow-haired boys.

ATSUKO: My daughter always goes to Setsuko-san's house. I've never been invited.

TERUKO: Setsuko likes her privacy.

ATSUKO: She invited you to tea.

TERUKO: Well, if you're not willing to be genuine with her, how can you share the honor of tea together?

ATSUKO: She invited Himiko, too!

TERUKO: Yes, even after the incident. Even though everyone was afraid.

A siren wails as a deafening gunshot echoes in the air and all lights black out. Atsuko and Teruko exit to the kitchen in the darkness. Himiko, without sunglasses, drifts from the darkness and stops center stage. The siren fades out and a spotlight fades up immediately on Himiko who crouches as if shooting a pistol. She smiles and rises gracefully. She speaks matter-of-factly to the audience.

HIMIKO: (*imitates the sound of shots, pronounced "bahn" like in bonfire*) Ban! Ban! Ban! Yes. I am Himiko Hamilton. The murderess. I married and murdered a gentleman from Oklahoma. And they let me go on self-defense. It took one shot—right through the heart I never knew he had. Now that he's gone, I can speak freely. Please listen. I wasted my life in Kansas. The state—of mind. Not Kansas City, but *Junction City*, a stupid hick town that rests like a pimple on an army base called Fort Riley. Where the army's resettlement policy exiled our husbands because they were married to "Japs."

Himiko indicates her own face as Chiz and Setsuko enter from opposite corners carrying food in a basket and furoshiki, respectively.

HIMIKO: They won't tell you that because they're real *Japaneezy* Japanese.

Chiz and Setsuko smile and bow formally to each other in greeting; Setsuko bows a second time.

HIMIKO: See what I mean? Well, . . . I'm about as Japanese as corn flakes, or so they say, and I killed my husband because he laughed at my soy sauce just one time too many.

Himiko smiles whimsically and turns away from the audience. Chiz and Setsuko drift down stage. They are unaware of Himiko's presence. Setsuko and Chiz stand outside of the house.

SETSUKO: Oh, Chizuye-san, I wish Himiko-san could have seen all the Japanese women at her funeral.

HIMIKO: (*to the audience*) All the Japanese women who were too ashamed to say hello to me in public because I was "no good."

CHIZ: (*adamant with characteristic exuberance*) Ever since she shot her husband two years ago, she's kind of haunted me. It made me remember that underneath my comfortable American clothes, I am, after all, Japanese. (*a quick smile*) But don't tell anybody.

SETSUKO: Well, after all, you were the one who went looking for her.

CHIZ: Someone had to. The rest of you were too afraid of what you would find. (*looks into space as she recalls*) I forced her door open and, there she was, paler and bluer than the sky over Hiroshima that strange August. She had pulled her kimono over her American dress, as if it might make her journey into the next life a little easier. But I took one look at her and I knew nothing was ever going to be easy for her, not in life or in death.

HIMIKO: I would have given anything to have tea with Japanese girls. I drank alone.

Setsuko and Chiz approach the house and remove their shoes. Setsuko straightens hers and Chiz's.

CHIZ: What'd you bring?

SETSUKO: Maki-zushi.

CHIZ: (*smiles to poke fun at her friend*) Figures. I brought spinach quiche, Sue.

SETSUKO: My name is not Sue. My name is Setsuko. Chizuye-san, I tell you many times not to call me by this nickname you made up.

CHIZ: But it's easier.

SETSUKO: Like "Chiz." (*pronounces it "cheese"*)

CHIZ: (*laughs; pronounces it with a short "i"*) No, Setsuko, like "Chiz." That's what my customers at my restaurant call me, but you can call me anything you like.

They enter the house and Chiz looks toward the kitchen.

CHIZ: Hello? Hello? Ah, Teruko! Hello.

Teruko appears from the kitchen with food, including fruit. Setsuko scurries to help her.

TERUKO: Hello! Hello! Look, Atsuko-san is here, too.

CHIZ: (*much surprise and a touch of contempt*) Atsuko?!

SETSUKO: Well, what an unexpected pleasure.

ATSUKO: Setsuko-san! I rarely see you, but you look younger every time I do. I was sorry to hear about your husband.

SETSUKO: Yes, well, it was his time to . . . to move on.

ATSUKO: Negroes don't live very long. The food they eat, you know.

SETSUKO: My husband ate almost entirely Japanese food.

TERUKO: Atsuko-san's husband hates Japanese food. (*giggles*) And he's Japanese Amerikan!

ATSUKO: He does *not* hate Japanese food! (*to Setsuko and Chiz*) Why are you both so late? We cleaned the kitchen already. And, of course, we must have tea.

SETSUKO: Oh, yes, tea sounds very good to me now.

TERUKO: Why, yes. Everything must start with tea.

CHIZ: (*laughs*) Tea is *just* a drink.

SETSUKO: Oh, it's much more than that.

ATSUKO: I couldn't live without tea.

HIMIKO: Yes, . . . it brings everything into balance.

ATSUKO: I think it improves my eyesight.

SETSUKO: (*laughing*) And my insight.

Teruko, Setsuko and Atsuko have a good laugh over this as Chiz looks on dead-pan. Finally she smiles and lights up a cigarette.

CHIZ: Hey, enough about tea. Who else is coming?

TERUKO: More than four would be too many. I stopped asking for volunteers after Atsuko-san spoke up.

CHIZ: How many were there?

TERUKO: At least fifty Japanese women!

CHIZ: Fifty? Jesus. You'd think it was a blue-light special.

SETSUKO: Chizuye-san! Shame, ne! After all, this is a difficult occasion for us: the first time a member of our Japanese community has passed on.

CHIZ: What "community"?

HIMIKO: (*again, to audience*) Yes, what community? We knew each other, but not really . . . We didn't care enough to know.

CHIZ: Who's got time to chit-chat, right, "Ats"? (*pronounced with a short "a," like "ahts"*) Now that I'm finally having tea with the great Atsuko Yamamoto, you get a nickname.

ATSUKO: Thank you, but you can keep your . . . gift. (*a beat*) It's obvious we're all from different neighborhoods.

SETSUKO: But we are all army wives—and we are all Japanese.

CHIZ: So what? That won't buy us a ticket to Nirvana. Let's face it, girls, after we get through dealing with our jobs and our families, we're ready to go to sleep. And, if any of us are willing to drive across town and have tea, we don't even talk about what's really on our minds—whether coming to Amerika was such a good idea. (*she smiles*) Countries last; love is mortal.

SETSUKO: But we're here today because we're Japanese.

CHIZ: We're here today because we're scared.

HIMIKO: Scared they will be next to die or their souls will be left in limbo like mine.

Atsuko can hardly contain her excitement at finally being able to ask a question she's pondered for years:

ATSUKO: Tell us, Satsuko-san. Is it true about Himiko being a dance hall girl in Japan?

SETSUKO: If that's what she said. I never really knew her until after her husband died. I would see her walking in the middle of a humid summer day in a heavy coat and the yellow-haired wig.

HIMIKO: (*reliving that day*) "Hello. I am Mrs. William Hamilton. May I have a glass of water? Oh, thank you, thank you. You are so kind."

ATSUKO: (*gesticulating that Himiko was crazy*) Kichigai, ne . . .

CHIZ: She was *not* crazy.

TERUKO: It is the Japanese way to carry everything inside.

HIMIKO: Yes. And that is where I hid myself.

ATSUKO: She came from Japan, but the way she dressed, the way she walked. Mah, I remember the district church meeting. She came in a low-cut dress and that yellow-haired wig, (*mocks how she thinks a Korean walks*) walking like a Korean.

SETSUKO: Atsuko-san, ne, we have something in common with all the Oriental women here, even the Vietnamese. We all left behind our countries to come and live here with the men we loved.

ATSUKO: Okay, okay. It's not that I didn't like Himiko-san. So many things she did were not acceptable. If she acted like that in Japan, people would think she was . . . well, a prostitute. Something was not right inside her head. I mean, whoever heard of a Japanese shooting her husband with a rifle? I told you that day at the cemetery.

Himiko, having had enough, rushes forward and the women freeze.

HIMIKO: (*defiantly calls them back into the past with a roll call, stamping her foot as she calls out each name*) Teruko. Setsuko. Atsuko. Chizuye.

Himiko exits through the kitchen as the music for "Taps" sets the mood. The women drift from the house as if answering the roll call. The lights fade out on house and fade up downstage. They stand as if around a headstone at a cemetery as Himiko enters. A black-veiled hat, black coat, and black pumps complete her widow ensemble. She carries a black bag out of which she pulls a can of beer. The women watch in shock as Himiko opens the beer and pours it over the "grave" by which they stand. Setsuko runs to her and takes the beer.

HIMIKO: Mah, there must be a thousand graves here!

SETSUKO: Shame on you, Himiko-san! Pouring beer on your husband's grave!

HIMIKO: I am celebrating. First Memorial Day since he "left me." He liked beer when he was alive. Why shouldn't he like it when he's dead.

CHIZ: Sounds pretty fair to me.

ATSUKO: Teruko-san, come. We've seen enough.

Atsuko pulls away a reluctant Teruko who beckons to Chiz. All three exit. Setsuko, concerned, lingers as Himiko suddenly looks up at an invisible object in great shock.

HIMIKO: I'm sorry, Billy. That's right. I forgot. You like Budweiser beer. This is cheap kind, brand X. See? (*points at the can*) Just B-E-E-R. Billy, what are you doing here? I believe in reincarnation, but this is a little soon. I planned on being gone before you came back. I'm sorry I didn't bury you in your favorite shirt. I couldn't fix the hole in it from when I shot you. No, no. I don't want to go with you (*fighting*) No, I want to stay here with our daughter. She's not mad at me for what I did. She says you deserved it. No, I don't want to be alone with you anymore. I don't want to kiss and make up. (*pushes away an unseen presence*) Setchan! Help me! Billy's going to take me away. (*the presence knocks her off her feet*)

SETSUKO: (*an antithetical picture of solitude, she draws near*) Himiko-san. Let's go home now. We'll make tea and talk.

HIMIKO: Help me, Setchan. He's going to beat me up again.

SETSUKO: Come, Himi-chan. You must go home and rest.

HIMIKO: There is only unrest. It is like the war never ended.

SETSUKO: (*sympathetically*) Oh, Himi-san. (*not knowing what else to do, she releases Himiko and bows her head sorrowfully*)

HIMIKO: (*enervated, to herself*) I wish I would have died in World War II. It was an easier war than this one.

Himiko exits offstage as Setsuko removes her shoes and returns to the tatami room and lights crossfade into Scene Two . . .

Lights up on the house where Atsuko stands wearing an apron over her clothing. Teruko sits at the table arranging three tins of tea, a porcelain tea pot, and the tea cups. Setsuko sorts through the trunk, removing such things as a photo album, materials, and green and purple crocheted poodle toilet paper covers. A tea kettle whistles loudly from the offstage kitchen. The noise jars everyone.

ATSUKO: (*to the offstage Chiz*) Chizuye-san. What kind of tea would you like?

CHIZ: I'm looking for coffee. Isn't there any coffee around here?

TERUKO: (*gets up, prepared to go*) I'll go to the store and buy some for her.

ATSUKO: Why do we need to waste time with that? There's tea.

SETSUKO: She just wants coffee. She's tired.

ATSUKO: She just wants to have coffee because we're having tea. She even brought egg pie. Ugh.

TERUKO: I like egg pie. (*on a look from Atsuko*) Sometimes.

CHIZ: (*enters holding up a jar triumphantly*) Instant coffee! What will we Americans think of next?

ATSUKO: Did you learn that at English class?

CHIZ: Why? You want to go to class with me, Ats?

TERUKO: (*interested*) What do you learn there?

CHIZ: English. (*a beat; smiling*) *You* should learn English.

ATSUKO: She knows English!

CHIZ: I mean real English. (*to Teruko*) Ever seen *My Fair Lady*? (*Teruko's face is blank.*) You know Audrey Hepburn?

TERUKO: Yes! Yes! *Breakfast at Tiffany*! (*a beat; excitedly but with surprise*) She goes to English class, too?

CHIZ: No, no, no. But in *My Fair Lady*, she starts out like you and ends up like me.

Chiz laughs, something Atsuko doesn't appreciate. Atsuko gets back to the matter at hand by tapping a spoon on the side of a tea cup.

ATSUKO: We have plain green tea, roasted rice tea, and just a little premium green tea.

TERUKO: Plain tea, please.

ATSUKO: Plain tea?

CHIZ: It's peasant tea, Teruko.

TERUKO: I like it.

ATSUKO: You have such simple tastes.

TERUKO: Makes life easier, yo.

SETSUKO: Well, roasted rice tea is fine.

ATSUKO: I like premium.

CHIZ: Of course.

SETSUKO: We'll let Atsuko choose.

Teruko starts to open the premium tin, but Atsuko pulls out a pretty tea tin from her bag and smiles like a reigning queen.

ATSUKO: I brought my own! Shall I treat you? (*Everyone but Chiz nods.*)

CHIZ: Once in a while I still drink green tea, but I choose my drink like I chose my husband: strong, dark, and with a lot of sugar.

ATSUKO: (*extremely offended*) Really, Chizuye-san!

CHIZ: Aw, loosen up, Ats!

ATSUKO: (*repulsed*) Did your husband teach you to talk like that?

CHIZ: (*ready to take her to the mat*) You don't know anything about my husband.

TERUKO: (*leaps into the conflict to avoid confrontation, hands each woman a plate of food*) Well . . . what do you think our husbands thought about us when they met us?

The other women look at Teruko with accustomed strangeness. Chiz isn't quite ready to relinquish her fight, but does so out of respect for Teruko and Setsuko.

TERUKO: I mean, there they were, in a strange land full of people they had never seen before. We were eighteen or nineteen, didn't speak too much English. Why do you really think they wanted to marry us?

SETSUKO: For the same reason we wanted to marry them. We were young and we fell in love. So many of us.

CHIZ: I don't think there were that many.

SETSUKO: Oh yes. My daughter read that over one hundred thousand of us married Amerikans after World War II.

CHIZ: That many?

TERUKO: (*with her customary amusing innocence*) That's a lot of love!

As the lights fade out on the house, Himiko, without sunglasses, enters and comes downstage center. She wears a pretty, youthful kimono. A light fades up on her and the song, "Don't Sit Under the Apple Tree with Anyone Else But Me," fades in to mark the postwar era in Japan. The other women drift downstage and occupy various background positions of the stage as they don pretty kimonos as well. Note: special kimono can be built with obi already attached.

HIMIKO: War's over. Strange-looking tall men with big noses and loud mouths are running our country. Our new supreme commander is called MacArthur, the great military saviour who will preserve our ravaged nation, . . . but who cannot preserve the common soul. (*a beat*) Last night, coming home from a wedding, I see my mother in her best kimono walking by the river. She takes off her geta and puts her feet in the water. Her face is peaceful. So lovely, like the moon in the shadows of the clouds. She slips her small hand into the river and picks up a large stone. Looking at it for only a moment, she drops it in her kimono sleeve. Suddenly, she begins filling both sleeves with stones. I try to stop her, but she fights. The same stones I played with as a child sagging in her kimono sleeves, she jumps into the currents. I watch her sink, her long black hair swirling around her neck like a silk noose. Her white face, a fragile lily; the river, a *taifun*. I wondered what it felt like to be a flower in a storm.

"The Wedding March" strikes up and the women move as if in an American ceremony toward center stage, all formally except for Himiko. All come downstage center looking outward, their expressions a varied repertoire. Setsuko smiles confidently. Teruko is meek, but decided. Himiko is arrogant. Atsuko smiles uncertainly. Chiz stands and joins them. The music rises to an uncomfortable pitch and ceases. Though facing the audience, the women share experiences happily as if stripped of inhibitions. Their demeanor and carriage reflect their youth.

TERUKO: (*a pert, cute bow*) I come from Fukuoka.

SETSUKO: (*an elegant, formal bow*) Me, from the great port city of Kobe.

CHIZ: (*a quick, crisp bow*) Yokohama.

ATSUKO: (*an official bow*) Nagoya.

HIMIKO: And me from the capital of the magnificent Empire of Japan: Tokyo. (*she bows, flipping her hair back*)

Lights widen. The women relax and take staggered positions. The lights focus from one to one.

TERUKO: We live in a small house next to my father's lumber business. I'm hanging clothes to dry as the white Yankee walks by. He says, "Why, hello, sugar pie! (*pronounced "shuga pie"*) Ain't you the purtiest thing!" I say no. He says yes. I say okay.

SETSUKO: And Father says, "Don't look at them! They'll rape you." He even confided to me they had tails. But on the way home from dressmaking school, the Yankee soldier's helmet falls off at my feet. What can I do? I give it back to him. For the first time, I look into the gentle eyes of a man the color of—soy sauce!

ATSUKO: (*removes a fan from her kimono sleeve and uses it girlishly*) Coming home from countryside to visit my aunt, I stop at market. Suddenly . . . there he is! A Japanese man in Amerikan uniform from California. He speaks bad Japanese. Sounds cute! He wants to give me a ride. (*sharply slaps the fan closed against her leg*) But I can hear my mother: (*speaks as if she's become her mother, an adamant and proud Japanese*) "Japanese Amerikans not Japanese anymore! They speak loud and marry foreigners. They don't even take a bath every night." (*again, the fan opens and moves girlishly*) He looked clean! But I say to soldier, "Sorry. No thank you, sir." (*bragging with joy*) He followed me all the way to the train station!

HIMIKO: It's tough in Tokyo after the Yankees take our country. I have six sisters. My father screams about all the daughters my mother left him with. "Too crowded, no money." If I want a new dress, I have to work for it. There is this cabaret. My girlfriend says let's go be dancers. I think she means onstage. Like movies, dancing in pretty dresses while people watch and clap. I find out too late it means dancing with Amerikans. Fifty yen-a-dance.

CHIZ: My mother died when I was born so it's always just Father and me. His best friend runs a restaurant that's pretty popular after the war with all the Amerikan boys. The first time I see Gustavo is there. Father and his friend—and his friend's marriage-hungry son—have me surrounded on all sides. But what they don't have covered is my heart.

All exit except for Teruko and Chiz. Music—"Tokyo Boogie Woogie"—sets the postwar mood in Japan again. Chiz immediately assumes the persona of an older, intrusive matchmaker. She stands behind the effervescent Teruko as if sneaking up on her.

TERUKO: Nineteen forty-seven. The business is picking up. We hold the yearly national barber competition and I win! First woman to win! Since the day he walked by my house, Master Sergeant Curtis MacKenzie comes to our barber shop again and again. He comes too much! Soon he will have no hair left!

CHIZ: Excuse me.

TERUKO: Yes.

CHIZ: That Amerikan. That nice-looking Texas man over there? He wants to take you to a movie. He's very nice. I cut his hair every week.

TERUKO: Explain to him.

CHIZ: Come on, Teru-chan, give him a chance. One little date. I won't tell anybody.

TERUKO: Tell him I can't be seen with a Yankee.

CHIZ: He said he will take you and a girlfriend to a movie. In fact, he said he will take everyone at the barber shop to a movie.

TERUKO: What? The four of us plus the three girls in back?

CHIZ: Yes. If that's what it takes to get a date with you. (*Chiz disappears in the darkness.*)

TERUKO: We walk on opposite sides of the street. Seven women on one side; you on the other. At the movie house, as if by chance, we sit next to each other. For a year, we go just like that, every week. Maybe fifty movies. Seven women. You spend a lot of yen, ne, just to get to know this silly country girl.

Blackout on Teruko; simultaneous spotlight goes up on Himiko who dances romantically to a slow American 1940s rhythm-and-blues song.

HIMIKO: It was simple; it was a job. "Good evening. Welcome, welcome. Fifty yen. Do you want a dance, soldier?" (*mimicks taking money and stands in surprise*) Five hundred yen! No, no. Too much. Take it back, please. (*offers it back*)

CHIZ: (*immediately appears and stands close to Himiko; the persona of the matchmaker continues, but in the style of a dykish, dance hall madam*) Girl-san. That Yankee soldier over there. He wants to take you to dinner.

HIMIKO: I don't leave with customers.

CHIZ: Ah, but one date won't hurt, will it, Himiko-san? No one has to know. (*touches Himiko sexually, who is taken aback by this*) After all, like he says, this is a dance hall.

HIMIKO: Yes. That is exactly what we do and all that we do—dance.

CHIZ: You'll never get anywhere thinking like that. (*Chiz disappears in the darkness.*)

HIMIKO: His name was Billy, a cute white boy from Oklahoma. He came back every week and danced only with me. Never said too much, but he brought me flowers every time. He taught me how to do the "lindy hop," (*she begins dancing and twirls around, finally stopping full of laughter; it settles into a smile*) . . . among other things. (*a beat*) It was my first time. (*a beat*) There was a teacher. Japanese. He taught at a university at Aoyama. He liked me. Truly. I was going to marry him. Good family. But I can't tell him I wasn't working at the trading company as an operator anymore. I can't tell him I am no longer respectable. So I just say I am sorry. I say my family won't accept the marriage. And I go back to the cabaret and wait for Billy.

Blackout on Himiko; spotlight on Atsuko and Setsuko, unaware of each other's presence. They come forward.

ATSUKO: We are shopping at the market.

SETSUKO: We are waiting for a train.

ATSUKO: Mr. Kazuhiro Yamamoto, the Californian, is buying fish. So cute his face. He says, "Buy. Fish. This one. (*indicates fish*) Kore," and looks at me for help with his Japanese—as the shop-keeper laughs and overcharges him! I say it's wrong to cheat him and protect my *Japanese* Amerikan fiancé.

SETSUKO: It begins to rain. Will the color of his skin wash off? I watch his wrist and wait, but (*to her pleasure*) it stays brown. He is a "military policeman" with great power. But he has gentle eyes; I don't know how he could have killed in the war. (*a beat*) Most of my girlfriends who married Amerikans are long gone. Creed goes, too, but we write—my bad English and his bad Japanese. He gets stationed in Tokyo after Korean war and, for five years, we date while I care for my mother. One August, I hold her and she dies in my arms. My bond with Japan gone, I can now leave. (*a beat as she smiles*) Creed and I marry. He says it's not like Dick and Jane getting hitched in Peoria.

The women address the unseen presences of their husbands.

TERUKO: You are so white, like a ghost, ne. How can I be sure you will never look at another woman? I hear you have many yellow-haired girls in Amerika. How can I be sure my black hair and different eyes will still be what you want?

SETSUKO: You say we may live the Japanese way wherever we go. I can't give up being Japanese even in your Amerika. This war drove my father to take his life. I gave up enough. I want peace.

ATSUKO: Well, you look Japanese. It isn't like marrying a real Yankee. Well, it isn't!

CHIZ: You keep telling me you're Mexican and that life isn't always easy in Amerika. I'm not sure what that means, but you have taught me this word "love" and I think that's what I feel for you. Life is short, Gustavo, and I have never felt like such a woman before. Take me with you. Hurry, before I see the tears in my father's eyes.

HIMIKO: My father doesn't want me to show my face at home again. "Look at your big belly," he shouts, "carrying Yankee-gai-jin baby. Shame. Shame." Billy, you have to take me to Amerika now. There's no life left for me in Japan. People whisper "whore" in the streets and spit at my feet. You brought the war into my heart. (*a beat, as if getting married*) Yes. I do. Until death do us part.

TERUKO: They are taller.

SETSUKO: And kinder.

ATSUKO: And cleaner.

HIMIKO: And richer.

CHIZ: Our men have lost their spirit.

TERUKO: It is hard after the war.

SETSUKO: We will soon be twenty.

ATSUKO: Soon too old for marriage.

HIMIKO: I am tired of living in the Tokyo the Yankees left us with.

They look outward and begin removing their kimono to reveal their original outfits underneath. They put the kimono away.

CHIZ: Father, forgive me. I should be here to take care of you when you're old.

TERUKO: Mother, please, stop crying. I'm not crazy. I love him.

SETSUKO: Dear mother, thank you for your blessing of Creed and me.

ATSUKO: My parents stop talking to me. I can't help it. He's the one I want to spend my life with. Forgive me. (*bows low*)

HIMIKO: Goodbye Father . . . (*regret and sadness*) . . . sisters. You shall never see me again.

CHIZ: Father weeps like a grandmother. "Write me, Chizu-chan!" he cries. "If you don't like it there, let me know and I'll come and get you myself." "Sayonara," he says, addressing me like a son. And I depart, my heart divided between two men like a dark, shameful canyon.

SETSUKO: We are a casualty the Japanese do not care to count.

CHIZ: Excess baggage Amerika does not want to carry.

TERUKO: And so the country watches as thousands of us leave Japan behind.

ATSUKO: And it aches.

HIMIKO: And it cries.

CHIZ: And it hopes we will not be lucky.

SETSUKO: Or brave.

TERUKO: Or accepted.

ATSUKO: Or rich.

HIMIKO: But between the hate they have for us.

CHIZ: The disdain.

SETSUKO: The contempt.

TERUKO: There is a private envy.

ATSUKO: Silent jealousy.

HIMIKO: Longing.

CHIZ: Yes.

SETSUKO: They want to wear our shoes.

TERUKO: Leave Japan and their war-ragged lives behind.

ATSUKO: Because the mess finally seems too much to clean.

HIMIKO: And Japan finally looks as small as it really is.

CHIZ: The war makes them see Japan is not the strongest or best.

SETSUKO: It makes us see—just once—beyond our tiny country and our tiny minds.

TERUKO: (*salutes, mocking an American army officer in a booming voice*) "Attention!"

ATSUKO: "All wives of American military personnel must wear pants on board ship during the entire fifteen-day journey."

HIMIKO: "Attention, all wives of American military personnel, socks and shoes must be worn at all times."

CHIZ: "I repeat socks *and* shoes."

SETSUKO: "Husbands and wives will be confined to separate sleeping quarters."

TERUKO: "That's all."

HIMIKO: (*as herself, quietly*) For now.

A single spotlight of interrogation grows tight, center stage, as the women are drawn to it as if by mandate. All crowd together and stand at attention. Himiko is less serious than the others. Teruko, unsure, follows Atsuko's movement and attitude. The women clear their throats. As they speak, they exchange looks which indicate unsure commitment to or a lack of understanding of the words. Setsuko and Atsuko raise their right hands. Teruko raises her left and then changes to her right, following Atsuko's example. Atsuko glances at Himiko who, with great boredom, raises her right hand. Only Chiz is confident, and she says the words well and with command.

WOMEN: (*in unison; with difficulty, stumbling over various words as this is the first time they have seen or read these words; some can say almost none of the words*) "I hereby declare, on oath, that I absolutely renounce all allegiance to any foreign state or sovereignty of which I have heretofore been a citizen; that I will defend laws of United States of Amerika against all enemies; that I will bear arms on behalf of United States; and that I take this obligation freely without any mental reservation: So help me God."

CHIZ: (*with pride and a sense of great accomplishment*) That's it.

ATSUKO: What? Did anybody understand any of that?

SETSUKO: Defend against all enemies? Aren't we enemy?

HIMIKO: Yes. Bear arms?

TERUKO: (*nodding at Atsuko for confirmation*) Freely?

CHIZ: Without *any* mental reservation!

SETSUKO: So help me . . .

ATSUKO: God?

Chiz sings "My Country 'Tis of Thee" and enjoins the others to sing along. Teruko is willing and joins in. They hold hands and smile and sing with joy. Setsuko softly sings the Japanese national anthem, "Kimi Ga Yo." Atsuko, after studying Chiz's choice for a brief moment, joins Setsuko and sings. But, as Himiko begins singing "My Country 'Tis of Thee" in a jarring, life-or-death manner, the women all grow quiet and sing the final lyrics with her, but with altered words. They sing with a sense of fear.

WOMEN: "Land where our souls will die. Land of our children's pride. From every mountainside, let freedom ring."

Crossfade to Scene Three as Chiz, Teruko, Atsuko and Setsuko return to the tatami and lights fade up. Himiko moves to side stage and observes.

SCENE THREE   Serving Tea

Atsuko pours tea as the others begin to examine the trunk's contents.

CHIZ: (*holds up her coffee cup*) Here's to fairy tales—and the dust they become.

HIMIKO: (*to audience, insistently*) No, no, they must drink for hope.

Setsuko, Teruko, and Atsuko lift their tea cups and sip. Teruko reacts if she burned her tongue.

TERUKO: A-cha-cha-cha-cha!

ATSUKO: Don't drink so fast, ne. Burn your mouth. (*tastes it*) It's not hot at all.

HIMIKO: It's hard to find the perfect temperature.

SETSUKO: It's fine. I like it this way, too.

CHIZ: Funny. You two like your tea the same way, your daughters are best friends, your husbands used to go hunting together—and you two probably haven't said a dozen words to each other over the last fifteen years. Is this the first time you've ever had tea together?

HIMIKO: It is, isn't it, Setsuko-san?

SETSUKO: I'm busy with my family. And I have so much sewing to do.

HIMIKO: What is your excuse, Atsuko-san?

ATSUKO: I keep busy with the church.

HIMIKO: And Teruko?

TERUKO: I try to visit everyone, but I like to play Bingo with my sugar pie. And, you know, three times a year we go to Las Vegas.

CHIZ: I don't have time either. After Gustavo left the army, we spent all our time together. Then . . . he was gone and, well, I started classes.

HIMIKO: Everyone has an alibi for silence.

CHIZ: (*smiles at the women to tease them*) Besides, no one ever invited me to take tea but Setsuko.

ATSUKO: I thought you didn't like tea.

CHIZ: Don't hand me that bull, Ats. You know damn well you didn't want me in your house because my husband was Mexican. (*slowly without hostility as she moves from woman to woman*) Atsuko believes she's the only pure soul left. But, Ats, I have to tell you, . . . you have no soul. (*Atsuko, taken aback, gets up and moves away. Chiz stands and walks toward her.*) Don't worry—I don't either.

TERUKO: Chizuye-san!

CHIZ: And, Teruko, you think your white husband buys you a position in town society, but, deep down at heart, you're still a "Jap" to them and you always will be. (*Setsuko looks away*) Setsuko, you live like a social worker. You've had to deal with so much prejudice you don't want *any*body else to feel pain.

SETSUKO: I enjoy taking tea. With any of you.

TERUKO: My husband doesn't like when we speak Japanese. He says it sounds like silverware dropping. So it's better if I take tea at someone else's home.

ATSUKO: Well, I'm not ashamed to say it: I only take tea with my very best friends.

CHIZ: Which is to say you don't take it very often. (*Atsuko boldly faces Chiz, who does not back off.*)

ATSUKO: Chizuye, there's no reason to spite me because my husband is Japanese Amerikan.

CHIZ: (*laughs*) Do you think I have any respect for Japanese Amerikans?

ATSUKO: (*quickly, adamant*) They're our people. My husband's parents died in a concentration camp in the California desert, just because they were Japanese.

CHIZ: They're not "our" people. They hate us more than Amerikans because we remind them of what they don't want to be anymore. They made a choice; most of us haven't. They don't like you either, Ats, because you're a "war bride."

ATSUKO: (*indignant*) I'm not a war bride. I didn't marry the war.

SETSUKO: Maybe we did.

CHIZ: And then we came here—to Kansas. Not quite the fairy tale ending you ordered, eh, Ats?

As Chiz laughs gruffly and darkly, the truth of this statement jars them. Clouded with discomfort, they lift their tea cups and drink, except for Chiz who stares off into the distance. Lights fade out on the tatami area. Downstage center, a spotlight fades up on Himiko. She wears her black sunglasses. A typically 1950s Kansas song— "How Much Is That Doggie in the Window?"—fades in as Himiko pirouettes and then speaks in the manner of a carnival barker. In the background in dim light, the others kneel as if just having arrived in Kansas. When Himiko addresses them, they smile, unaware that they are the joke.

HIMIKO: "Welcome, welcome, to the Land of Milk and Honey, the Bible Belt; the land of great, wide plains and (*with pride*) narrow minds. On behalf of the tourism bureau, we'd like to welcome you to Kansas, the Sunflower State. We know all about you people. We read the magazines. We saw the cartoons. We saw *Sayonara*.

Himiko bows ridiculously and the women respond sincerely with bows; Himiko returns to her own persona.

HIMIKO: It was more than racism. It was the gloating of victor over enemy. It was curiosity about our yellow skin, about why in the hell their red-blooded Amerikan boys would want to bring home an "Oriental." (*she indicates the other women*) Some of them liked us; most of them didn't. (*exits; the music fades out, and the others move downstage.*)

ATSUKO: Tell me, miss, do you have a Japanese restaurant here? I want to surprise my husband. No Japanese restaurant? *Ara!* What kind of restaurant do you have? Steak? Barbecue? (*pronounced bah-bee-q*) What is barbecue?

SETSUKO: Excuse me. We are looking for a hotel. What? Interracial couple? What does that mean? You reserve the right to refuse service? But what did we do wrong? My husband works for your government. We just need a place to stay for the night. I *am* speaking English!

TERUKO: (*fearfully*) Please stop staring at me like I am an animal. I just want to buy groceries. (*less fearfully*) What? You want to be my friend? Oh, how . . . how nice! (*She mimicks shaking the person's hand, something she finds strange. She bows at the same time and then, uncomfortable, draws her hand back without malice.*) You have such beautiful yellow hair. Like the color of Japanese pickles!

CHIZ: (*determinedly and to the point*) Listen, lady, you give me a hard time about opening a checking account just because I'm Japanese, and I'll give you more hell than you bargained for. I'm an American citizen now. (*but she slightly mispronounces the word "citizen"*)

TERUKO: I miss sashimi!

CHIZ: It would be nice to bite into o-manju.

SETSUKO: I can taste the crisp nashi.

ATSUKO: Sasa-dango.

TERUKO: Kushi-dango.

CHIZ: Hot oden.

SETSUKO: Kaki. There's nothing like Japanese persimmons.

ATSUKO: He never told me there would be no Japanese food.

SETSUKO: He never told me about "we reserve the right."

CHIZ: I never thought he would die and leave me here to be an American without him.

TERUKO: I never thought they would be scared of us, too.

The shrill whistle of a tea kettle blasts through the air, bringing the women back to the tatami room. Himiko enters and drifts. Periodically, she rests and rubs her feet as if they are sore.

TERUKO: More tea.

HIMIKO: (*to audience*) Yes. Please. They *must* keep drinking.

ATSUKO: You didn't mix up the tea cups, did you?

The women react to Atsuko's idiosyncrasy.

TERUKO: I think this one is mine.

SETSUKO: This one is mine.

Teruko serves fresh tea to everyone and Teruko freshens Chiz's coffee.

CHIZ: Now, Ats, take it easy.

ATSUKO: She talks just like the women at the grocery store.

TERUKO: Yes, but she gets through the checkout line faster than any of us, too.

SETSUKO: She's always adapted faster than us.

ATSUKO: So, ne, I could never even get used to Amerikan bed. In Japan, I always sleep right on the edge of the blankets so my nose could smell the sweet straw of the matting. I come to Amerika and every night for months I fall out of bed!

SETSUKO: One day—I am so embarrassed—Creed sees me in the bathroom. He says, "Setsuko! You're standing on the toilet! Sit down." So I sit—facing the wall. Next time, he laughs and says, "Honey, you're sitting on it backwards. Turn around."

TERUKO: You know this car wash on Sixth Street? I want to surprise my sugar pie by washing the car for him. So I drive through about twenty-five miles an hour! The machines scrape the car. When I come out of there, there are bumps all over and I tell that manager he better pay me for the damage. He just laughs and calls my husband.

SETSUKO: (*looks at the placid Chiz*) Was it always so easy for you?

CHIZ: Well, I live *here*. I make the best of it.

SETSUKO: Japan. Amerika. Maybe it doesn't matter where we go. Back home, country papa-san says to me when my first is born, "Bring *it* here for me to see." He wants to see how ugly she is. But she is pretty, and the Japanese crowd and stare. She doesn't look Japanese, they say, and she doesn't look Negro. And I am glad because I have created something new, something that will look new and think new.

CHIZ: (*a chuckle which she knows will irritate Atsuko*) Hybrid Japanese.

TERUKO: Mixed Japanese kids at school are very smart. Teachers say they've never seen anything like it.

ATSUKO: That's only because they're half Japanese.

CHIZ: Ats, may your daughter marry a Mexican.

Atsuko almost chokes on her tea at this remark.

TERUKO: Japanese Mexican girls are pretty.

ATSUKO: I don't expect Chizuye to understand the importance of being Japanese.

CHIZ: Oh, Teri's (*notes Teruko*) all right because her daughter came out looking Japanese. Buddha was good to her for chanting all these years. (*rubs her hands together to make fun of chanting*)

ATSUKO: At least none of our girls turned out like Mieko Hamilton.

HIMIKO: But they are like Mieko. They're between two worlds. We put them there.

ATSUKO: Mieko was just like her mother.

HIMIKO: Yes. And like her father.

ATSUKO: Himiko was crazy and she drove her husband crazy.

CHIZ: And I think you're crazy, so it's all relative, Ats.

TERUKO: It's nice to be together again, ne.

Crossfade lights from tatami to downstage center as women march quietly in military formation to a period military song and drumbeat. Himiko comes center stage.

HIMIKO: Our husbands didn't know what they were getting into. They brought us to Kansas: their Japanese wives dressed up in Amerikan clothes. We were little, breakable dolls to them. I don't think they ever really understood us, but they loved us. Even when the memories of the war crashed through their heads like an endless nightmare, they tried hard to keep on living like normal people and to be the husbands they had dreamed about being when they laid their lives on the line for their country.

As the women file into place and stand at attention, Himiko joins them. They appear rigid, stoic with the carriage of men. Setsuko breaks line and takes on the persona of a gentle, urban Negro.

SETSUKO: Uh, Baby-san, why are you staring at the washing machine? The clothes should have been done an hour ago. Yes, I said you don't have to do a thing. Yes, I promised it's all automatic. But, honey, even when it's automatic, you have to push the button to turn it on.

Setsuko falls back into formation. Atsuko takes on the persona of a mellow, California nisei and steps forward.

ATSUKO: Hey, Atsuko, where'd you put my hammer? I gotta finish these shelves and I know you never put it back when you use it. Now don't get upset. I'm not trying to say you don't ever do anything right. I just want my hammer. Are you on the rag or what? (*the imaginary hammer comes flying through the air and he barely catches it*) Okay, okay. Sorry. I didn't mean it. Aw, honey, please don't make me sleep on the couch. (*apparently, Atsuko has hit him on the head*)

Atsuko falls back into line. Chiz falls out.

CHIZ: Hey, Chizuye. I'm happy you've learned to cook Mexican food, but can you cook some Japanese food for me? The paella is fine, but I love Japanese food. What do you say you teach me how to make yaki-soba?

Chiz falls back into line. Teruko breaks line and takes on the persona of a robust, swaggering Texan.

TERUKO: You did *what* to the car at the car wash? Shit, Teri, ain't you got any sense in that little Japanese head of yours? You don't drive *through* the car wash. You just sit in the damn car and let the machines roll the car. I'll be damned, my new car lit'rally gone down the drain. (*reacts to a crying Teruko, softens*) Now, honey, don't cry. We'll just have to get the car fixed. (*falls back into formation*) Again.

HIMIKO: (*falls out of formation with the persona of a scrappy Oklahoman with an edgy, rural voice*) Himi, I didn't stay out late. I told you. I was fishing with Kaz Yamamoto. Okay, okay, so I fished all night and only brought home two fish. What can I say? I'm a bad fisherman. You want to go out for ice cream? There's a Peter Pan store right up the street. I'll get you some Oregon blackberry. I'll bet you never had that flavor before. What? Wait a minute, these ain't frozen fillets from the grocery store. Shut up before I knock your fuckin' teeth in, you hear me, Himi?

Himi falls back into formation. The "men" break line and ad lib hearty greetings. Two go through the motions of cleaning and loading rifles; two open the beers and mimic drinking. Campsite activity ensues.

TERUKO: Yo, beer.

ATSUKO: Yeah.

HIMIKO: Ain't nothin' like a huntin' trip to clear out the lungs, ain't it, boys?

TERUKO: Kinda like shooting at Japs again. (*men look at him*) Oooooooops. I didn't mean it that way. Y'all know how it was during the war, "do this to the Japs," "do that to the Japs." Sorry. Slip of the tongue. 'Course mine always has been kinda swingin' on a loose hinge. (*as he pats Atsuko on the shoulder*) I mean, you know I got a good heart. (*he turns and mimics shooting a basket*) Two points.

ATSUKO: (*he takes his turn at shooting, makes the basket and ad libs victory*) My friends said I married one of my own kind. Uh-uh. I spent my life trying to be American, not Japanese American. Being American was better.

Atsuko and Setsuko exchange a handshake of fraternity.

SETSUKO: I grew up hard in New York. I had chicks throwing a lot of fast words and a lot of fast ass in my face for years. When I met Setsuko, I knew I could live the quiet life I love, and she'd be right there with me. Forever.

TERUKO: Before World War II, I never dated anything but white tomatoes. When I laid my eyes on Teri, I said to myself, "Fella, you are just about to cross the big boundary line." And I crossed it and there ain't a yellow rose in all of Texas who'll ever turn my heart like her.

CHIZ: (*he shoots a basket and misses; the other "men" kid him*) I never even saw a Japanese until the war. I just fell in love with this strange girl. She happened to be Japanese, and she happened to be pretty ballsy and bright. She may be less Japanese now, but I think that's her way of survival. I hate to think what a loner I'd become without her, and vice versa.

ATSUKO: (*mimicks urinating with back turned to audience*) Ats and I are a good example of opposites attracting, but she's the only person who calls me Kazuhiro . . . just like my mom used to.

TERUKO: Aw, well ain't that cute.

Teruko and Atsuko mimick tagging each other, shooting two baskets competitively.

TERUKO: Two points. Whoosh.

ATSUKO: (*joking*) Wimp. (*shoots and revels in victory*)

Teruko and Atsuko do a quick "Three Stooges" exchange.

ATSUKO: Women. You can't live with 'em and—

HIMIKO: And you can't shoot 'em. Not anymore. Even though they're Japs. (*dark, reverberating laughter that disturbs the other "men"*)

ATSUKO: (*approaches Himiko*) Hamilton, I'm tired of hearing that word. What should I call you? White trash?

HIMIKO: I'm the only real American here. (*with pride*) All-American mutt. (*more somberly, threateningly to Atsuko*) Fightin' Japs . . . marryin' Japs. Yellow skin and slit eyes. Just like the man in the jungle. Wanting me to die so he could live.

TERUKO: I remember the time your wife ran out of your house wearing a slip. She said you'd had a fight and you told her you wanted to kiss and make up. (*a beat as the others relive this, too*) And you kissed her, all right—and bit off part of her lip. They had to sew it back on.

HIMIKO: What can I say. There's nobody like her. Never has been. (*a beat*) Never will be. She's the only fuckin' prize I ever won.

The others eye him like a jury and Himiko laughs.

SETSUKO: What did you expect, Hamilton? You'd bring her home and she'd sprout blue eyes and whistle "Dixie"?

HIMIKO: (*anger simmering just under the surface and finally busting loose*) Hey, what do you want me to do? Huh? She crawls under my fist like an orphan beggin' for love and my knuckles come down like a magnet. Like a fucking magnet, man. I got eight younger brothers and sisters and I lived in a trailer the size of a pencil box, working three jobs while you guys was jabbin' broads in the alley. Fuckin'-ay man, give me some room to breathe in.

Himiko spins away as lights blackout on the "men." Spotlight simultaneously fades up on Chiz, downstage left.

CHIZ: Gustavo always said, "Chiz, you're gonna love Kansas. It's real slow, I know, but we'll have a house and a business, and Mama's going to spoil you rotten." He was going to teach me how to build a snowman, our project for that first winter in Kansas. So the snow came and we waited. He said it had to be just the right wetness so we could pack it tightly, so we could make a snowman who would outlive all other snowmen. A *perfect* snowman. That afternoon, Mama Juarez and I were making cinnamon hot chocolate for when Gustavo came home. Snow was falling around the steaming window. The icy streets looked like a distorted mirror. And, somewhere where I couldn't hear him call, where he couldn't grab my hand for help, Gustavo was sliding into another world, thinking only of me as the ice cut into his beautiful face. The next day, the snow was perfect for building our snowman. But I didn't know how to build anything without Gustavo. And I told myself I would never not know how again. (*a beat, a vow to herself*) Perfect.

Setsuko enters the light and hovers over her.

SETSUKO: My youngest takes home economics. She taught me how to make cookies and milk. I'm almost done. The phone rings. "Mrs. Banks?" the army doctor says, "We regret to inform you Sergeant Banks passed away at fourteen hundred thirty-two hours." The nightmares of war had chased his heart away. (*a pause*) The girls come home, their sloe-shaped eyes full of the sun. I ask them if they want to go "home"—to Japan. Or to California, where there are more (*smiles*) "hybrid Japanese." They say they want to go with me. That I am home. And so, I have a family to raise and my house. I'm staying right here and I dare anyone to move me.

CHIZ: Setsuko.

Chiz holds onto her, a move that makes Setsuko uncomfortable at first but then becomes necessary for both of them.

SETSUKO: Yes.

CHIZ: (*with unbitter puzzlement*) It wasn't perfect.

SETSUKO: But at least it was. At least we had it. Once.

Lights dim on them with an immediate spotlight up on Himiko.

HIMIKO: (*with quiet, determined dignity without a shred of anger or self-pity*) No, we didn't. We never had it. All we had filtering through our fists was the powder left when a dream explodes in your face and your soul is left charred with the memory of what could have been if there was no war, if there was never a drink to help him forget, never a place like this where our dignity was tied to a tree and left hanging for strangers to spit on.

Himiko exits as Chiz and Setsuko return to the tatami room and lights cross fade into Scene Four:

SCENE FOUR Cold Tea

The women reflect exhaustion and contemplation. They appear to be sitting closer, except for Atsuko, who is distant both physically and psychologically.

SETSUKO: The tea is cold.

ATSUKO: Well, we must make a fresh pot. (*exits to kitchen to do so*)

TERUKO: We've been talking so much.

SETSUKO: Yes, things get cold when neglected.

TERUKO: (*checks Atsuko's tea tin and calls out to Atsuko*) We're out of your tea, Atsuko-san. May we drink "peasant" tea?

ATSUKO: (*from the kitchen*) Have what you want. (*Atsuko returns with fresh hot water for tea.*)

TERUKO: I've been in Kansas so long, I don't know good tea from bad.

CHIZ: Oh, Teruko, come on. You've adjusted the best; you're an entrepreneur. You and Curt started from scratch; Japanese barber comes to Kansas.

TERUKO: Curtis wants to stay here. Maybe buy a farm. I think that's okay. Setchan, what about you? Do you think you'll marry again and stay here?

SETSUKO: If a nice man comes along . . . maybe. I will be fine.

CHIZ: How many Kansas rednecks are there who can think of a Japanese as anything but a geisha or Tokyo Rose? Even the most beautiful Japanese in the world couldn't find a redneck for miles who'd see her as a real person. (*a beat*) I don't want to love again. It hurts too much when they go away.

ATSUKO: Well, I suppose you all envy me, thinking I'm the lucky one. (*the women react to her again*) But my husband promised he'd leave the army and we'd move to California. He's still in the army and we're still here. (*a beat*) It's so unfair that I have to die in Kansas.

TERUKO: (*tired of Atsuko's ridiculous fears*) Atsuko-san, you're going to live a long time.

ATSUKO: So? What difference does it make? When we're dead, no one will remember there were Japanese in Kansas.

TERUKO: What will happen to the last one? Who will bury her?

ATSUKO: When it comes down to it, we're alone. Just like Himiko. She died alone.

SETSUKO: But she's not alone now. I am with her.

ATSUKO: Oh, spare me. She's dead. Who cares about death unless it's happening to you?

HIMIKO: They must care. If my journey leaves me stranded here, they, too, will have no passage.

TERUKO: I am with Himiko-san, too.

ATSUKO: Well, I'm not and I never was. (*starts gathering her cup and goodies*) In fact, I'm ready to go home. I've wasted my day and, let's face it, all the cleaning in the world isn't going to change Himiko's life or help her find a new life that's any better.

SETSUKO: Maybe it's really not Himiko's life you're worried about. Maybe it's yours, Atsuko-san.

Atsuko looks outward. Her eyes lock with Himiko's for a moment. Himiko bows her head toward her invitingly. Atsuko shakes her head as if she has seen something and then turns to the women again. She is uneasy and caustic.

ATSUKO: Come on. Let's be honest. Since when has anyone really cared about Himiko Hamilton? We've always known she was crazy. Poor Teruko, you had to live in the same neighborhood as her. You couldn't even go into your front yard without her bothering you. Of course, Himiko was scared of Chizuye so she didn't bother her too much. She admired you, Chizuye. Yes. You had become a model Amerikan. She used to talk about your "perfect Amerikan" accent. Said you sounded just like a television star.

CHIZ: Atsuko, shut up before I lose my temper. I've been saving it up for you all these years, so if it gets loose . . .

TERUKO: (*gently, again trying to deter confrontation*) It *was* Chizuye who finally came to check on Himiko when she disappeared. She found her here. Sleeping.

CHIZ: Dead. For at least three days. To think of it.

SETSUKO: No. She died many years ago. Of a broken heart.

ATSUKO: Oh, you all make me laugh. Such tragedy in your eyes. I can just hear the shakuhachi playing in the background as you weep for her spirit.

SETSUKO: That's enough, Atsuko-san.

ATSUKO: Enough what? Enough laughter for the joke the war played on my life? Enough tears for having no allegiance except what I practice in the silence of my soul? Excuse me for not being strong like you, Setsuko. We all have our own problems to worry about. Maybe you think you can bear the weight of the world, but I can't.

CHIZ: What you can do for me is shut up. You've always been a mean, selfish bitch, Atsuko.

ATSUKO: (*quite taken aback, she tries to collect herself*) Teruko let's go! (*Teruko shakes her head firmly*) Teruko!

TERUKO: (*highly upset, the words spill out uncontrollably*) Atsuko, I know you're afraid because the first of us is dead. Maybe you think soon we'll be having tea like this after you die. And maybe that is what will be. You can't control that. But you *can* control how you treat people.

SETSUKO: And the respect you owe the dead.

ATSUKO: Oh, just leave me alone. I wish I'd never come here today.

CHIZ: But we did, didn't we? Like the good Japanese ladies we are. (*a beat*) We're not here because we have to be. Japanese manners don't require us to pay homage to some loon of a woman, even if she *was* Japanese. No, we're here today because we hurt inside like we never have before. Because when the first of us goes so violently and it's all over the papers, it wakes us up. For the first time in our lives, we gather together all the pieces of our used-up hearts and come running here hoping we'll find some kind of miracle that will glue it all back together and send us into our old age with something to hold onto.

TERUKO: But today we *have* all gone a little farther with each other than we ever have before.

CHIZ: Tomorrow it'll be status quo again.

SETSUKO: No, it won't ever be like it used to be again.

ATSUKO: Speak for yourself. (*a challenge, desperately trying to maintain the control she has always enjoyed over Teruko*) Are you coming, Teruko? (*She begins to move toward an exit; she is full of anger and suppressing tears. She turns once again to look at Teruko. Setsuko stands supportively behind Teruko. The words bite out of Atsuko's mouth.*) Teruko . . . this is your last chance.

To her shock, Teruko even more firmly turns away. Devastated, Atsuko moves toward the door and then, defeated, falls to her knees; Himiko immediately comes to her side.

HIMIKO: Atsuko-san, stay. If you leave now, no one will rest.

Himiko stands in front of Atsuko and, without touching her, helps her to stand and balance using her hands as delicate guides. Atsuko fights with herself and then turns back to the women. She bows in apology to Teruko who bows back. She turns toward the door again, but Setsuko bows to her. Feeling better, Atsuko returns the bow. Still uncomfortable, Atsuko glances at Chiz who motions kindly for her to sit down. She does and the other women follow suit, except for Teruko.

TERUKO: The only time we have taken tea together is whenever something bad happened to a Japanese "war bride." We have the best tea and realize how little we understand about each others' choices: in husbands, in raising our children, in whether or not we choose to embrace Amerika. Amerikans don't want us. Japanese Amerikans too busy feeling bad themselves. We can't go back to Japan. That's why I say family is the most important thing. What makes us the most happiest? Our children. Our children.

Chiz exits as lights crossfade to the tatami area and music—"Runaway"—fades up rapidly. The women dance onto the tatami area as young girls. The "girls" assume positions as if enjoying themselves at a slumber party: manicuring, Teruko rolling someone's hair, putting on cosmetics, etc. Atsuko mimicks smoking. The women are playing their daughters. They sing the "wa-wa-wa" lyrics of the song and burst into laughter.

ATSUKO: Can you believe it? My mom won't let me go out for cheerleading. She said it's too "sexual." (*imitates mother's accent*) "Don't do skiing. Japanese don't ski. Don't do motorcycle. Don't do skydive." She even thinks life insurance guarantees you don't die. When I was born, she bought me a hundred thousand dollar policy.

SETSUKO: My mother worries about life, not death. (*imitates mother's accent*) "Did you eat your raw egg and fermented soy beans today? Did you have bowel movement?" (*she laughs*) Mom's so funny. We were separated in a store and, over the intercom, I heard: "Japanese mother lost in dry goods. Will her daughter please claim her?"

TERUKO: My mother doesn't worry about anything except my dad. When she starts licking the bottom of his shoes and gets that look in her eye, (*mimicks her mother doing this*) I can say, "Mom, hi, I'm going to join the Marines, become a lesbian, screw the football team." She'd just say, (*imitates mother's accent*) "Okay, Linda. That's good. Have to fix dinner for sugar pie now."

ATSUKO: (*does breast exercises*) Man, the only thing that really bugs me after all these years is having to take my shoes off in the house.

SETSUKO: I thought I was going to die when my date picked me up for the homecoming dance. While he waited for me, my mother put shower caps over his shoes!

Except for Himiko, the "girls" laugh and ad lib sounds of embarrassment. Himiko is eerily silent.

TERUKO: Mieko, what about *your* mother? (*Teruko can't help giggling, although she tries hard to suppress it. It is contagious.*) She came to our house wearing that blonde wig. She slurped her tea and crocheted those green and purple poodle toilet paper covers. Ugh.

All but Himiko laugh nervously, unable to restrain themselves, despite Himiko's cold stare.

HIMIKO: (*without feeling, no sense of bitterness, with an eerie smile*) I hate the world. (*fresh laughter from the other "girls"*)

ATSUKO: So take a number, Mieko.

HIMIKO: You guys don't know anything about what life really is. Life is about relationships. Relationships with guys.

TERUKO: Oh, Mieko. We all date guys.

HIMIKO: It isn't about dating guys. It's about being *fucked* by guys.

Their laughter is cut short by Himiko's remark. Whatever they are doing, their motions grind to a halt: Teruko in the middle of putting on lipstick, Atsuko in the middle of a laugh, and so on. They are shocked at this language and eye one another uncomfortably. Mieko seems to enjoy this power.

HIMIKO: In fact, it's about being fucked by everyone: your mother, your father—and even yourself. (*a beat as she looks away from the girls and then she hits the table with the palm of her hand, frightening the other girls*) Don't ask me about my mother. Because then you're asking me about myself . . . and I don't know who the hell I am.

She spins away from the other girls, moving to one side of the stage and folding herself into a ball and the other "girls" exit quickly. A light fades up on Himiko, now having reassumed the persona of Himiko, the spirit.

HIMIKO: I was born in a storm and it's never stopped raining. My only blessing is Mieko, my half-Japanese girl. I love her so much, but she was born in my storm, too. For years, I tried to talk to her, but she wasn't ready. (*a sad laugh*) Mieko is so fast, I only know what she looks like from behind. Because she's always leaving, her big Japanese *o-shiri* swaying like a flower, out looking for dreams she thinks men are going to give her. So it was a Saturday in May. Mieko wants to make me worry, so she *hitchhikes*. She's gone three days. Then the big policeman comes. "Do you have a daughter named Mieko? When's the last time you saw her, Mrs. Hamilton?" (*breathes hard and fast; forces composure*) The last time I saw Mieko is in the dusk. She looks so Japanese, her shoulders curving like gentle hills. "Perfect kimono shoulders," her grandmother would say. (*a beat*) Mieko came home today. Someone made her dirty, stabbed her in the chest many times and then raped her as she died. Left a broom inside my little girl's body. Her brassiere was shredded by the knife. (*a beat*) There is no one for me; there never was. Even my sisters of Japan cannot bless me with sandals to cover my blistered feet as I prepare for the longest journey. (*looks around*) Billy, is that you? Before it's too late, tell me the truth. You loved me, didn't you? Once. Once there was nobody like me. Now that I know, I can go on without you, Billy. I see you there, waiting in the mist, your strong arms ready to hold me for one last dance. But I'm going another way. Like bamboo, I sway back and forth in the wind, bending but never breaking. Never again. The war is over. Mother? Is that you? Are you waiting for me, too? (*brief, absolute delight, addressing Mieko when she was five*) Mieko-chan, I see you dancing in my best kimono: all light and laughter and . . . clean! (*the delight fades*) No, you all have to let me go now. I have a long walk ahead of me. All ties are unbound, as completely as if they never existed.

She exits as lights dim and we bridge into the next scene. Wind chimes tinkle in the darkness:

SCENE FIVE   Perfect Drinking Temperature

SETSUKO, ATSUKO, CHIZ, TERUKO: (*from various corners of the stage, they chant in the style of Buddhist chanting; in English the ancient poem means:* "I don't care / What anybody says / I will never stop / Loving you.") *Hito wa dono yo ni, i oo to mamayo.*

SETSUKO: *Tsunor'ya*

ATSUKO: . . . *suru to mo* . . .

TERUKO: . . . *yami* . . .

CHIZ: . . . *wa senu.*

SETSUKO: *Hito wa dono yo ni . . .*

ATSUKO: *. . . i oo to mamayo . . .*

TERUKO: *Tsunor'ya suru to mo . . .*

CHIZ: *Yami wa senu.*

SETSUKO: Himi-chan.

ATSUKO: Himiko.

TERUKO: Himiko-san.

CHIZ: Searching.

SETSUKO: For peace

TERUKO: Finally free.

CHIZ: Himiko-san.

As if drawn to the power of their harmony, Himiko enters dressed in resplendent kimono. She moves gracefully, winsomely, and comes center stage as the chanting continues.

SETSUKO: Your sisters call.

TERUKO: Come.

ATSUKO: Come unto us.

ALL: Come to tea with us.

They study each other thoughtfully and then surround Himiko with warmth. Himiko kneels before them, facing the audience and bows her head low.

ALL: (*a whisper*) *Gan'batte.*

SETSUKO: (*a whisper in the shadow of "gan'batte"*) Persevere.

The women return to the tatami room, wind chimes marking the transition. Himiko follows and watches them.

CHIZ: I am glad I came here today. Somehow, I feel at home with you women, you Japanese women. (*smiles*) Today.

SETSUKO: We should have let anyone who wanted to help come over. Today, even taking tea is different.

ATSUKO: Yes, even tea tastes different.

CHIZ: Maybe we will have tea again. All of us?

SETSUKO: Yes, Chizuye-san. Soon.

TERUKO: As you wish it.

SETSUKO: Atsuko-san?

ATSUKO: (*looks around the room as if she senses a ghost; answers slowly*) Yes? (*a frightened beat*) Himiko is here, isn't she?

TERUKO: Oh, please, you're scaring me. Let's not talk about ghosts.

ATSUKO: But maybe that's the fate that awaits us all. A black space where the war dead and us, the war wounded, must sit out eternity.

SETSUKO: If it is our destiny, then—

CHIZ: Then it is our destiny.

TERUKO: So, ne.

SETSUKO: (*The women look solemnly at one another as Setsuko bows in honor of Himiko*) Okagesama de.

CHIZ: (*takes a cup for Himiko and acknowledges her*) In your honorable shadow. (*Chiz puts a fifth cup on the table.*) Please join us for tea.

The women sit for a last drink of tea. Himiko joins them. They lift their cups simultaneously and slightly bow their heads to one another. Himiko forms a cup with her hands and drinks from it in unison with the others. She looks happier.

HIMIKO: Perfect.

The minute that word is uttered, the women pack up their things, ad lib farewells in Japanese—"sa," "ikimasho, ne," "mata, ne," "ato de denwa shimasu," etc.—except for Chiz. She is the last to speak and says "bye-bye" and Teruko responds with "bye-bye." They exit in different directions. Setsuko lingers as if trying to absorb Himiko's energy from the air. She bows deeply. Then she, too, exits as traditional Japanese music fades up. Taking each cup of tea and bowing to the woman who left the tea before, Himiko pours the remnants into her cup. She gathers strength from this and moves downstage center where she kneels. Holding the cup outward, she bows gracefully to the audience and then drinks the tea with extreme thirst that appears to be satisfied from the drink. She sets the cup down in front of her and smiles a half-smile, perhaps like that of Mona Lisa, to the audience. She bows low, all the way to the floor. Black out.

THE END

WALLS

❋

JEANNIE BARROGA

In the late 1940s when Jeannie Barroga was born in Milwaukee, Wisconsin, Vietnam was a French colony, fighting a perennial battle for national independence. By the 1960s, however, as she came of age, Vietnam was the setting for an American war that raged at the periphery of her daily life. "I grew up with Vietnam inundating my senses through the media. It got to the point where I felt every waking moment there was something horrible happening—not just on foreign soil, but on the streets of our nation."[1]

It was not until 1985, when she was already six years into a career as a playwright, that she began to think about the Vietnam War and its legacy as subject for a play. The notes she collected for the project were used for the basis of a play called *The Night Before the Rolling Stones Concert 1981* which Barroga describes as "a comedy, sort of like *The Big Chill*." When the play was given a staged reading she was surprised by the intensity of the audience response to a scene where a returning veteran confronts his friends and asks, "Why didn't you even write me while I was there?" "It was a short bit, didn't last more than two to three minutes on stage, but the reaction to those few minutes was volatile. It really surprised me that the audience should pick that one scene to get riled up about."

Barroga filed the draft of that script and pondered over the unresolved and conflicting feelings the veteran scene had raised within her audience and herself. Two years later she ran across Jan Scruggs's *To Heal a Nation*, a book of photographs with text about the Vietnam War Memorial.[2] "I was paging through it and I just urst into tears. . . . I knew it was something I could transfer onto stage and have people feel the way I felt. . . . That's when I went into high gear and started doing the research."

While her investigation included interviews with veterans and research in the Library of Congress, she continued to return to the penetrating images in Scruggs's book. The photographs became the inspiration for several key characters and plot scenarios. The characters of Sarah and Morris, for example, were based on a photograph of a nurse pushing a disabled veteran down Constitution Avenue. "From the photos I got these 'what if' story lines. What if [Sarah and Morris] had just met at the Wall and somehow had gotten to a point where he felt comfortable enough for her to roll him down Constitution Avenue? . . . I wanted the stories to happen right in front of the Wall as opposed to peripheral areas."

As a counterpoint to the multiple scenes and subplots that occur at the Wall, Barroga chose to probe the controversy surrounding the monument's design and construction by including its architect, Maya Lin, as a character. A Chinese American, Lin was born in 1959, the year of the first American casualty in Vietnam. As a twenty-one-year-old Yale student, she competed with a national field of professional and amateur artists to have her design selected over 1,421 other entries. Her model became the center of a heated controversy, its construction opposed by veterans and veterans organizations which found its abstract lines too austere and alienating. Some wanted the competition open only to veterans, others felt the monument should be realistic and figurative.

Over sixty plays have been written by American playwrights about the Vietnam War experience including plays that deal with the veteran experience such as *Tracers* by John Difusco, *Back in the World* by Stephen Mack Jones, which details the experience of African American veterans, and *Honey Bucket* by Mel Escueta about the participation of Asian Americans. *Walls* is typical of this genre of American plays in that its point of view is American and its primary focus is the effect of fifty-eight thousand American lives lost as opposed to the two million Vietnamese casualties. However, Barroga adds a unique perspective through the inclusion of the Maya Lin subplot. "To me it's a woman's viewpoint on a male war. Specifically a woman of color's viewpoint on an essentially racist war which to this day I don't think people want to recognize. [In the case of Maya Lin] they reacted to a design and then a designer as if the war was still on. . . . it couldn't help but be racial as much as everyone denied it. It was . . . the fact that she's Chinese, she looked like the ones they died fighting."

During her research phase Barroga attempted to contact Lin in hopes of an interview, but she received no response. In the original draft of *Walls* the Lin character's dialogue was completely invented, a decision that proved disastrous in the first reading of the play. "It just didn't ring true . . . so I went back and researched everything she ever said in interviews and devised scenes around her words." Using quotations from interviews that had appeared in *National Geographic* and the almost daily articles detailing the controversy in the *Washington Post*, Barroga devised a way for Lin to address the art war that surrounded her design while revealing the unspoken racial tension underpinning the controversy.

The examination of racism has been a major focus for Barroga, not only in her plays, but in her personal life as well. Her father, a Filipino musician who followed the lounge circuit along Interstate Route 66, settled with his Phillipine-born wife in Milwaukee, where Barroga and four siblings were born and raised. Although her parents spoke Tagalog and Visayan they did not teach their children their native languages. "They figured being in America, you're an American." Barroga was raised in an all-white neighborhood and vividly recalls the experience. "We were the family that brought the neighborhood down. We were the first family of color they had ever seen. It was a trial by fire—I had to prove myself at every turn. I felt like I had to explain myself every time I did something; I'd walk into a store and clerks would follow me. I'd ask for something in a public place and they'd talk to me real loud as if I didn't understand English. It makes for a very tense existence. . . . I was a very angry child—in retrospect I can see I was reacting to cultural differences."

Her anger continued through a rebellious adolescence and her college years at the University of Wisconsin, Milwaukee, from which she graduated in 1972 with a degree in fine arts. After graduating she moved to Northern California where her anger began to subside in an environment where, for the first time, she was not an oddity: "I felt a sense of relief—to just walk down the streets of San Francisco and feel I blended in." In 1979 her father's death prompted her to write her first play, *The Pigeon Man*. "It was about a white midwestern family. I didn't even think then that writing for ethnic roles or my own culture was possible. I just assumed it would never be produced."

It was not until 1981 after she had written her second play, *Reaching for Stars*, which was also written for Caucasian actors, that she was encouraged to tell her own story. The director, Judith Abend, suggested she write a story about her own culture. When Abend asked Barroga, "Don't you have a story about what it was like in the midwest?" Barroga responded, "Who wants to hear a story about a Filipino musician trying to pass himself off as a Hawaiian raising his kids in the midwest?" The moment she answered the question she realized the comic potential of such a play and set to work on *Eye of the Coconut*, a comedy with serious undertones which has been embraced by Filipino communities in productions in Seattle, San Francisco, and Los Angeles.

Subsequently she also saw a production with Asian actors for the first time. The play, *State without Grace*, by Linda Faigo Hall had been produced by the Asian American Theater Company in San Francisco. "All of a sudden doors opened for me—she was a Filipino playwright; it was a Filipino story, there were Filipino actors. It gave me a whole new insight into the possibilities."

In addition to writing for the theater Barroga has been an active creator of theater in several other capacities. In 1983 she founded Playwrights Forum, in Palo Alto. In its first two years the forum read or staged some fifty new works by California playwrights, eventually coming under the umbrella of Palo Alto's TheatreWorks in 1986, where it continues to function as The Discovery Project. Barroga served in 1989 as the literary manager for the Oakland Ensemble Theater and returned in 1990 to serve as literary manager for TheatreWorks. In 1990 she encountered what she considers to be her most rewarding work in the theater, both professionally and personally, when she was invited to be the Associate Artistic Director for TNT—Teatro Ng Tanan (Theater for the People)—a San Francisco-based Filipino youth theater. The group began when Chris Millado, the artistic director of P.E.T.A. (Phillipine Educational Theater Association), was invited to conduct theater workshops with a Daly City youth group of recent Filipino immigrants. Their laboratory resulted in a series of stories, which Barroga, along with four other Filipino writers—Luis Syquia, Presco Tabios, Oscar Penaranda, and Mars Estrada—were asked to adapt for the theater. The play, *Kin*, opened at the Cowell Theater in San Francisco in 1991 and has toured in the Northwest. Following the success of that play Barroga was asked to assume the associate artistic directorship.

Working with a group of predominantly Phillipine-born actors age twenty-five and under has caused Barroga to appreciate the differences and affinities between what she terms "Fil-Fils," Phillipine-born Filipinos, and "Fil-Ams," Filipino Americans. "At times I'm envious of them—at least they know what a Filipino life style is. The more I learn the more I know there's still much more I need to learn. I wish I could close the gap faster. Despite that, I feel more at home than I have in my whole life. Being in touch with my culture has permeated every branch of my career and personal life."

Notes

1. Editors' interview with Jeannie Barroga, Amherst, Massachusetts, 17 October 1991.
2. Jan Scruggs and Joel Serdlow, *To Heal a Nation* (New York: Harper Collins, 1985).

205

Jeannie
Barroga

WALLS

JEANNIE BARROGA

Time: 1982 to 1984
Place: The Wall, Vietnam Veterans' Memorial Fund
office, press conferences, various settings

CHARACTERS

TERRY, vet, white, remains onstage throughout the play as lone color-bearer
DAVE, African American, Stu's buddy, never served
STU, Asian American, posttraumatic shock syndrome
JULIE, white (or any), protested in the 1960s
SARAH, African American, former nurse
MORRIS, African American, paraplegic
VI, Asian American, news reporter
RICH, any race, Vietnam Veterans' Memorial Fund representative
MAYA, Asian American, twenties, architect
SCRUGGS, white, foremost promoter for memorial to veterans
CARHART, any race, vet opposing the Wall
DAN, Asian American, twenties, a ghost in fatigues
JERRY, any race, twenties, also a ghost in fatigues
various OFFSTAGE VOICES, SOLDIERS 1 and 2, MAN, WOMAN, WWII VET, HIPPIE

ACT ONE   Scene 1

(VOICE:) They shall not grow old
   As we, that are left, grow old
   Age shall not worry them
   Nor years condemn.
   At the going down of the sun
   and in the morning—
   We shall remember them.

Scene 2

TERRY: For Jimmy-boy, for Mark, for Stevie, and Joe. . . . Here we go boys. (*He hoists flag into place.*)

DAVE: Come on, Al, cover for me, okay? . . . Just tell the man Dave's uncle died or Dave's sick, I don't care. . . . Stu and me are in Washington. . . . Something I gotta do, man, so tell him, okay? Tell him that for me.

JULIE: I'm leaving our class picture with this letter at the wall for everyone to read. Two boyfriends gone, two reasons for pain and regret. And someone's got to know that. Someone's got to tell me why that is.

SARAH: Baby, you be home on time after school. Carrots, celery, cookies, lemon pound cake. No messing around, you hear? Going to the Wall. . . . I'll be back by supper.

VI: "Event: Announcement by the Vietnam Veterans' Memorial Fund of winning design of a memorial to be placed on the Mall to honor Vietnam Veterans. Location, American Institute of Architects, 1735 New York Avenue Northwest, Washington, D.C."

VOICE: The material used for constructing this memorial is polished black granite imported from India. Approximately 150 panels were cut into three-inch thick blocks, the shortest panel being eight inches tall, the highest ten and a half feet, the largest panel weighing three thousand pounds.

The memorial was conceived in 1981 and eventually built over the next two years, 1982 to '84. In comparison, the Lincoln Memorial to your right took sixty years to complete. The landscape was leveled, and the apex of the wall reaches a depth of almost eleven feet. Notice the mementos left by those who visit: medals, pictures, flowers, helmets, photos of teenage boys frozen in youth, of babies never seen by their fathers.

This represents an entire war a nation meant to forget.

WWII VET: What are you, a coward?

HIPPIE: No, I'm not a coward! Just cause I won't fight in a war we don't belong in—

WWII VET: We fought wars in my day! Bunch of commies, burning draft cards, standing on the flag.

HIPPIE: A commie! Not fighting has nothing to do with commies.

WWII VET: You don't want to fight, go to Russia.

HIPPIE: Oh, great, now he's talking about—

WWII VET: I got the Congressional Medal of Honor and you dirty hippies won't even lift a finger to help your country.

HIPPIE: Big deal—a medal. This is bullshit!

WWII VET: Don't you curse at me, you punk! I'm an American, not some dope-smoking flower child who's nothing but a coward.

HIPPIE: You're a murderer. I'm not a murderer, and I'm not a coward.

WWII VET: Soldiers aren't murderers. Soldiers do their job.

HIPPIE: You go fight if you want a war.

WWII VET: I don't have to fight, I fought my wars. And I'll fight you, you lazy hippie punk. I'll fight you!

HIPPIE: Hell no, we won't go! Hell no, we won't go!

VOICE: No matter how many monuments, or statues, or stones . . . the wars go on.

Scene 3

DAVE: Lord, look at this. Stu, move on up, look at all this. We're here. We are actually here. Look at all these names, man. Every one of them carved in, every one. Like one big, black gravestone, you know? That book of names maybe four, five inches thick, you see that? Stu? That's like thousands of names, tens of thousands. You know there's one man to every ten women our age now? I read that. I read all about that. You wanna know anything, you ask ol' Davey Lewis.

Stu and Terry nod at each other.

Yeah, just ask me. Or tell me. You gonna introduce me to your buddy?

STU: I don't know who he is. He was just there, Dave. That's all.

DAVE: Oh, I get it. Something between you all, huh? Something somebody like me don't know nothing about, right? Stu?
I can't take this silent treatment no more, Stu. I can't all the time be reading your mind, you dig? You gotta talk to me. Why we come here, huh? Why? Not so you could eyeball me every time I want an answer. That's not why I came here, that's for sure.
Say something, man. Tell me to shut up, tell me I'm full of shit. Say something.

STU: You don't know why we're here.

DAVE: Okay, Mr. Knows Everything, then you tell me.

STU: Just a boondoggle to you.

DAVE: Right. I take off work, pay for two tickets out here. Yeah, just some joyride for me. Tell me something I don't know. Tell me what happened to you. Tell me that.

STU: We don't belong here. I sure don't.

DAVE: Aw, man, don't be starting that again. We here so we can get back to the way we were, hear what I'm saying? You lost some years I don't know nothing about. And I want to know. Cause I'm your buddy. Not like that dude holding the flag back there. He ain't been through shit with you like I have. And I lost some years, too. So it's time we both get back on track.

STU: What, we're gonna be punks again? Dream on, Dave. We're nobodies.

DAVE: Don't you be calling me a nobody, Stu. Nobodies look like you. You the nobody. Know why? You lost your bite, man. You lost every bit of that street tough I pounded into you. Where is it, man? Here, in your pocket? Or your jacket, huh? Or here, in your shoe, huh? That where it is? Cause it sure ain't in your head. And it ain't here neither. (*grabs his crotch*)

STU: Fuck you.

DAVE: No, it ain't anywhere now. It's gone. And you gone. Call me a nobody, I'm not a nobody, cause I'm here. And you as gone as they can be. Nothing left of that street punk I used to know. Uh-uh, ain't nobody there.

STU: Grow up, Dave. Street punks are dead, they're nothing. Being a punk didn't help me one bit.

DAVE: Yeah? Well, it did you just fine when you were some cow-licked ten year old scuttling down some back alley. I'm the punk that saved your yellow ass, remember?

STU: You gonna lord that over me the rest of your life, aren't you?

DAVE: Ain't much to it if that's all I do. I'm trying to do more, Stu. What'd you do over there, man, you come back like this? You kill kids? Women? You shoot at other Chinese, what? Just say it, man. I'm not gonna judge you. Me? Hell, I didn't even go. You survived the streets and you come out of the war, that's twice more than me, now what's that say? You even survived that one time I coulda beat you to a pulp pushing me off the mountain—that garbage pile we called a mountain. 'Member that?

What's it gonna take, Stu? Another five years of running? Another bout in rehab? Another war? What? You tell me. Cause I'm getting tired of running my mouth off to somebody who ain't listening. And we stay here till that somebody tells me what I wanna know. You ain't the Stu you were before, dig what I'm saying? You

Jeannie

Barroga

ain't the buddy I knew back then. I want my buddy back. I want to know if he's with our world, or theirs. What's it gonna be?

STU: Let me think, Dave. Let me just look at the Wall.

Scene 4

Julie wanders on during the following speech.

TERRY: Douglas Mericle, Corporal, Bravo Company, 2nd Battalion, 49th Infantry . . . Doug, Dougie . . . Timothy McGurty, Private First Class, Bravo Company, 2nd Battalion, 49th Infantry. . . . The Gurt, Big Gurt, Tim-Boy . . . Randolph Larson, Private First Class, Bravo Company, 2nd Battalion, 49th Infantry . . . Randy . . . William Tanner, Sergeant, Bravo Company, 2nd Battalion, 49th Infantry . . . Donald Fischer, Private First Class, Bravo Company, 2nd Battalion, 49th Infantry . . . Don . . . Smithy, Private First Class, Bravo Company, 2nd Battalion, 49th Infantry . . . Bravo Company, Bravo Company, my own goddamn Company.

Sarah approaches.

What're you looking at?

SARAH: Man on guard duty. Right? Been doing this a long time?

TERRY: Long enough.

SARAH: I got people here, too.

TERRY: We all do.

Sarah approaches Julie.

JULIE: Oh!

SARAH: Scare you?

JULIE: No, I was just . . . Class picture, 1969.

SARAH: You in there?

JULIE: Yeah. And so are they.

SARAH: Young looking, ain't they?

JULIE: They'll always look that way to me.

SARAH: (*referring to book*) Can I see that?

JULIE: Sure.

SARAH: Got some nurses here I want to look up. You one?

JULIE: No. I just went to school with these guys.

SARAH: Some reunion, huh?

JULIE: Yeah. They're here, you know. They are here, I can feel them.

Dan and Jerry enter.

DAN: "Bird, bird, bird, bird is the word. Bird, bird, bird, bird is the word."

JERRY: Shut up, you spaz.

DAN/JERRY: "Ba-ba-ba, oom-maw-maw, ba-ba-oom-maw-maw."

JERRY: (*noticing Julie*) Hey, spaz, would you get a load of this.

DAN: That's some really nice put-together little—

JERRY: Oooh, baby, you remind me of some sweet young thang back home.

DAN: Since when do you talk like some jiveass dude all of a sudden, huh? Hick like me from Missouri.

JERRY: Since we were in the army. Spaz!

DAN: We were in the army?

JERRY: Hey, honey, what's your phone number, huh? Boy, I would love to get you on some lonely back road in a convertible—

DAN: Jerry?

JERRY: —Under the stars on a moonlit night.

JULIE: Jerry.

SARAH: You say something?

JULIE: One of them was Jerry. And Dan.

JERRY: I'm busy, Dan.

DAN: When did we ever join the army?

A moment of realization, they stare at each other.

JERRY: (*waving hand in front of her*) See. You forgot.

JULIE: I guess I was in love with one of them, or was it both?

DAN: Hey, Jerry, you know who this is?

JULIE: It couldn't have been Dan. He loved that awful song, what was it? "Bird, bird, bird is the word."

DAN: I always thought she got a kick out of that song.

JERRY: Julie, twelve years from now. Or back. Whatever.

DAN: And that's us down there, huh?

JULIE: Well, it was Dan for a while as a sophomore and a senior. Then it was Jerry as a freshman and a junior. It varied.

SARAH: Kid stuff.

JULIE: Yeah, I guess it was, always kidding around, joking. Jerry was always the corny one.

JERRY: Come on, let's make like a tree and leave. First she don't like your song, then she says I'm corny.

DAN: Naw, man. I want to hear this.

SARAH: Yeah, my daughter's going through that right now. Can't make a commitment at fifteen. At that age, you play the field.

JULIE: I did.

DAN: She sure did.

JULIE: I'm sorry, you don't want to hear this.

DAN: I do.

JERRY: I don't.

DAN: She's hurting, Jer, I can feel it.

JERRY: Come on, I feel like moving.

DAN: You always did.

JERRY: What's that mean?

DAN: That's why we're here.

JERRY: I just jumped out of the foxhole.

DAN: And I jumped after you.

JERRY: So why did you, huh? You could still be alive, you know.

DAN: Cause I had to, you spaz. You're my buddy.

JULIE: They did everything together.

JERRY: Did I really get us here?

DAN: You really forgot, didn't you?

JERRY: I remember we were born, we went to school, went to war, and we died. Some legacy.

DAN: And we left Julie.

JERRY: Yeah . . . damn.

JULIE: Was it Dan or was it Jerry?

DAN: Hell, she can't even remember. Which one did she love?

JULIE: Maybe both.

SARAH: Both what, honey?

JULIE: I loved them both. I miss them both so much. So much . . .

JERRY: Come on, let's make tracks.

DAN: Ghosts don't leave tracks.

JULIE: I would've protested something like this back then.

TERRY: Shit.

SARAH: You'd protest this wall? You mean, the building of it?

JULIE: I protested anything acknowledging the war. I mean, the way I saw it, kids my age shouldn't have been fighting in a senseless war, you know?

TERRY: Terrific.

JULIE: Oh, Dan and I got into it in letters. I mean, I argued that he'd be mistaken for the enemy cause he was Chinese—

DAN: American!

JULIE: Well, he was American. Anyway, I wrote that all of them looked alike over there.

DAN: American born and bred. We go through this every time.

JERRY: Cool your jets. What difference does it make arguing about that stuff now?

JULIE: God, did I really do that?

SARAH: Do what?

JULIE: Did I really use the time I had left with him arguing?

SARAH: Whole bunch of arguing back then. You weren't the only one.

JULIE: Sometimes I'm reminded of how young I was and self-righteous. Even dating Dan, his being Chinese. I knew what people were saying. I knew everything. Not that I regret anything I said about the war. Just what I said to Danny.

JERRY: What about me?

Jeannie

Barroga

JULIE: Jerry never wrote letters. He was good for the both of us, that joker. He'd just size us up and wave us off. He'd play around and never let something like war get to him. He'd ... He'd ...

SARAH: Go ahead, remember.

JULIE: I guess I wonder why I'm here and they're not. Me protesting, them fighting and both over the same thing, really. I need to know why, you know? Why I feel sorry. And why I should tell someone that, someone who was there.

Morris rolls in—in a wheelchair.

SARAH: Well, maybe this is just the place to do just that.

JULIE: I don't know.

SARAH: We're still here. They're still here. Talking don't hurt anyone.

JULIE: I can't. Not that way.

SARAH: I can. I did.

JERRY: Boy, I'm glad they built this thing. To us, buddy, and them. In twenty years we'll be history.

DAN: Spaz, you're history now.

Sarah approaches Morris.

SARAH: (*pushing chair forward*) Let's get us a close look here.

MORRIS: What're you doing?

SARAH: Got it on lock, huh?

MORRIS: What the hell you doing to my chair?

SARAH: Where you from?

MORRIS: What's it to you? And leave my chair alone.

SARAH: Come all the way from somewhere to see this wall. Well, let's see it.

MORRIS: Let me be.

SARAH: Don't worry. I pushed lots of chairs like these.

MORRIS: I don't want it pushed. I want to sit here.

SARAH: Now don't be that way.

MORRIS: This is my visit, I'll handle it the way I want to, now leave me alone.

Scene 5

RICH: Ready Vi?

VI: As I'll ever be. How's my hair?

RICH: Always perfect. It's amazing how you manage an invitation to these things. Normally they'd pick a more established newscaster to announce something this important.

VI: Ah, but Dan Rather is not female. And Walter Cronkite is not Chinese. And your winner is both. And so am I. To me, it's great PR.

RICH: You mean, for you. You only pull out "being Chinese" when it's to your advantage.

VI: That's it, Rich, stop right there.

RICH: An Asian war, an Asian interpretation in art form.

MAYA: My name is Maya Ying Lin.

VI: Ironic, isn't it?

MAYA: I'm from Athens, Ohio.

VI: A midwesterner? I didn't think they knew anything about art.

MAYA: I graduate in June.

RICH: She's studying architecture at Yale.

VI: Ah, so that's why it's so modern.

RICH: Very modern. Two black lines.

VI: Pretty controversial stuff. Maybe she had a brother over there, or some other relative.

MAYA: I was too young to know anybody there. My dad did, a friend of his.

VI: Fraught with possibilities if we can find anything. Is she rich? Beautiful? Is she a Valley girl? A radical? A dyke? A pothead? A nun? What is she? Is she even real?

MAYA: I don't like to talk about myself.

RICH: She's pretty private, Vi.

VI: Well, being private does not news make. If I have to dig up one more anecdote about the hostages, I'll scream. They've been back two months, and they're still front page.

217

Jeannie

Barroga

RICH: How about Agent Orange? With this memorial coming up, anything on the vets would be—

VI: Rich, read between the lines. The public doesn't even want to acknowledge we were there, in spite of the memorial.

RICH: There is a tie-in, Vi: this, the vets, even you.

VI: Yeah, well, with a tight-lipped young architect, it'll be hard in coming, won't it? Will she ever say more than the pat answers she's been giving the press? Will a story come out before this thing is built? Will she?

MAYA: All I can say is: the design speaks for itself.

VI: (to Maya) Nervous?

MAYA: A little, yes.

VI: Don't worry, you'll do just fine. If Rich has done his job, you should have no trouble at all. Just answer the questions the best you can, okay? Oh, and honey—

MAYA: Maya.

VI: Sorry. Maya. This is the start of a public image. You know: interviews, television, radio.

MAYA: I know.

VI: Lots of repetitive questions and lots of dirt-digging. Did you know that, too?

MAYA: Yes.

VI: We might even ask you things you've already been asked. You see, the public in general has the attention span of a fly. They see a face . . . they may remember, however, they usually don't. So we prod memories by asking the same questions—or pointed ones.

MAYA: I take it you don't like the public much.

VI: Hey, honey, they're my bread and butter. And they love me.

MAYA: Maya. My name's Maya.

VI: Of course.

MAYA: Chinese?

VI: American.

MAYA: Of course.

Scruggs enters.

VI: Ah, and here's the man of the hour. Hi, Jan, how are you doing?

SCRUGGS: Hey, how're ya doing? (*to Maya*) And you're the girl from Yale.

VI: Yes, this is Maya Lin. (*to Maya*) Jan spearheaded this whole thing.

MAYA: Hi.

VI: The monument's his idea. The chosen design however. . . .

SCRUGGS: Well, they told me they were a little worried how I'd react. Unlike some, I have a personal stake in this.

Rich enters.

VI: Oh, there's Rich. Excuse me.

SCRUGGS: I must admit it looked pretty weird.

MAYA: Oh?

SCRUGGS: Yea, I thought maybe a third grader had won. All this work and the thing looks like a big bat.

MAYA: I hadn't thought of it that way, myself.

SCRUGGS: You're not a third grader, that's for sure. How old are you, anyway?

MAYA: I'm twenty-one.

SCRUGGS: 1959. The year of the first American casualty in 'Nam. So you were only four when Kennedy was assassinated.

MAYA: Just around kindergarten, maybe.

SCRUGGS: And the marines landed in Da Nang four years later.

MAYA: Where?

SCRUGGS: Da Nang. In 'Nam? Do you know these places? Did you know anybody there?

MAYA: No . . . well, maybe one.

SCRUGGS: One, huh? Well, I had practically my whole company blow up right in front of me! I saw parts of buddies lying all around me, and you know what I had? One band-aid. One lousy band-aid.

MAYA: I'm sorry.

SCRUGGS: You weren't even ten years old when we were over there getting blown to bits. And I come back and work my ass off to get this whole project going, and the judges choose a bat for my bud-

219

Jeannie

Barroga

's to be remembered by. I mean, if this is the way I feel about it,
can imagine what others like me think.

A: The requirement was that the memorial avoid a political
nent and begin a healing process.

SCRUGGS: Yeah, well it's a little hard for me to think that I, or any
other guy who's been there, will stand in front of something like
that and think, "Yeah, I feel better now."

MAYA: I thought all you vets approved the jury's choice.

SCRUGGS: What else could we do, huh? Hey, in 'Nam, I had a
machine gun leveled at me for four hours. I know when to move
and when not to move. We're this close, and I sure as hell ain't
gonna blow it. But I want some honor here. We'll get around this
design if we have to. Between you, me, and "The Wall," we could
have done better. But I'll back the Fund now. Just expect some
changes, that's all I'm saying.

Vi and Rich approach.

VI: Have a nice chat?

MAYA: Yes. Very interesting.

RICH: You all set, Maya?

VI: Okay, We're on.

She steps up to podium.

VI: Ladies and gentlemen of the press, the moment you've all been
waiting for. We're here to announce the winner of the National
Contest to design a Memorial to Veterans of the Vietnam Era. The
contest's deadline was March 31st of this year, 1981, and during
the week of April 26 through the 29th, our seven judges—com-
prised of prominent sculptors and landscape artists—deliberated
on 1,421 entries. The unanimous vote chose Entry Number 1,026
as the winner.

MAYA: (*to Scruggs*) I'm not the Viet Cong, you know.

SCRUGGS: I don't care what you are. No one even knew your name
till the envelope was opened.

VI: The designer whose proposal most clearly meets the formal
requirements of the program has created a place of quiet reflection,
where the simple setting of earth and sky pay tribute to those who
served their nation in difficult times. Ladies and gentlemen: Miss
Maya Lin.

Maya has not only won first prize, but she has also been given a position as consultant on the project. The cash award for first prize is twenty thousand dollars.

Say a few words, Maya.

MAYA: Well . . . thank you.

VI: Let's take this opportunity to introduce another prominent figure in all this—

VET 2: (*whistling loudly*) Yo, Jan!

VI: Well, I guess you already know him. Former Army infantry-man, the mover and shaker for the Vietnam Memorial, Corporal Jan Scruggs.

SCRUGGS: (*aside to Vi*) Is this really going to go over?

VI: We're about to see. (*to audience*) Ladies and gentlemen, the Vietnam Veterans' Memorial.

Maya slides the cover off her model. Silence.

VI: Maya, is there anything you'd like to say about your design? Anything at all?

MAYA: Yes, I just want to say . . . I just want to say this memorial is meant to be reflected on. People should be mesmerized. They should face it, approach it, perceive the names before they read them. Touch them and realize in the black reflection they've touched something in themselves.

They shouldn't just see a bunch of names or even a political statement.

Even the process of killing the grass in order to build this is important. I meant to show what it's like to die.

VI: This all started as one man's dream. Let's hear what he thinks.

SCRUGGS: Well, uh . . . Uh, I, really . . . really . . . I really like it . . . it's a great . . . uh, wonderful memorial.

Scene 6

Terry and Julie, she watches him.

TERRY: What? What are you doing?

JULIE: I was just . . . I don't know.

TERRY: I'm busy, lady.

JULIE: Well, I know, but I. . . . Can we talk for a minute?

TERRY: What about?

JULIE: When I was talking to that woman over there, she's a nurse and—

TERRY: Yeah, yeah, we met. And?

JULIE: Well, I thought I heard you say something when I mentioned protesting to her, and—

TERRY: Oh, for Chrissakes.

JULIE: Yeah, something along that line.

TERRY: I said, "Shit." Okay? Got that loud and clear? Want it in writing?

JULIE: No, that's all right. That's pretty much what I heard the first time. Thanks.

TERRY: And you can take that back to all your other antiwar, hippie-flower-children, touchy-feely—

JULIE: Whoa, this sounds a little trite—

TERRY: Listen, I don't really care what you all think. You can call me anything now and I don't give two flying fucks. So I'm a baby killer, so what, huh? So I'm some crazy Vietnam Vet that had nothing better to do than collect ears.

JULIE: Listen can we start over? I'm Julie. (*No response.*) Okay, we'll start another way.

TERRY: Why bother?

JULIE: Why? Because very few people have. Nobody I know. I came to Washington all by myself because I read all about the Wall—

TERRY: Great, another armchair revolutionary.

JULIE: Yes, I do that. I read a lot. Anyway, I came across some old diaries of when I was at the university boycotting. And you know what?

TERRY: What, lady?

JULIE: Julie.

TERRY: Well, what is it?

JULIE: Well, I read them over and, I feel a little silly now. I mean you can read till you're blue in the face about all sorts of things and not know a damn thing about any one of them. Twelve years now, and I'm wondering if what I did made any difference, you know?

TERRY: How should I know.

JULIE: All I know is I need to talk to someone who was there. Because I wasn't. Maybe that someone can help with an answer. Like why are two of my friends just names carved on a wall? And what can I do about that?

TERRY: Don't ask me, lady.

JULIE: Julie. (*She extends hand.*)

TERRY: Terry. Look, I can't, this flag's heavy. Two hands. . . .

JULIE: Oh, yeah, for sure.

Dan and Jerry enter. Jerry is singing.

DAN: Could you let go of that stupid song, spaz? I'm sorry I ever started it.

JERRY: I can't help it. It's on the brain, now. You know how that goes. "Bird, bird, bird, bird is the word."

DAN: Weren't you even blown away by the beauty of that place? Didn't it even affect you at all?

JERRY: Hey, man, I let go of all that stuff when we got here. You should too.

DAN: 'Nam was always pretty in the spring. Course it looks different, all built up and everything.

JERRY: One thing about being dead, you never have to deal with travel agents.

DAN: And that Vietnamese woman standing where we, you know. . . .

JERRY: Just say it.

DAN: Died.

JERRY: Bit the big one.

DAN: Okay, okay. We're back in D.C. Now how did that happen?

JERRY: Cause she's here.

JULIE: They're here, you know? Feel it? Not just names. Them.

TERRY: I suppose.

JULIE: Doesn't that ever hit you? You're here and they're not?

TERRY: Course it does. Every day, every hour, every minute I stand here. But I'll see this through because . . . because. . . .

JULIE: Because?

TERRY: I got a job to do.

JULIE: We all had jobs to do. I'm so sick of hearing what we've got to do and never hearing why. Dan and Jerry did a job and it killed them. You're doing something and you can't even say why. I did my job, and we're still—

TERRY: Oh, yeah, sure. Wearing a red bandanna, sitting in the streets, getting out of class, real hard.

JULIE: Hey, wait a minute. Don't discount what I did back then. I fought off nightsticks and tear gas for you guys. Yeah, me and the others, we got you out of the jungle faster. We helped pull you out of Saigon.

TERRY: Don't think you did anything for me, lady.

JULIE: Julie!

TERRY: You think we were mindless out there? We didn't have a thought in our heads, huh?

JULIE: You were grunts—

TERRY: Damn right we were grunts. Yes, sir, no, sir. We did what we were told. Know why? It wasn't our turf, that's why. You do what you're told and look out for each other cause one wrong move and you're dead. Just like your goddamn friends. I did what I was told, and now I'm here. I'm not just some name on a wall.

JULIE: Bothered you, didn't it?

DAN: Tell her, yes.

TERRY: Yes! I mean. . . .

JERRY: Hey, don't.

DAN: First we're fighting Vietnamese, then we're fighting Cambodians.

TERRY: First we're fighting Vietnamese, then we're fighting Cambodians. They change the players on us. We fight who they tell us, but we get back here and you spit on us.

DAN: She'd never do that.

JULIE: I never did that.

JERRY: Like stereo, man.

JULIE: Just admit they used you, and it bothered you.

TERRY: Know what really bothers me is that all of you with your peace signs and beads and flowers really thought you knew what was going on. You really thought you knew it all.

JULIE: So tell me.

TERRY: Huh?

JULIE: Tell me what was going on? Was I wrong to want my friends alive? Were you wrong to fight? Who's wrong here?

TERRY: This is a twenty-year-old argument, lady—

JULIE: Julie! I have a name. You have a name. We can both say them. We're not reading the two of them off some wall, either—

TERRY: Two. You got two on this wall. I got twelve. And I'm doing this for them.

JULIE: Well, so am I. For your twelve, and my two. Does that still put us on opposite sides?

JERRY: Are we having fun yet?

DAN: The war's here, Jerry. It's still going on. I won't let this all be for nothing—I won't.

Scene 7

VI: We are interviewing Maya Lin, winner of the nationwide contest to design the Vietnam Memorial to be built right here in Washington. How are you, Maya?

MAYA: Fine.

VI: First of all, you're twenty-one? A Yale architect student?

MAYA: Yes. I graduate in June.

VI: The top of your class, I imagine.

MAYA: Well, uh, no. I wouldn't exactly say that.

VI: Tell me, Maya, what did you personally think of the Vietnam War? Were you opposed to it? Or did you think we were right?

MAYA: Uh, well . . . I don't know.

VI: Well, you must have some opinion, one way or another.

MAYA: I was pretty young.

VI: Well, for a young woman, you came up with an amazing tribute to soldiers who served in Vietnam. Now, you do realize that, don't you.

MAYA: Yeah, yeah, I do.

VI: Are you a Democrat?

MAYA: Uh, well, I don't know.

VI: An independent, is that it?

MAYA: No, not exactly.

VI: Playing it safe, I guess. Tell me this then, Maya: are you happy?

MAYA: Yes . . . I'm happy.

VI: And we're happy, too. The memorial is a bold artistic statement, one that should affect anyone who sees it. Already some controversy is giving it coverage not only on T.V., but on some radio talk shows, and of course, the newspapers. (*to Maya*) What do you think of all that, Maya? Not even built, and the whole nation's reading about it. Any comment?

MAYA: I don't read newspapers.

VI: We've been interviewing Maya Lin, designer of the Vietnam Memorial, fast becoming a national controversy. We may be seeing a lot of both Maya and the Wall. Back to you. . . .

Scene 8

WOMAN: Look at all the people, John . . . John? . . . Hold me.

Our son's name. Nineteen years old and war takes him away from us. Takes his youth, his ideals, his life. I wanted a son who would visit us with grandchildren, who would grow up as we grow up and live into our old age.

Memories, John. I wanted memories with my son. But this is what I have, what we have. A name to look at in the black stone. And your face. Your face as his would have been, looking back at me. His and your face . . . John? John?

Scene 9

Scruggs watches from the side.

PRESS 1: Why is the wall black?

MAYA: Well, it's more reflective. This isn't new, it's been used before. People should be entranced by its reflective quality. The depth doubles and triples dimensions—as I've told you before.

PRESS 2: How come it's underground?

MAYA: That way it's like the earth itself is a wound, and pushing out from it are the names of those who have descended into it and have emerged to remind us they were even here.

PRESS 3: I guess I'm not visual. These drawings need a lot of explaining. It looks like two black lines—

RICH: It says exactly what we want to say about Vietnam—absolutely nothing.

PRESS 1: Okay, so there are names and dates, right?

MAYA: Names and two dates: 1959 and 1975, beginning and end.

PRESS 2: Where does it say Vietnam?

RICH: Does the Washington Monument say Washington?

PRESS 3: Are they alphabetical, the names?

MAYA: No. Chronological, by the date they died.

PRESS 3: So how does anyone find anyone?

RICH: We're in the process of addressing that very issue.

PRESS 1: Alphabetical's easier, don't you think?

MAYA: I think of it as a Greek poem: at the height of battle, the most names. The sheer number should astound people.

RICH: Maya—

MAYA: Finding the names by the date they died is like finding the gravestone on the field.

RICH: Let me handle this—

MAYA: All the victims in one place on one day, the last day of their lives.

RICH: Don't play this up—

MAYA: Reading the names, like a bell, tolling in your head.

RICH: Again, as I have said, we have not yet made a final decision on that. Next.

PRESS 2: What's construction on the monument going to cost?

RICH: Well, we've projected that all together we'll need about seven million dollars.

PRESS 2: Got your work cut out for you, Rich.

RICH: We can do it.

PRESS 1: We've heard unanimous votes have pushed the memorial this far. Who's involved?

RICH: Well, the judges, of course. Then the vets themselves approved the judges' choice. Then the Fine Arts Commission unanimously approved the judges' and the vets' choice. And finally the National Capital Planning Commission voted unanimously to approve everyone's choice . . . Maya's.

PRESS 3: And Secretary Watt? He still has power to veto?

RICH: Only if he acts within ninety days. And frankly, he's been pretty quiet. Our time is up. We'll inform the media again of any follow up. Thank you.

Maya exits.

SCRUGGS: Rough?

RICH: Not bad. I didn't want to touch that alphabetical listing, though. Not one bit.

SCRUGGS: She got all dressed up for a garage sale, I see.

RICH: Aw, come on, Jan. Lay off her. The press thinks she's cute.

SCRUGGS: You know if she can't change for us, she should do it for her design. As long as she looks like a hippie, she'll be treated as one.

RICH: Okay, okay.

SCRUGGS: It's not just her image, you know, or her design. We're seen through her. I pick up a newspaper and see her face and how she dined somewhere in Georgetown and there's nothing about us vets, or Agent Orange, or unemployment—

RICH: Jan, what's the problem here, huh? What is it, really?

SCRUGGS: Aaah, this whole design. So what are we going to do about the alphabetical listing? We can't do a thing till we know what order they'll be in.

RICH: Between you and me, we're thinking we'll index them in a separate book nearby. With the panel number, and the line number. And for multiples—Smith, Jones—they'll all have the home state as well.

SCRUGGS: It just seems to me—

RICH: The Defense Department has a listing two inches thick, five point type, and six hundred are named Smith. That's practically a whole panel by itself. So that's a pretty sound argument to me why not to go alphabetical. She thought of that, you know.

SCRUGGS: I just want my buddies remembered. I don't want them screwed again. I'm not going to argue about minimalism or modernism or figurative art. It's beyond that now. As far as I'm concerned, every name of every vet who served is going to be on that wall—one way or another.

RICH: We haven't addressed if it will be everyone, yet—

SCRUGGS: I'm addressing it. There's got to be a separate inscription for those who didn't die.

RICH: We're working on a prologue and an epilogue. You know that.

SCRUGGS: She didn't go for that.

RICH: She's been told there'll be changes.

SCRUGGS: Well, good, then . . . good.

Scene 10

DAVE: Want one? (*offers a beer*)

STU: No . . . not here.

DAVE: Where, then? When?

STU: Later.

DAVE: Everything's later for you.

STU: Don't you like some peace and quiet sometimes? Just some silence. Is that ever in your realm?

DAVE: "Realm?" You barely say two words to me in five years, and now you say stuff like "quiet" and "realm?" Shit—

STU: I've talked to you.

DAVE: Sure, bullshit about Hawaii. That's all I know you did. Ain't no action in Hawaii.

STU: You're wrong there.

DAVE: So tell me.

STU: I told you. Americans like me in the hospitals getting operated on last cause they look Vietnamese. I told you that.

DAVE: So, they shouldn't have signed up.

STU: We had to. We volunteered cause we were loyal. And our families backed us. My father's grateful to this country. I wanted to show I was, too.

DAVE: Yeah, well, you Chinese have a thing about that stuff anyway.

STU: What does that mean?

DAVE: Well, see, you Chinese and all you Asian types—Japanese, too—you got this family honor thing that keeps you going. I mean, you got things you still paying dues for that happened dynasties ago. And this fuels you, you dig? Like we don't have that shit. Me, man, I wait till they drafts my ass, then I think of all kinds of shit to make me something other than the kind of soldier they want. See, I don't have generations to answer for. It's just me, man. Just me, that's why I fight; not cause I'm gonna lose face by saying I made a mistake, you dig? See, that's what this whole country did. Too chicken shit to say they made a mistake. They shouldn't have gone over there. And they sure shouldn't have stayed.

STU: So I "saved face" for my Dad, huh?

DAVE: I don't know, man. Maybe your grandfather, too. Didn't he work on the railroad or something, laying the track cross-country or some such shit. Well, see, both your father and your grandfather are thankful they got to make something of themselves in America—even though it sounds like your grandfather was pretty much of a slave. But anyway, they stayed and done good and now American-born Stewart Lee is gonna do them proud serving his and their time and coming back crazy.

STU: I'm not crazy.

DAVE: Well, you ain't exactly all there, either.

STU: You don't know what I've been through.

DAVE: No I don't. Look I packed away three beers already and all you been telling me is how you met some other Chinaman from the States.

STU: I wouldn't expect you to understand.

DAVE: That's like me going to Fifty-seventh Street in New York and bringing back snapshots of me and Al from the warehouse. We didn't meet nobody. We just fucking around, goosing each other.

STU: That's not the same at all. You know it isn't.

DAVE: I just wanna get past the tourist shit, that's all.

STU: Tourist shit, huh? Amazing how you have an opinion on just about everything, you know that?

DAVE: I'm a knowledgeable man—

STU: You're bullshit, that's what you are.

DAVE: What're you really mad at, huh?

STU: You stand there and dribble on about what you read or what you heard. But how could you know, huh? You weren't there. Too fucking chicken shit to serve, that's what you were.

DAVE: I ain't afraid of nothing.

STU: Bullshit. You're afraid of being left behind, that you might have missed something over there. Yeah, those of us who were there might have something over you, might know more than you for a change.

DAVE: Am I hearing you right? Here I am doing you a favor—

STU: Don't bother.

DAVE: I think we're going to get down and be the friends we once were, but no. Stu Lee don't need nobody. Don't need me, anyway.

STU: Truth hurts, don't it?

DAVE: Don't fuck with me. I should've just let you wimp around, feel sorry for yourself, sleepwalk the rest of your life. No, I should just beat the shit out of you, just to see if you can feel anymore. Thinking—no, believing—that my bringing you down here is gonna give you a reason to talk, and a chance for me to listen—

STU: As if you could shut up for a minute.

DAVE: You know what I think you did over there? Huh? Nothing. Cause that's all you ever did. Always hiding behind mama's apron, then hiding behind me. Always hanging back in the shadows: theirs, mine. Come on, admit it. You did nothing, and you came back a mess. You came back a fucking loser.

Stu jumps him, then backs off.

231

Jeannie

Barroga

DAVE: Okay, hotshot. We're long overdue, anyway. Come on, come on. Come on you dumb shit.

Stu attacks Dave. Dave eventually subdues him.

STU: Sure big man. Some big ass punk who'll never grow up. The gangs are gone. Handshakes, secrets, rules—all gone! Rules don't do anything for anybody over there, and I know, cause I was there. I saw them! I know!

DAVE: What did you do, man?

STU: I hauled body bags, you dumb shit. Nothing glamorous, Dave. You want war stories, I don't have any. I didn't walk point, I didn't frag any officers. I wasn't a grunt, okay?

DAVE: Okay . . . okay.

STU: I put these guys on their last plane rides home. You know how that feels? Well, I do. I thought about it all the time I was there.

Scene 11

RICH: I don't know what he's going to say. I don't even know who he is. Who's this Tom Carhart?

SCRUGGS: A vet. In fact, he entered the contest.

RICH: Is he vindictive because he didn't win?

SCRUGGS: Naw, Tom wouldn't do that.

CARHART: (*at press conference*) A black wall of shame! I, for one, can't live with this. A lot of vets wanted to celebrate a monument to Vietnam Vets, we were hoping to glorify it. Memorials, I was brought up to believe, should be white. And if there's any honor in-volved—which I had hoped this memorial would have—it should also be above ground. Vets are being put on the back burner again. Vets, like me, are being screwed—again. I, for one, am personally entering my veto on the choice of the design to honor Vietnam Vets.

RICH: Can you get to him?

SCRUGGS: I know him, we toss down a few—

CARHART: I invite all vets who feel as I do to join me in resisting the ultimate insult in an already underacknowledged tribute to fellow vets.

RICH: He knows how you feel, then?

SCRUGGS: Hey, we talk.

CARHART: I hope the key people in power—in positions critical shaping the right decisions—will join me, too. Thank you.

RICH: The phone will be ringing off the hook after this.

CARHART: Hey, Jan! Some turnout, eh?

RICH: Talk to him. Tell him.

SCRUGGS: You tell him. (*to Carhart*) Tom, what are you—Tom, this is Rich. He's with the fund, Tom.

CARHART: One way to block this intellectual abstract bullshit, eh?

RICH: Tom, not everyone liked it, but—

CARHART: Well, Jan don't. At least he didn't the other night.

SCRUGGS: Not in public, Tom.

RICH: Listen, let's just get it done and—

SCRUGGS: We can add our own little ideas later.

CARHART: Why? It's not even built. Let's just nip it in the bud. Hell, it would save everybody a lot of time and money.

SCRUGGS: You don't understand. There are a lot of politics involved here.

CARHART: From a twenty-one year old Chinese girl? Come on, Jan, we can handle her.

RICH: She won, Tom—

CARHART: And I didn't. Don't think I don't know what people are saying. A vet should have won. A statement should've been made in the name of all vets by a vet. Twenty years of denying we were even there. Someone there should be the one to blow that whole damn secret wide open! Someone who still carries the scars. Us, Jan, you know that.

SCRUGGS: Lots of other people didn't win, either, Tom.

CARHART: Hey, don't get me wrong. I never claimed to be an artiste, a sculptor, or anything. I can take rejection. I have before. But what they picked can be changed, can't you see? We're in Washington. There's power here. There's money, too. Can your fund say that?

RICH: Who's backing this, Tom?

CARHART: I'll give you a hint—

233

Jeannie

Barroga

SCRUGGS: Just tell us.

CARHART: He financed the whole contest to begin with, the first mailing. He paid with his money, and he don't like the results.

SCRUGGS: Perot?

CARHART: "Make it inspiring," he said. "High, white, and rising." Perot don't like it, Jan, it's as simple as that. He said, you've all made a mistake—a big mistake.

RICH: Well, we've got big guns of our own. Tell him that.

CARHART: Yeah? Who? You're being funded by nickel-and-dime organizations all around the country. The very people who spat on us as we got off the plane. They won't come through for you, Jan, they didn't before. Call me, we'll do lunch.

Scene 12

SARAH: (*begins to wheel Morris closer to the monument; he applies brakes*) Sorry.

MORRIS: Should be.

SARAH: Bad habit from my nursing days, trying to get my boys to open up. A place like this kind of does that to folks, you know. Helps them open up.

MORRIS: Listen, do me a favor. You go be a nurse someplace else. I want some quiet, understand what I'm saying? I deserve it. I heard enough noise over there. "Open up." Someone else can "open up." I'd like some nice closed peace and quiet.

SARAH: Well, excuse me.

MORRIS: You're excused.

SARAH: I swear, I get so sick of ornery cusses like you. (*indicates Terry*) First him, now you. Got a handicap, don't take it out on me. I didn't give you that handicap. Just giving you a hand, that's all. Just putting my hand out there, that's all I did. Cuss. An attitude problem, a bad one, too. Don't want no company? Stay home, you feel that way—

MORRIS: What you got here, huh? You got some man or boy on this here wall that you can come up to me and roll my chair wherever you want, huh?

SARAH: I got a right to be here.

MORRIS: Well, I got more rights.

SARAH: Oh, you do, huh?

MORRIS: Yeah, I do. In the seven men I'm paying my respects to. Wiped out in one day. I lost a wife, a son—both ashamed of me— and I lost the use of the two legs under me, so there. I told you how I earned my rights. So you think about yours.

SARAH: Hey, it's 1984, cuss, how long you gonna keep up this kind of attitude, huh?

MORRIS: I'm fine the way I am without the preaching, thank you.

SARAH: What're you doing at this wall, you ever ask yourself that? Cause you better, if it's not for people to talk to you—

MORRIS: I know what I want.

SARAH: —And while you're asking, ask yourself just how fine you really are coming here, staring into space. Ask yourself how long you want to keep up this I-don't-need-nobody attitude you so proud of, cuss—

MORRIS: The name's Morris.

SARAH: —Ask why you take it out on the likes of Sarah Mitchell, cuss.

MORRIS: Sergeant Lee Morris!

SARAH: —And another thing, Lee, I got eight nurses on this wall. And I got close to fifty-eight thousand mothers and daughters and loved ones I stand with looking at it. And you won't see our names up there, and you won't see our wounds. Hell, you won't even see what part of us we really lost. But we got rights to be here, all of us. We paid, just like you. And we survived. Just like you. You talking peace and quiet? No, sir, you talking respect. And I deserve some of that, too. All of us here do. I earned it.

MORRIS: Oh, you did, huh?

SARAH: Yeah, I did.

MORRIS: Well, okay, then.

SARAH: Okay.

MORRIS: I had plans, I guess . . . expectations coming here. Arguing with a nurse wasn't one of them.

SARAH: Talk to me then, Lee. Especially me and the others here like me. Know why? Cause you and me is color. All the more reason we need to tear down those walls we build to buffer ourselves against the world out there, against all them other wars. That make any sense to you?

MORRIS: Every day's a war to me.

SARAH: Whose damn fault is that, huh? Okay, there are daily wars. Take them on, then, one day at a time. Like I am, with you. Hey, I've seen lots of attitudes like you. And I deal with them cause it's important to me. Cause all you are is a voice crying in the dark. And I hear you no matter how much you say I don't. How's that for nursing?

MORRIS: You must have been a great nurse.

SARAH: Shoot, I was a beautiful nurse. Beauty don't last long under all that stress, though. Probably better for all those boys they rolled in—crying, unconscious. Probably better for them we did look so dragged out. I remember one, though, head all bandaged, his eyes gone. We knew he'd never see again. But he took hold of my hand, and I kept telling him, "It's all right, baby. Everything's all right." And he settled down and said, "You're all beautiful, aren't you? Tell me you're the most gorgeous women on earth, right at my side. Tell me!" And we looked at each other, all us tired, overworked, under-slept nurses doing our jobs. And we patted his hand and said, "Yeah, we're the most beautiful women in the whole wide world, baby." And they wheeled him away, this sightless boy never to see that whole wide world again. And I'm here, remembering him . . . them. But it's time to come home now.

MORRIS: I thought coming home meant I didn't have to talk about that war no more.

SARAH: When you're at home with yourself, that's when the war's over, cuss.

MORRIS: I ain't no cuss! Talk about respect, I told you, they called me Sergeant.

SARAH: If we be talking respect, then you call me Lieutenant. You respect me, and I'll respect you, Sergeant Cuss.

MORRIS: Well, I'll be damned. I'll be goddamned.

Scene 13

MAYA: What changes?

SCRUGGS: Well, that's what we should talk about—

MAYA: You announce on national television that changes would be made in the design to bring vets together again. What changes, Jan?

SCRUGGS: There's going to be a flag.

MAYA: And? What else?

SCRUGGS: The statue, somewhere. It won't screw up your design, really it won't. Maya, we need to start construction, especially now that we've told them that on T.V. Fight it later, but not now we're so close. We meet in two months to review all the figurative statues in the original contest.

MAYA: You voted, and I wasn't there?

SCRUGGS: We had to think fast.

MAYA: The memorial, no matter what, is that it? Your kind of memorial?

SCRUGGS: Our memorial. Who has final say is not the issue here.

MAYA: Oh, of course not.

SCRUGGS: I'm backing the fund. I told you that.

MAYA: Yeah, I remember.

Rich enters, waving piece of paper.

RICH: I can't believe this.

SCRUGGS: What now?

He hands Scruggs the letter.

Oh, great! This screws up everything even more. I can't believe he'd do this.

RICH: We're being railroaded.

SCRUGGS: We're backstepping.

MAYA: What does it say?

RICH: Carhart's lined up that Republican from Illinois—Hyde. He's circulated a memo accusing some of the jury members of being communists. His Christmas offensive, he calls it.

MAYA: Well, when did this arrive?

RICH: They're dropping like flies. Even Carter's left, and he signed the two acres over to us. We're losing our support.

SCRUGGS: Listen! "In view of the controversy surrounding the construction of a monument to honor Veterans of the Vietnam Era and as Secretary of the Department of the Interior, I, James Watt, hereby declare the execution of such monument on hold until a suitable compromise is reached or until further notice." On hold—

RICH: All our work.

SCRUGGS: —till further notice.

Carhart enters.

CARHART: I warned you. I warned all of you. Numbers, Jan. You forget we always had the numbers. We'll get more, too. We'll always outnumber you.

ACT TWO   Scene I

"Puff the Magic Dragon" plays. Eventually, Stu joins in, singing.

SOLDIER A: Chrissakes, folk songs in Hawaii? Hey, turn that down. Do Hendrix or the Stones. Smarmy kid's song. Come on, put on something we can all enjoy. Hey! (*to Soldier B*) What's wrong with him?

SOLDIER B: He's high. He's a little . . . you know, spooky.

DAVE: Spooky? Why'd they call you that? Hey, man, I knew you smoked, but—

SOLDIER A: How spooky is he? If he jumps me, I'll whip him good.

SOLDIER B: Listen, this guy can't whip cream.

DAVE: You let them talk about you like that, man? You could hear them, and you didn't do nothing to defend yourself?

SOLDIER A: This job sucks.

SOLDIER B: Yeah? Wait till the show starts.

STU: (*reading dog tag*) Staff sarge, first name William . . . Bill.

SOLDIER B: Yep, ol' Stu's seen 'em all.

STU: My dad's name was William. I've found my two uncles' names, my cousin's, I even found yours, Dave.

DAVE: You always this ripped, then?

SOLDIER B: Yep. Ol' Stu's not long for this world himself. Are you? Gone, man—gonna lose it soon.

STU: Private First Class . . . Jeffrey . . . Jeff. . . . My middle name's Jeff.

SOLDIER B: He's starting up again.

DAVE: Too many names, man.

STU: Sorry, sarge, but it looks like you're on the bottom for this ride.

DAVE: I'm not feeling too well.

SOLDIER B: You asked for it, man. You wanted to know.

DAVE: Okay, okay. I know I did.

SOLDIER A: How long has he been here?

SOLDIER B: Too long.

DAVE: Ten months. I remember.

STU: Knew it all back then, didn't I? Thought I had it made! (*He begins to laugh.*)

DAVE: Go on, man.

STU: Yeah, got it made! Honolulu. Blue ocean, grass skirts, naked women. Got it made. (*to Soldier A and Soldier B*) Let's get a move on here! Chop, chop! Get it? Chop, chop?

DAVE: No one's laughing, man.

STU: Come on, throw 'em on. Planes to fill, boys. Lots of planes to send home. It's okay, they're light, see? Sorry, Jeff, old buddy. This won't hurt. But I gotta dump you on the sarge over there. Ol' Bill won't mind, will you, Bill?

SOLDIER B: He's working up to a real good one this time.

An agonized scream is heard offstage.

SOLDIER B: They must be moving the live ones to the hospital.

STU: They're all the same, those here and there. These don't cry, that's all.

Scene 2

SARAH: How goes it?

JULIE: I feel I'm back in '69.

SARAH: I hear you. Stubborn, huh?

JULIE: It's not him, it's me. I feel I'm always apologizing! Why should I apologize? I didn't start the war.

239

Jeannie

Barroga

SARAH: I know, I know.

JULIE: I didn't draft him. I didn't give him that chip on his shoulder.

SARAH: Okay, okay now.

JULIE: I tell him how silly I felt recently reading those naive journals of mine, and then I end up feeling even sillier. I'm trying to say something here, and I'm ending up all thumbs.

SARAH: Well, if we would just admit it to ourselves, we're all trying to find something from back then. Get back to that moment just before the world went crazy.

JULIE: And then what? Change it?

SARAH: In a way.

JULIE: But it won't, will it?

SARAH: You tell me. See if—in spite of that big old war—you can both somehow stop the little ones.

JULIE: Oh, what's the difference?

SARAH: I don't know. It's a long way to come just to bang out the same note, it seems to me.

JULIE: I'm sorry I started this.

SARAH: No you aren't.

JULIE: (*indicating Morris*) And him? How's it going?

SARAH: We're in a holding pattern.

Scene 3

RICH: You've got to be kidding.

CARHART: We've got to incorporate the symbols that it should represent and doesn't.

RICH: The names are the symbols. Why can't you understand that?

CARHART: A flag, Rich. We want a flag—there. (*He points to the left end of the wall.*)

RICH: No!

CARHART: The statue—there! (*He points to apex.*)

RICH: No!

CARHART: Well, then I'll be back.

MAYA: The design is different. Just because it's not blaring, because it's not loud, doesn't make it any less beautiful.

CARHART: We have conceded. We will push to have the flag there instead. (*He points to the right end of the wall.*)

RICH: Are you crazy? No!

CARHART: And the statue there. (*He points to the left end of the wall.*)

RICH: It won't do, Tom. It's not working out at all.

CARHART: We'll just have to get back to you again.

MAYA: The wall doesn't scream; it wasn't meant to. It evokes feelings, thoughts, emotions. It's strong in its understatement. It's strongest in its simplicity.

CARHART: Okay, we've weighed all the choices.

RICH: Good.

CARHART: And we've decided the flag is here—(*Center, top of the wall.*) And the statue, here. (*At apex, in front of wall.*)

RICH: I swear, you've all got your sense of art up your ass.

CARHART: Well, what do you want us to do? Hide it in the woods nearby?

MAYA: If we have to have either the flag or the statue, it should be harmonious . . . integrated. . . .

CARHART: Here.

RICH: No!

MAYA: Harmony. . . .

CARHART: Here.

RICH: No!

MAYA: Integration . . .

CARHART: Symbols, Rich. Figures.

MAYA: Is anybody listening?

Scene 4

CHAIRMAN: I hereby declare this meeting still in session after this short recess. May I remind you that we have voted to change the agenda of this meeting and have now debated for hours on the placement of the flag and statue, and have yet to return to our original plan of reviewing eighty slides—

RICH: Mr. Chairman, again, I repeat we don't need to adorn the memorial with a lot of political claptrap. I repeat that the flag is an obtrusive object next to this design.

VET 1: I object. We don't have to have some modernistic art piece as our memorial, either. Put art where it belongs—in museums. Put honor back in memorials.

CHAIRMAN: You're both out of order.

RICH: Maya, you designed it. Where do you think we should place a statue if we have to have one?

MAYA: I think—if you really have to do this—that it should be integrated with the original design. It should be harmonious. That's all.

SCRUGGS: All right!

VET 2: We all heard her. She wants the flag, too.

CHAIRMAN: Order! Order!

RICH: Now, wait a minute, everybody—

MAYA: That's not what I said—

SCRUGGS: So, come on, let's get this show on the road. We've made our compromise.

VET 2: Let's just build it and get it done.

MAYA: —what I meant was—

SCRUGGS: Let's get that permit.

RICH: Maya, I knew what you meant.

MAYA: They don't. They never have. I'm taking off for a while. I just want to be far, far away.

RICH: Once those shovels are in the ground, this episode will be history, Maya.

MAYA: When construction begins, I'll do what I have to do.

Scene 5

DAN: (to Terry) Getting hungry? Boy, a cookie would taste good right about now. Aah, well, what the hell, just call out to her. Say,

"Hey, if I give you a quarter would you give me a cookie?" Come on, you just want to talk to her. You know that. Just admit it. I bet you don't even know what it is that puts you off about her, do you? This is an opportunity for both of you, don't you know that? Come on! Don't be so mule-headed! Call out to her. Say, Julie ... Julie ...

TERRY: Julie?

Julie turns as Scruggs enters. Jerry follows.

SCRUGGS: Mister?

TERRY: Sir.

DAN: (*to Jerry*) What are you up to?

JERRY: Just thought I'd join the fun.

SCRUGGS: Just got a question for you. See, they're going to do a special ceremony here—

TERRY: Yeah?

SCRUGGS: You want to move your flag off the Mall?

TERRY: No, sir.

SCRUGGS: I see.

JERRY: Ask how long he's been here.

SCRUGGS: How long you been here?

TERRY: About two days now, sir.

DAN: Julie, look.

SCRUGGS: Take off work, huh?

TERRY: Some things are more important, sir.

DAN: Vouch for him, Jules, come on.

JULIE: Determined man you have here.

SCRUGGS: I see.

JULIE: Always tell a determined man by the set of his mouth, his posture even.

SCRUGGS: Is that right?

Jerry goes to Morris, whispers in his ear. Morris wheels closer.

DAN: Guy deserves respect.

JULIE: Man that determined deserves some respect, don't you think?

SCRUGGS: Mmm-hmm.

JERRY: (*to Morris*) He's not going to make him move that flag, is he?

MORRIS: Hey, you gonna make him move that flag?

SCRUGGS: Well, I thought I was.

MORRIS: Yeah? Then I'll hold the same flag right there for another two days. See if I don't.

JERRY: (*to Scruggs*) He's got a job to do.

SCRUGGS: Mister!

TERRY: I'm just trying to do something here—

SCRUGGS: Corporal, Infantry.

TERRY: Private First Class, Infantry.

MORRIS: Sergeant.

TERRY: I have to do this, don't you see? I have—

SCRUGGS: A job to do. I know.

JERRY: Good show.

SCRUGGS: Good job.

Scruggs exits. Morris and Terry exchange a glance, then move apart.

JULIE: Wow, two days.

TERRY: Yeah, like "wow," hey.

JULIE: Please, don't make fun of me.

TERRY: What do you want now, a thank you?

JULIE: I just want to say I really am impressed. I mean, you're being here two days.

TERRY: It's not to impress you.

JULIE: I mean, you must be tired or hungry even—

TERRY: I'm fine.

JULIE: Well, good!

TERRY: You can go "do lunch" now.

JULIE: Why are you so, so damn—

DAN: Mule-headed.

JULIE: Mule-headed! Okay, so we don't see eye-to-eye on some things, we probably never will. I'm just saying . . . I don't know. You got this flag—not a small flag, either—and this . . . what is this anyway?

TERRY: Holster.

JULIE: Holster thing and you set yourself up when you knew you'd be questioned. You knew people might bother you—like me.

TERRY: You didn't bother me. Nothing you do affects what I'm doing because I would've done it anyway. Look, I don't have much going on now, but when I heard about this, I had to do something. It may not be much to anybody else, but right now it's all I have. And it's—

JULIE: For them, I know. I just wanted to tell someone I'm sorry . . . and thanks. That's all.

DAN: Julie!

JULIE: Yes?

TERRY: Huh?

JULIE: Did you say something?

TERRY: No.

DAN: Come on, buddy, talk to her. (*to Jerry*) What's wrong with people, Jer? Life's too short, don't they know that?

JERRY: Well, sometimes the magic works, and sometimes. . . . She said what she wanted to say, didn't she?

TERRY: For Billy, Matt . . . and from someone named Julie, thanks . . . to Walker, and Tom, and Stuart, and Chuck. . . .

Scene 6

VI: Anyone know a good round? Rich can start, Jan goes next, and—

RICH: Eighty-six that, okay?

VI: Just trying to liven things up around here.

SCRUGGS: You sure there's not another delivery?

RICH: This came at three, and the next mail comes at nine in the morning. And this is the last day to get that permit.

SCRUGGS: We've done everything Watt wanted. We should've gotten that permit a week ago.

VI: Timing, Jan. It's all timing.

SCRUGGS: It's my ulcer, that's what it is. What time is it, now?

RICH: Jan, why don't you go home, relax, turn on the tube—

VI: Yeah, Jan. We'll call you.

SCRUGGS: No, siree. I'm staying right here. I want to see with my own eyes how he sat back on his monkey's ass and let a whole dream die in one afternoon.

RICH: (*pulling out champagne*) And I brought this especially for today.

SCRUGGS: An optimist. There's one in every crowd.

Maya enters with an envelope, unnoticed.

SCRUGGS: If there's one thing I can't stand, it's a pie-eyed optimist.

MAYA: There was a messenger out there from the Department of the Interior.

RICH: From the Secretary of the Department of the Interior, addressed to the Vietnam Veterans' Memorial Fund—

VI: Open it, Rich. Don't start reading the postmark.

RICH: I am, I am.

SCRUGGS: Well, say something.

RICH: "Enclosed is the formal permit to build in a specified two acres of the Constitutional Gardens a monument honoring Veterans of the Vietnam Era."

SCRUGGS: We got it! We got the goddamned permit!

VI: I'm so relieved! This is wonderful!

RICH: I can't believe it! The eleventh hour!

SCRUGGS: Where's that champagne, optimist?

RICH: Oh, yeah. Get some paper cups, in the hallway by the water—

VI: Happy days, Rich. No one can stop you now.

RICH: Listen, I'm sorry if I was a grouch.

SCRUGGS: "Happy days are here again. The skies above are clear again—"

RICH/SCRUGGS: "—So let's sing a song of cheer again—"

RICH/SCRUGGS/VI: "Happy days are here again!"

RICH: (*pouring champagne*) Our troubles are over, folks. We're on our way now. Hey, ladies first. Maya, some champagne?

MAYA: A little.

RICH: All right. . . . Oops, have a little more there, just a smidgen more—

MAYA: Really, that's enough—

RICH: (*to Scruggs*) And you, take that! (*to Maya*) And just a little more—

MAYA: No, please. I know my limit.

RICH: Okay, but listen, when we have the real ground-breaking, you gotta celebrate just as much as the rest of us, got that? (*He drinks*) Whoa! Bubbly!

VI: Well, guys, I got a story to get out. Congratulations, everyone.

SCRUGGS: I gotta call my wife.

RICH: I better call that foreman. Tell him to dig and dig now. Make that lawn look like a B-52 hit it.

MAYA: Does he know where it goes? Where the angle should be? Has he seen the plans?

RICH: Don't worry, we got it all under control. He's a vet, too. He won't screw it up.

MAYA: Rich, we need to talk. While I was gone, I was thinking about some legal advice regarding the flag and all—

RICH: Just a sec, Maya. . . . Hello?

MAYA: I don't know if we've done everything we could do to protect my design—

RICH: Guess what? This is Rich, and you have the go-ahead. . . . That's right, tear into it. . . . Yeah, meet you there. And if anybody stops you, tell them I'll be right there with the piece of paper . . . Just keep those bulldozers working. . . . Let them call the National Guard. I'm not waiting one second more.

VI: Checking out the scene of the crime?

MAYA: Hello, Vi.

VI: Mind if I ask you a few questions?

MAYA: Please, no interviews now.

VI: Oh, this isn't an interview, if you say it's not. I just want to get a few things straight.

MAYA: They've added an inscription, a flag, and a statue. You know as much as I do.

VI: It's what they call an art war, Maya. Speaking of which, have you talked to Frederick Hart?

MAYA: We talk through newspapers. Everyone quotes what we say to each other, but we've yet to speak in person.

VI: Well, he was led to believe his design would be used in the first place, you know.

MAYA: But mine won.

VI: Well, that's what I've said all along.

MAYA: It's unethical, what he's doing.

VI: Can I quote you on that?

MAYA: No. You know, you've been making a big deal of my being a female and Chinese. Do you realize you're doing that?

VI: All I do is report the facts—

MAYA: I mean, doesn't it bother you having "our kind" brought up all the time? You must get a lot of that. I sure have since this started—

VI: I said, no.

MAYA: I don't believe you.

VI: All it is, is news, Maya. This is history in the making.

MAYA: I don't want to be in history. I just want someone to be on my side.

VI: Talking to the press helps.

MAYA: You mean, you.

VI: I know a lot of people.

MAYA: I know. You get your stories that way.

VI: I told you and Rich from the start how it would be. Questions, more questions, and—

MAYA: Dirt digging. Yeah, I know. I just want my design done as planned. How can I get them to do that?

VI: It's simple. You start your own campaign. You issue a statement to the press announcing you've found legal help. I know just the person.

RICH: *The Washington Post*, for God's sake!

SCRUGGS: Let me read it. "I have to clear my conscience. This farce has gone on too long." It's a farce all right. If we hadn't picked her design in the first place.

RICH: Read on, read on.

SCRUGGS: "It's not worth compromising. The wall is not worth getting built if I have to sell out my own design. I'm kept uninformed, in isolation—"

SCRUGGS: (*to Maya*) We'll can it now, if you don't go along with us.

MAYA: It's disheartening to see the democratic process subverted and to see politics win out over art. I thought this war was fought for freedom. This includes, I thought, freedom of expression. In essence, Frederick Hart is drawing moustaches on someone else's work. An artist with any integrity would never do that.

SCRUGGS: What can we do?

RICH: No statue, no permit.

MAYA: It's been mentioned—many times, in fact—the fact that me as the designer of a memorial to an Asian war was upsetting. I'm a young woman, a student. And I'm Chinese American. We're all lumped together, us "gooks."

SCRUGGS: We never made an issue of that.

MAYA: All I can say is, I entered a contest. I was given a number. I followed the requirements, and by all technical standards, I won. And someone, if not some group, should abide by that decision.

SCRUGGS: I can't believe she'd jeopardize her own—

MAYA: The ground-breaking was a really tough time for me, knowing my design had been compromised. As you know, I wasn't there. I admit I ran away. I see now I should have fought. I'm fighting now.

249

Jeannie

Barroga

SCRUGGS: Let's do something. We can't stand here.

RICH: Okay, we got the permit, then we dug up their manicured lawn, next step . . .

SCRUGGS: Let's get a panel in place right away.

Vi enters.

RICH: I can't believe you did this.

VI: Me?

RICH: Yes, you. We were together on this and now we're split apart.

VI: Listen, let's go get a drink.

RICH: Are you kidding? Haven't you done enough?

VI: I just told her about a lawyer I knew, that's all—

RICH: Ten months till dedication day. There's no way we'll make it now, with this injunction. How did you think we could get anything done in that time, huh? How do you think we do things around here?

VI: Okay, okay. I'll admit there's a story now. Vets praising the wall is boring, vets attacking it is something else. Vets attacking other vets, art versus establishment, Maya jeopardizing her own design, now that's news—

RICH: The news is you've been playing both sides of the fence, that's the news. Weaving your little web of intrigue—

VI: Intrigue?

RICH: —I'm surprised you didn't throw in what you did in the war. Did you do anything? Even protest?

VI: I was busy being an A-student.

RICH: Oh great. That's why you're so perfect now, right?

VI: Stop it. Stop saying my hair, "as usual," is perfect. That I am perfect. You don't mean it, anyway.

RICH: Oh, but I do. Anyone middle-of-the-road—

VI: Yes, that's right. I didn't make waves or make any radical political statements. Know why? Because I'm from a family that says success above all: be brighter, do better. And I did, I achieved. And if you don't think that was a struggle, then you try it.

RICH: Try what? Pretending I'm not what I am? Putting on a face in front of millions of viewers and ignoring the fact that I look like the ones this war was fought against? An Asian face.

VI: Stop it!

RICH: You think people don't notice that? Can't you see the irony in all this?

VI: I'm sick and tired of—

RICH: You're the story, Vi. Maya knows that. And if you'd admit it, you do, too. Both of you. You're part of what this memorial is supposed to represent. Can't you see that? What do you got to say about that? What words will express what now will never be carved on that wall, huh? How do you feel about that, or do you feel? Is the facade too thick now?

VI: I'm not doing anything that anyone else wouldn't do to get where they are. I've paid big to get here. Rich, someone makes the news, others report it. Someone has to stay impartial, unaffected, despite what they may feel—

RICH: No, Vi, you don't feel—

VI: I do feel, Rich!

JERRY: —Impartial, unaffected, yes. You're definitely that. But, you forgot heartless, Vi. Look it up.

VI: That was unfair. That was cruel.

RICH: You got your story, Vi. The vets are riled up, Maya is riled up. You should be happy now.

Scene 8

SOLDIER B: Don't even take care of himself anymore, you know? Don't wash or comb his hair. Always talking to himself. Look at him.

SOLDIER A: One oar in the water, if you ask me—

SOLDIER B: Bats in the belfry—

SOLDIER A: —Not dealing with a full deck—

SOLDIER B: Something's scrambled—

STU: I'm sorry!

DAVE: Stu?

STU: I said I'm sorry!

SOLDIER B: Come on, the next plane's in.

STU: (*regarding bag*) One hundred forty pounds. I can guess the weight of any body now. Still intact. Blonde. See the zipper? You try.

DAVE: No thanks, man.

STU: I know 'em all before I see 'em. Sometimes I look at 'em, too, you know?

DAVE: Why, man?

STU: To read the dogtags jammed into their teeth.

DAVE: Oh, God, Stu . . .

STU: Yeah, you get to know them all real good.

DAVE: Like a bad dream that don't stop.

STU: Like the "Twilight Zone," man. Like maybe this tour's not just two years . . . it's forever.

Stu reads tag, recoils.

DAVE: What is it, man? What'd you see?

STU: Four! That makes four this week. Not cousins or uncles or fathers anymore. They're named Stu. They're all named me.

SOLDIER B: Okay, Stu, settle down.

STU: It's me I'm sending off. Little parts of me in every bag.

SOLDIER A: He's been getting worse all week.

STU: And two went back to Illinois. Illinois for Chrissake!

SOLDIER A: What's so great about Illinois?

STU: I'm from Illinois, dipshit. My name's Stewart, and I'm from Illinois. Just like them.

SOLDIER A: This guy's wacko.

Stu stumbles over bag.

STU: I'm sorry. I'm sorry. Okay?

SOLDIER A: We gotta get him out of here.

SOLDIER B: I think you're right.

SOLDIER A: Hey, Stu, come on. You need a break.

STU: Don't touch me. Just leave me alone.

SOLDIER A: I'm going for help.

STU: I'm sorry I tripped. I'm sorry I threw Jeff. I'm sorry they went and I didn't. I'm sorry I lived. Oh, God, I'm sorry I did anything to anybody. I'm sorry, I'm sorry, I'm sorry . . . (*He unzips bag. Screams.*)

DAVE: What'd you see, man. Stu, what'd you see?

STU: Meeeeeee!

DAVE: I'm still with you, Stu, don't you worry. You're back and you never going off again. You here with me now. You back in one piece, and when we get back, we go see that dude you were seeing once, you hear? We ain't done yet, buddy. We're gonna get more help. Welcome home.

STU: Kept me for six months, and I tuned out. Kept the pain out and reality. And I can't get back. I don't know how to get back.

Scene 9

RICH: Hey, Jan, is that you?

SCRUGGS: Hey, Rich. What are you doing here?

RICH: Thought I'd come imagine the rest of the wall already up.

SCRUGGS: Like this first panel? You know, there were only four families, at the unveiling Rich. Four families and eight color guard. Six hundred and sixty-five names were on that one panel. It seems every one of them should have been represented. That says something, I guess. I'm not sure what.

RICH: They'll be here, Jan. Four months from now, in November. Vets Day, Dedication Day. Boy, that'll be the time to celebrate.

SCRUGGS: Yeah, we'll see. Hey, I got a call from my old sarge last night. He say "Jay-un, ya'll got a tiger by the tail up thar in Washington. Get that 'ol Watt out of the way. And you keep fighting. Get the names of those boys on that wall."

RICH: He's right, you know. We will, too.

SCRUGGS: You know, this panel is the damnedest thing.

RICH: Pretty amazing, isn't it?

SCRUGGS: I saw something yesterday. It struck me somehow. See, this black isn't black, you know, like a chalkboard. It's like . . . it's like a mirror.

RICH: Well, you knew that.

SCRUGGS: Yeah, I saw samples, but this is about eleven feet high, five feet wide. I can see my whole figure in it. And in the sun, it was warm. It radiated warmth. And I found myself . . . it's hard to explain this.

RICH: Try.

SCRUGGS: I found myself reaching out to touch it, touch the names. It's different, Rich. It's really different.

Scene 10

SARAH: Well, I found 'em all. And Liz Jones. You talking yet?

MORRIS: You still here?

SARAH: Sure, cuss. Planned a whole day.

MORRIS: It's just too much.

SARAH: Yeah, a lot of boys in one place.

MORRIS: (*referring to book*) Look here: over two million sent. Two hundred and ninety thousand in '69 alone. Twenty-five thousand in just one week. Seventy-six percent were, what they call "lower class." You know what that means—mostly black. Breaks down to two black men to every white.

SARAH: A numbers man.

MORRIS: Hell, everybody knew that—everybody black. That's all we talked about. Can't give us jobs or a place on a bus, but they sure can find a spot for us on the front line.

SARAH: Got that right. (*She takes out lunch bag.*)

MORRIS: You gonna eat right here?

SARAH: Why not? There's grass, a clear sky, something to look at, people to watch. Sure, I'll eat here. Why?

MORRIS: Never mind.

SARAH: Got some celery, cookies, oh, and lemon pound cake.

MORRIS: What you all got in there, girl? Gonna stay the night?

SARAH: Told you. I planned for a lot of time here. Picnic with my friends. In Victorian days people would pack picnic baskets and sit near the graves of their loved ones, spend the whole day. Like me. Didn't want the dead left out just because they're dead. They'd want it that way. Come on, have a carrot stick—on them.

MORRIS: Rabbit food.

SARAH: Oh, take one.

MORRIS: Where'd you say you served?

SARAH: I didn't say, but I was stateside. San Diego.

MORRIS: Oh.

SARAH: Hey, now. Don't be "oh-ing" me. I had a job to do here, too. Not all the war was in the jungle.

MORRIS: I didn't say nothing.

SARAH: No? What's this "oh" then, huh? That "oh" said, "Just San Diego, huh?" Not front line like real nurses, that's what that "oh" said to me. Don't think I don't know where I was and where they were. Okay, so they were braver than me. They volunteered. I did what I could, where I could.

MORRIS: You gonna let that cake go to waste?

SARAH: Why? You want it?

MORRIS: Yeah. Pass it over. Got something on your mind, Sarah?

SARAH: Upset stomach is all. Not your concern.

MORRIS: Never said it was. Seems to me, you the one all fired up not being at the front.

SARAH: I don't want to talk about it.

MORRIS: Hey, you the one park yourself at my wheelchair, not the other way around.

SARAH: (*referring to Julie*) Talking to that girl over there by the flagman earlier?

MORRIS: Yeah?

SARAH: She said she felt they were here, these boys she knew from school. Like maybe us talking about them brings them back, you know? Like ghosts. Not just human ghosts, though. Ghosts I thought were dead and buried coming back to haunt me again. Shadows of things I should've done—and didn't.

MORRIS: Like what? Volunteer?

SARAH: Maybe.

MORRIS: Like carry a gun, see real action?

SARAH: I ain't telling you nothing.

MORRIS: Hey, you didn't miss anything. Let me tell you, that was no "picnic" back there, no sir. I wouldn't go back if—

SARAH: No, that's not what I mean. I could've gone. If it weren't for excuses. Always excuses. We were given a choice to volunteer, a bunch of us, Liz included. All of us agreed we'd draw straws, see. And I didn't even show up. I couldn't even do that.

MORRIS: Wish it had been that easy for us.

SARAH: See, that too. You guys served. You had to. Me, I knew I could stay home. I was gliding, you know what I mean? Grumbling to myself every time I turned over some body in bed. Saying I don't want to do this anymore. I don't want to be here. I don't want to touch anyone, and I don't want anyone to touch me. And I could carry that out if I wanted to, just up and leave everyone on his own. But they took it further. Every time another nurse was killed in action, I felt bad, you know, but I also felt relief.

MORRIS: Cause you weren't the one.

SARAH: Yeah. I would pat myself on the back for being so smart when they were so—

MORRIS: So what? Huh? Go ahead, say it. What were all of us who went when we didn't have to?

SARAH: What do you call it? What do you call any of it? Telling boys everything's all right when it's not. For believing we all heroes over there, when we're not. For thinking I was better off a black nurse than a black maid in some cheap hotel. You see what I'm getting at? We all congratulating ourselves on how we so much better off than the poor unfortunate next to us. And when you do that, you ain't nothing. We all just poor souls. We ain't men and women, or black and white, or whole and broken. We ain't nothing. We just walking sins of pride. We just fools.

MORRIS: Pride, huh? Yeah, we all proud back then. Hell, I thought I'd come back a hero, medal and everything. I'd be marching down the middle of the street every Vet's Day, chest out, people waving and cheering. And I'd be walking. I'd come out of that war whole. You know, maybe that's why we're both here, reminding each other of our pride. What you say to that?

SARAH: Nothing. I got nothing to say.

MORRIS: Like a damn movie. The woman won't talk, but she won't leave either.

SARAH: I ain't leaving. I got just as much right—

MORRIS: So talk or leave. You stay here, you on my time.

SARAH: I went to a movie that night, the night of the straws. Some old war movie. John Wayne, a soldier, and Maureen O'Hara, a nurse. Boy they white, ain't they? I was only half-listening. I was thinking if it hadn't been a movie, it'd have been something else. Laundry, letter writing, something. I didn't want to go, that's all. I didn't want to put me in a position to go. That's my ghost, Lee.

MORRIS: So bury it.

SARAH: How?

MORRIS: What's in your feedbag there?

SARAH: What're you looking for?

MORRIS: Straws.

SARAH: Oh, I don't think—

MORRIS: Here. Two juice cartons. Each with them little straws wrapped around them. (*He breaks one, holds both in fist.*) Okay, draw.

SARAH: This won't prove anything . . .

MORRIS: I'm a numbers man, remember? Let's try this out. Draw. See, by my calculation, I was meant to go, you weren't. It's the numbers. Same thing could happen with dice. Fate, Sarah. You'll draw the long straw. Now prove me right, or prove me wrong.

Sarah takes the long straw.

SARAH: Oh, Lordy . . .

MORRIS: See? Let's bury this right here at the base of Liz Jones's panel. You weren't meant to go, Sarah. You were meant for something else. You got kids? Maybe that, then. Or to stand here years later feeding rabbit food to one who did come back. Now, where's some more of that lemon pound cake?

Scene 11

MAYA: I appeal to the Commission to protect the artistic integrity of the original design. What is realistic? Is any one man's interpretation better able to convey an idea than any other's? Should it not be left to the observer? The original design gives each individual the freedom to reflect upon the heroism and sacrifice of those who served. It is symbolic of the freedom this country stands for. It is a Living Park, a symbol of life—the life of the returning veteran who sees himself reflected within the time, within the names.

What is also memorialized is that people have not—and still cannot—resolve that war. Nor can they separate it from the issues, the politics, or even their inner wars.

CHAIRMAN: It is the decision of this court to move a styrofoam model of the three statues around the Mall until a mutually agreed upon position by both parties is reached. It is understood that the composition be located and designed so as not to compromise nor diminish the basic design of the memorial as previously planned, and that it will not hamper, obstruct, or in any way damage the aesthetics of one or the other. The same shall be done for the placement of a flag representing these United States of America. This hearing is adjourned.

RICH: (*to Vi*) We got it. We got the permit, a flag, a statue, and the Wall. Maya's through with us, though. If you see her, I'd appreciate it if you would . . . oh, never mind.

Scene 12

Vi enters. Lights match. Scans wall for name. Match goes out. Lights another match. Scans wall for a name, finds it. Pulls out photo, and leaves it at the wall.

DAVE: My buddy, Stu, wanted to light ten candles at the wall. They kept going out. Me and a bunch of vets nearby stood around and formed a windbreak. I want to thank someone for this day, man. That's all.

TERRY: I came alone. I've been alone, and I thought it would stay that way even here. But guys came up to me, and I edged over to them. And we did what we were afraid to do. We cried.

SCRUGGS: I left 'Nam thirteen years ago wounded by shrapnel. When I saw *Deerhunter* back in '79 I couldn't sleep. Since then, I've been swearing, arguing, fighting with myself and others. I kept thinking, "I gotta say something." People gotta know we were there, and I didn't think they ever would. But at that panel, I found myself remembering my buddies alive—now dead. And all those memories choking me for years inside me, they come out, and I feel free of something. We were there. It did happen, and they're remembered. I remember them. And I miss 'em. I feel better knowing they're on the wall, but I still, oh God, I miss 'em.

MAYA: All the people, all the letters of support. I'm a little overwhelmed. I'm really touched. I never expected it to be painless. It's not meant to be cheerful or happy, but to bring out in people the realization of loss and a cathartic healing process. A lot of emotion is let go when you visit the memorial. A lot of people were afraid of that emotion; it was something we had glossed over.

VI: We of the '60s knew about Vietnam through T.V., newspapers, and radio. But it numbed us instead of sensitizing us. We dissect that era as dispassionately as we watched it happen. For one decade a whole nation denied its involvement. A decade later, it honors its dead. There is still today, division. I myself still fight a war, one of prejudice and indifference. We are victims of that war as we are the enemy because walls do exist. Walls are still built. Let's hope this Wall will be the last. This has been live from the memorial to Veterans of the Vietnam Era, Washington, D.C.

MORRIS: Here's my medal. . . .

WOMAN: So warm, as if it's living. . . .

SARAH: I feel I'm sharing. . . .

RICH: I feel I've stopped. . . .

VET 2: Like death itself. . . .

WOMAN: Fathers looking for sons. . . .

STU: All the lifeblood. . . .

JULIE: A waste. . . .

MORRIS: Here's to you guys. . . .

VET 3: Here's to half my platoon. . . .

RICH: Here's to this wall. . . .

JULIE: To never age and never grow old. . . .

STU: Here's to me.

They all say names* and continue into a whisper as lights fade.

* DAVE: panel 32 east, line 93 (David Fischer)

SARAH: panel 5 east, line 47 (Elizabeth Jones)

JULIE: panel 41 west, line 47 (Dennis Jerdet)

259

Jeannie

Barroga

STU: panel 29 west, line 49 (William Tanner)

TERRY: panel 19 west, line 3 (Randy Larson)

MORRIS: panel 22 east, line 68 (Jimmy Earl Carter)

VI: panel 10 west, line 109 (Glenn Hung Nin Lee)

RICH: panel 34 west, line 46 (Dougie Mericle)

SCRUGGS: panel 30 east, line 98 (Joel Matusek)

MAYA: panel 1 west, line 75 (Peter Chan)

VET 1: panel 66 east, line 12 (Tim McGurty)

VET 2: panel 37 west, line 43 (Blair Two-Crow)

WOMAN: panel 27 west, line 90 (John McDonald)

THE END

LETTERS TO A

STUDENT REVOLUTIONARY

❀

ELIZABETH WONG

Although Elizabeth Wong's *Letters to a Student Revolutionary* culminates in the events of the Chinese student uprising in Tiananmen Square in the spring of 1989, at the core of the play is a friendship between two women of widely disparate cultures who have in common their youth, gender, and race. During the course of a ten-year correspondence between Bibi, a Chinese American, and Karen, a Chinese, Wong explores the issues of personal identity and individual freedom through women living under systems of government that define freedom in widely divergent terms. The women serve as mirrors of their respective societies, reflecting the gap between ideology and reality from the perspective of individuals who neither hold power nor possess great ambition, but simply aspire to have choices.

Wong's play is an unraveling of aspects of her own history and is in large part autobiographical. Born in 1958 in Southgate, an industrial area of Los Angeles, California, Wong like her character Bibi hails from working-class, first-generation immigrant roots. Both her parents were born in mainland China. Her mother is a hospital kitchen worker and her father, like Bibi's, owned a small family grocery store before he died. Although he was trained as a chemical engineer at the University of California at Berkeley he never worked in his profession. According to Wong, "My mother tells me it's because no one would hire him . . . because he was Chinese."[1]

Despite her firsthand knowledge of the barriers encountered by Asians attempting to enter certain professions in America, Wong, again like her character Bibi, made a bold career move with the decision to become a playwright. For nearly ten years she had worked as a journalist, writing for the *San Diego Tribune* and later for the *Hartford Courant* after having studied journalism at the University of Southern California. But in 1988, tired of merely reporting the facts and maintaining a professional objectivity, she "came to a point where I decided I couldn't be objective anymore, I couldn't be neutral, I needed to express who I was—who I am." This career shift corresponded with a period of intense self-examination and revelation. Though raised in Chinatown, Wong had spent most of her life escaping her origins. "I didn't want to have anything to do with all these people who talked with accents, who didn't read the things that I read or see the movies that I saw. . . . I didn't have anything in common with those people. . . . I didn't feel like I was like them, I didn't want to be associated with them, and I didn't know why. . . . it wasn't until I became a playwright that I began to like myself the way I am."

As a journalist Wong had felt she was a token if asked to report on an Asian subject. "I always used to blanch when they sent me to do the Vietnamese-arriving-from-Vietnam story. I resented it. I always thought, oh they're only sending me because I'm yellow. I didn't make those connections that maybe I could . . . learn a different type of sensitivity." Wong asserts that negative film and television images of Asians were key factors in what she terms "a process of brainwashing." "I think you just learn to hate yourself. I think I hated myself for a long time and didn't even know it."

Coming into contact with the Asian American theater was pivotal in reversing Wong's way of thinking. Although she had always had a passion for the theater, she had a particularly pointed reaction to seeing Wakako Yamauchi's *And the Soul Shall Dance,* which she saw in its television version. Seeing the play affirmed her identity and experience, much in the same way Yamauchi herself had been influenced by writer Hisaye Yamamoto some three decades earlier. Wong remembers, "I really felt opened up by Wakako's play to the possibility that I could explore my own world and other people would find it interesting. . . . I had grown up in Chinatown and it was always imperative to get the hell out. I didn't think that my story was that interesting. That's why I never wrote about it. I had always wanted to be a writer but I was preconvinced that what stories I had to tell weren't going to be interesting to anybody." Wong also acknowledges playwright David Henry Hwang as a major influence, "I think that David's play *FOB* gave me a lot of courage. I knew the places that he was talking about. I knew San Gabriel. I knew the language that he was speaking in. I also felt that was only part of the story. I knew I could tell a different story from my own experience as a woman and as an Asian American woman coming from a ghetto experience. . . . even though I was trying to get out of Chinatown all my life I've sort of come back to it."

It is this sense of a cycle, of coming to know oneself by looking at "the other" that is a dominant theme of *Letters to a Student Revolutionary*. Written in 1989 during Wong's first year at New York University's M.F.A. Playwriting program, the impetus for the play came from her correspondence with a young Chinese woman she had met in 1984 while on a tour of China with her family. The Wong family was among those Chinese Americans who sought to reestablish ties to their relations in China following the 1979 normalization of diplomatic relations with the People's Republic of China.

In June 1989, Wong, like countless other Americans and people around the world, found herself mesmerized by the television coverage of the student uprising in Tiananman Square. "I sat in front of the television set and was horrified by what I saw. It was ugly and disturbing and tragic. I felt a kind of overwhelming connection because I was Chinese, or I thought I was Chinese. . . . I felt it on two levels. . . . One, I was aghast and appalled that a country could destroy its own children. . . . But on another level . . . being Chinese American, seeing people who looked like me, really made me feel endangered in some way. I made that leap across the miles. . . . the things happening in China made me reflect on what is happening here in America and whether I, as a Chinese American, had any power to speak out and move my government."

The following autumn, after moving to New York City, Wong came across a stack of letters from the young Chinese woman she had corresponded with since 1984 but not heard from since the June massacre. Reexamining the correspondence, Wong was struck by the longevity of their correspondence despite the language barriers. "Her English was very poor, my Chinese nonexistent, so basically we exchanged life style. Information about the life style she led there and I led here. The first letter did discuss politics. She did make a plea for me to bring her to the United States. She thought that I could probably support her, that she would pay me back. . . . [She wrote that] life there was very oppressive to her. She didn't have an opportunity to express who she was and that was something that stayed in my mind when I began to write the play. Also I wanted to find a way to really talk about my own feelings about what happened in China." Wong's attempts to read between the lines of her correspondence and understand China continuously forced her to examine assumptions she had made as a Chinese American. "One of the things Bibi realizes when she goes to Tiananmen Square is that she's really American, she's not Chinese.

Both Bibi and Karen make the mistake that they think they can forge a friendship based on a shared heritage, when in fact . . . they don't have a lot of similarities."

In Wong's actual correspondence her Chinese friend eventually abandoned her desire to come to the United States. "It was only in the last year and a half, maybe the last two years [of the correspondence] that she stopped making references to the possibility of coming to the United States and the probability of working, staying in China. . . . The play is based on what I imagine her life would have been like and what I know from research of what life was like there during that period. It was an exciting period of tremendous hope for the students . . . but at the same time China has a history of opening up and cracking down. My friend was exceedingly hopeful when she made that decision to stay in her country."

The confirmation of Karen's and Bibi's respective Chinese and American identities unfolds in *Letters to a Student Revolutionary* as the exchange of personal information consistently leads each woman to define her individual and national concepts of freedom. Bibi cynically exhorts Karen to come to America and participate in "retail therapy."

> BIBI: I can see you now Karen—at the altar of The Church of Our Lady of Retail—Nordstroms, Lord and Taylor—kneeling beside me at the cash register as it rings up our sale. *Fifty percent off*—the most beautiful three words in the English language. Now that's America.

Wong inverts the original dynamics of Bibi's and Karen's relationship: whereas Karen originally yearned to leave China and live as an American, eventually she is confirmed in her Chinese identity as she glimpses more and more of Bibi's life in a constantly shifting, alienating society. As Karen gains a sense of purpose and a greater confidence in her vision that China can change, Bibi's American glibness diminishes, and she begins to question a freedom that increasingly is revealed as hollow and false. Wong says, "I think the play was trying to reflect on what it means to have freedom. . . . I really do think that the definition of democracy in America has been mutated—equating democracy and capitalism."

Subsequent to *Letters to a Student Revolutionary*, Wong wrote a second full-length drama, *Kimchee and Chitlins*, another highly topical work reflective of her journalistic background. Written in 1990, the play explores the conflicts between African Americans and Korean Americans in New York City. When it was read at the Mark Taper Forum in May 1992, the *Los Angeles Times* called it a "prophetic drama," noting the date it was written and the climate of the city at the time of the reading. Coming as it did on the heels of the worst urban rioting of this century, the play's issues extended far beyond the city of its setting. Aside from her objective grounding as a journalist, Wong approached the work with a certain empathy as an Asian American. "As an Asian I have experienced not being served by a white person in a restaurant. I also know what it's like to be spit on by a Chinese man for walking down the street of Chinatown holding the hand of a white boyfriend. *Kimchee and Chitlins* deals with that type of deep-seated racial prejudice which we all have."

Among her current projects is a three-act play *China Doll* which looks at the life of America's first Asian film "star," actress Anna May Wong. *China Doll* is Wong's response to the *Miss Saigon* controversy through a dramatic fictionalization of the experience of a media figure with whom Wong shares common origins. Anna May grew up in Chinatown, Los Angeles, and Wong draws an immediate parallel, "I can really relate to her because she lived in Chinatown and found she couldn't relate. . . . she was more interested in climbing onto a bus, just like me, and going to movies on Sunset or Hollywood Boulevard. At age eleven Anna May Wong began her acting career, contrary to the wishes of her parents. Her portrayal of a slave girl in *The Thief of Baghdad*, starring Douglas Fairbanks, brought her notoriety, although she was continually frustrated by her "B-movie" status in America. The play is a celebration of Elizabeth Wong's life-long love for the cinema, and a commentary on the racism of the movie industry. As she does with *Letters to a Student Revolutionary* and *Kimchee and Chitlins*, Wong chronicles the social problems and cultural nuances of an era through the lives of her characters. Her summation of *China Doll* aptly characterizes the body of her writing: "It explores the passion for work and personal self-expression, and the need to remake images, as well as remake personal mythologies."

Notes

1. Editor's interviews with Elizabeth Wong, New York, 22 February 1991 and 30 August 1991.

LETTERS TO A STUDENT

REVOLUTIONARY

ELIZABETH WONG

Time: 1979–1989.
Place: China and the United States.

CHARACTERS

BIBI, a Chinese-American woman in her twenties.
KAREN, a Chinese woman in her twenties.
A CHORUS of four (three men and one woman), in the following multiple roles:

CHARLIE/LU YAN/CHORUS ONE
BROTHER/FATHER/INS OFFICER/CHORUS TWO
SOLDIER/BOSS/CAT/JONATHAN/CHORUS THREE
MOTHER/MEXICAN LADY/CHORUS FOUR

There is no intermission.

PRODUCTION NOTES

The play is mainly stylistic and presentational in nature. It is imperative the actors follow the stage directions.

SET: The play consists of two separate areas representing China and the United States respectively. The center space is a neutral territory wherein the rules of time and geography are broken. The chorus is stationed upstage center. Minimal props are used to suggest occupation and/or location.

CHORUS: Remain on stage throughout. Their movements should be militaristic—crisp and clean.

COSTUMES: Clothes are suggested by the text. The Chorus should be wearing drab, loose-fitting garments similar to the Mao jacket and trousers, preferably in navy blue or grey.

SPECIAL EFFECTS: Slides of the Tiananmen Square Massacre.

The Chorus is frozen in time, upstage center.
Spotlight on Bibi, extreme downstage. Bibi is warm, humorous, melodramatic, fond of games and outwardly very self-possessed.

BIBI: (*to audience*) Day thirty-five. I *rebelled* against breakfast. The hotel dining room was hushed. I pushed myself away from the table. The chair went flying like a hockey puck. I struck a defiant Bette Davis pose.

Bibi does her best Bette Davis impression. Chorus One unfreezes, approaches, mimes offering her a bowl of rice porridge.

(*to Chorus One*) "Get that slop away from me, you pig!" (*to audience*) Actually, what I said was a polite (*to Chorus One*), "Ahh, another bowl of oriental oatmeal? No thanks." (*to audience*) My parents were appalled at my behavior. But I couldn't help it. The ghost of . . . James Dean, I told them. So, for thirty-five days, wherein I wished I was in the Bahamas instead, I was Kunta Kinte of the new Roots generation. Touring China with Mom and Dad.

Chinese opera music clangs the air. Bibi grimaces, writhes, clamps her hands over her ears.

Loved the music. Also, loved the toasting of the honored guests (*intones*) who have come back to their homeland to dedicate a new high school in the village of their humble beginnings.

The Chorus mimes a salute, with drinks in hand.

CHORUS (ALL): Gom bei!

BIBI: (*disgustedly joins in*) Gom bei! (*pause, to audience*) Oh sure, I loved the *endless* tours—the jade factory, brocade factory, carpet factory. But breakfast! Gary Cooper, John Wayne wouldn't stand for it, so why should I? They would shoot the damned cook, yep, who was probably a Chinese guy, anyway.

Every morning, every day, for thirty-five days, I was bored to . . .

CHORUS ONE: (*patiently finishes her sentence*) . . . death, which comes in the shape of an innocent bowl.

BIBI: (*to Chorus One*) Thank you. Very succinctly put.

Chorus One returns to Chorus. Bibi abruptly runs upstage. The Chorus comes alive briefly. They are the people of Tiananmen Square, going about their daily business. They freeze in a tableau. No one reacts as Bibi runs about the stage among them.

BIBI: (*to audience*) I took to the streets of Beijing, half crazed. Wandered into Tiananmen Square—a hungry look in my eyes, a vain hope in my heart. (*to Chorus Four*) You there, sweeper. Yes. Could you please tell me where I might locate a golden oasis of fast food. . . . (*to Chorus Two*) Hey there brother, can you spare an American down on her luck. . . . (*to audience*) Someday, right next to the mug of Chairman Mao, there'll be a golden arch and a neon sign flashing—billions and billions served. Open 24 hours. No place is truly civilized without Mickey D and a drive-up window. (*runs back upstage, to Chorus Three*) 'Scuse me Mr. Soldier, can you possibly direct me to the nearest greasy spoon?

Chorus Three slowly turns to look at Bibi. Both freeze.

269

Elizabeth

Wong

[handwritten margin note: chorus always miming]

CHORUS ONE: (*to audience*) Summer 1979. Tourism was still so new in China.

Karen enters the square pushing a bicycle. Karen appears tentative, soft-spoken, shy, frightened.

KAREN: (*to audience*) I am on my way home from the factory. End of the graveyard shift. Is this the correct phrase? Yes, graveyard shift. This morning, there is much mist. But it is already hot like hell. Do I say that right? Yes, I think so.

CHORUS FOUR: (*to audience*) I sweep. I sweep. Everything must be clean.

KAREN: The square is very crowded, very many people everywhere. But I see a girl. She looks like me. But her hair is curly like the tail of a pig. She wears pink, lavender, indigo. She is a human rainbow.

Karen steps toward Bibi.

CHORUS FOUR: (*to Karen*) I sweep *you* if you become unclean. Sweep you right up. Watch out for contamination! (*whispered, to Chorus One*) You, you there waiter.

CHORUS ONE: (*overlapped whisper, to Chorus Two*) Watch out! You, you there brother.

CHORUS TWO: (*overlapped whisper, to Karen*) Watch out! You, you there sister.

Intimidated, Karen backs away from Bibi.

CHORUS FOUR: (*to audience*) My duty to sweep all day. My duty to sweep all night. My back hurts. But I have duty to perform.

KAREN: Don't be a silly girl. What harm is there to practice a little English?

Chorus Three looks sharply to Karen.

CHORUS THREE: (*to Karen*) I am watching her, and . . . (*to audience*) I am watching you.

BIBI: (*to audience*) Oh look. Grandmothers with ancient faces. Pushing bamboo strollers like shopping carts. Aw, sweet little babies with wispy fuzzy spiky hair.

KAREN: (*to audience*) Look, there is a butcher I know. He carries chickens upsidedown, hurrying to market. He does not see me.

BIBI: (*to audience*) Pictures bigger than billboards on Sunset Boulevard. What's playing? O.K. That's the Mao matinee. That's Le-nin. Stalin. Is that guy Marx? Yeah, I'm sure of it. Give the girl a piece of the pie.

KAREN: (*to audience*) There, a big strong worker shoulders his load of bamboo for scaffolds. He helps to build a hospital. He is too busy to notice me.

BIBI: (*to audience*) Bricklayers push a cartful of bricks. A man carries a pole balanced with two hanging baskets. Filled with live fish. Great smell! Bicycles everywhere in the square.

CHORUS ONE: Yes, a busy morning in the square.

The Chorus, one by one, create an impenetrable human wall between Karen and Bibi.

CHORUS FOUR: (*to audience*) I am not you and I am not me. I *am* a good citizen of the state.

CHORUS TWO: (*to audience*) With so much going on, so many people, who pays attention to an inconsequential girl on a bicycle?

all about "the state"

KAREN: I will go up to her and speak to her. Right now. We will make beautiful sentences together.

CHORUS FOUR: (*to audience*) I am watching too. Watching everything. It is my duty as a good citizen of the state.

CHORUS THREE: (*to audience, overlapping*) Anarchy will *not* be tolerated.

CHORUS TWO: (*to audience, overlapping*) Even a spark of spirit will be squashed.

CHORUS ONE: (*to audience, overlapping*) Wild behavior will not be permitted.

CHORUS THREE: (*to audience, overlapping*) Wild thinking will not be permitted.

CHORUS ONE: (*to audience, overlapping*) Any messes will be cleaned up.

CHORUS TWO: (*to audience, overlapping*) This is what a broom is for.

CHORUS FOUR: (*to audience, overlapping*) This is my sword. My broom.

CHORUS: (*to audience*) We must have cleanliness. The state will insist.

Karen tries to penetrate the wall.

KAREN: Hello.

BIBI: (*to audience*) Like in "Vertigo." Jimmy Stewart climbing the steps, looking down from the tower. *Everything* going in a woozy circle. I see me and I see me and I see me. Faces like my face, like my mother's face, like my father's face. But not really, you know. I don't fit in, not at all.

Karen breaks through the wall, crosses over to Bibi.

KAREN: Hello.

Bibi doesn't hear. Karen steps closer. The Chorus steps into a line and turns their back to the audience.

Ah, hello. Excuse me.

BIBI: Oh hello.

KAREN: Are you?

BIBI: (*chuckles*) I am. How can you tell?

KAREN: Ahh. (*pause*) Your hair.

BIBI: Completely unnatural, I know. It's called a permanent. Why something's called permanent when you have it redone every six months I'll never know. More like a temporary, if you ask me. Go figure.

KAREN: Go to figure.

BIBI: Right. It's like every time I go to the salon, they want to give me the same old, tired thing—the classic bob and bangs, exactly like yours. So I plead, "Please do something different." Understand? But every time, without fail, I end up with . . . you know . . . (*indicates Karen's hair*) *that*—bland and boring, like breakfast.

KAREN: Like breakfast.

BIBI: Right. They tell me, "But oh no, you look so cute. A little China doll, that's what you are." Make me *puke*. So I say, "Aldo baby darling, perm it. Wave it. Frizz it. Spike it. Color it blue." So if you look in the light. See. Not black, but blue . . . with red highlights, tinged with orange.

KAREN: You want haircut like me? That easy. Very simple. I do it for you.

BIBI: Sorry. I know I talk too fast. I'm what is known as an energetic person. I have so much energy, I sometimes think I'll leap out of my clothes.

KAREN: No, I'm sorry. My comprehending is very bad. My English is too stupid. But I wish to practice. I would like to have hair curly like yours. Can you do that for me?

BIBI: Sure, you come to California. And I'll set you up with Aldo. But I warn you, he'll poof and pull and snip, and you think you're going to be a new woman, but you get banged and bobbed every time.

Karen starts to touch Bibi's sleeve; then withdraws shyly.

KAREN: Here we have only a few colors. Grey and blue and green.

BIBI: Grey and blue and green are good colors.

KAREN: May I ask what is your name?

BIBI: Bibi. My name is Bibi.

They reach to shake hands, but before they touch, Bibi and Karen freeze.

CHORUS THREE: It was nothing. Conversation lasted two, three minutes tops.

CHORUS FOUR: (*overlapping*) Anything can happen in two, three minutes. Did they touch?

CHORUS ONE: (*overlapping*) Was there a connection?

CHORUS TWO: (*overlapping*) Did they touch?

CHORUS ONE: (*overlapping*) Did she have a newspaper?

CHORUS THREE: (*overlapping*) A book?

CHORUS TWO: (*overlapping*) Was there an exchange?

CHORUS FOUR: (*overlapping*) Did they touch?

CHORUS THREE: (*overlapping*) Watch her very closely. Such encounters might be. . . .

CHORUS FOUR: (*overlapping*) Dangerous.

CHORUS ONE: (*overlapping*) Dangerous.

CHORUS (ALL): (*whispered*) There is no you. There is no me. Only people. People must prevail. There is no you. There is no me. Only people.

CHORUS FOUR: Watch her for signs of contamination.

CHORUS TWO: Yes, I'll watch my sister, very carefully. I'll watch.

The Chorus freezes. Bibi unfreezes.

273

Elizabeth

Wong

BIBI: (*to audience*) Our conversation lasted about two, three minutes tops. It was a fleeting proverbial blink of the eye. We didn't have a pencil or even a scrap of paper.

Karen unfreezes; she moves away from Bibi.

BIBI: (*shouts*) That's Los Angeles, California. U.S.A. 90026. Can you remember all of that?

KAREN: Yes, I will remember. Yes. Yes, I remember it.

BIBI: (*to audience*) She didn't even tell me her name.

The Chorus addresses the audience, overlapping. They recite matter-of-factly, as in a news report.

CHORUS THREE: The girl peddled away.

CHORUS TWO: Merged with the other bicycles merging together.

CHORUS ONE: Bibi couldn't distinguish one rider from the other.

BIBI: I went back to the hotel, hamburgerless.

CHORUS FOUR: Then Bibi and her parents boarded the train to Hong Kong.

CHORUS ONE: Where she ate a fish filet at the McDonalds on Nathan Road.

CHORUS TWO: Where she also found a Pizza Hut.

CHORUS ONE: She stopped in every store and she shopped from dawn til dusk.

BIBI: Now that's freedom. Shopping from dawn til dusk.

CHORUS (*whispers*)	BIBI (*to audience*)
There is no you and there is no me.	But China is changing
There is no you and there is no me.	KAREN
There is no you. There is no me.	But China is changing

CHORUS THREE: Nowhere is a hint of anarchy tolerated.

CHORUS ONE: Not here, not there. Not anywhere.

CHORUS TWO: Bibi went back home to California, U.S.A. And that was the beginning.

CHORUS THREE: The beginning of what?

CHORUS ONE: The beginning of a most uncomfortable correspondence.

Lights out.

Hong
Kong

274

Letters to

a Student

Spotlight comes up on Karen sitting in her bedroom.

KAREN: (*writes*) Summer 1979. My dear American friend. . . . (*scratches out, starts again*) My dear new friend. . . . Greetings from Beijing.

Karen sits back, stares into space. Lights up on Bibi lounging on the beach.

BIBI: (*to audience*) Summer, 1979. *This* is Venice Beach. I have my chair, hunkered down in the sand, positioned for maximum good tanning rays. The pier to my left. The muscle boys to my right. The surfers in their tight black wet suits. Life can't get better than someone muscular in a tight black wet suit.

Charlie, a virile young man, brings on a blaring radio playing "Good Vibrations" by The Beach Boys. He lipsyncs the song. He is shirtless, his trousers are rolled up at the ankles—he's California cool.

Speaking of which, my friend. A cross between Frankie Avalon and Louis Jordan, which I guess makes me a cross between Annette Funicello and Leslie Caron.

CHARLIE: Limon? Ma cheri Gidget Gigi?

BIBI: (*to audience*) Not bad. But temporary. I mean this guy thinks "Casablanca" is a fine wine. He does try though, and he brings me lemonade? So here we are, me and Casanova under an umbrella of blue sky, hoping for a beach blanket bingo state of mind. But I admit, I've been a bit preoccupied.

Bibi shows a letter to the audience.

CHARLIE: (*to Bibi*) Preoccupied nothing. You've been downright morose. Whatsa matter punky pumpkin? You been bluesy woozy all day.

BIBI: You mean I've been in a nonverbal, pissed-off mood, and you want to know what in the hell you've done. Turn that thing off.

CHARLIE: Okey dokey, cupcake. Still suffering jet lag, ma cheri?

Bibi ignores him, reads her letter.

BIBI: I've been back a month.

CHARLIE: It's a known fact, these cases of extended air terminus, jetum laggus, dipso facto, ad hoc air baggum in vomitus—something to do with NOT paying enough attention to your boyfriend. Moi!

Bibi permits a slow smile. Charlie is triumphant because he's won the game. Her smile is the prize, and the audience should see it—sunny and winning.

BIBI: You are so easy to please. (*sighs, self-mockingly*) I, unfortunately, am not.

CHARLIE: My lady Cleopatra, Queen of the Nile, command me. I live to serve.

BIBI: Oh, put a lid on it. (*to audience*) Like I said. He tries. (*to Charlie*) Caesar, look on this.

Bibi shows him a letter. He takes it, examines it, reads it.

CHARLIE: Nice stamp.

Lights up on Karen.

(*reads*) Summer 1979. Dear Bibi, greetings from China. Do you remember me? I am the girl with whom you have shared a conversation. (*to Bibi*) Looks like you've got a pen pal. I think it's very sweet.

BIBI: Keep reading.

CHARLIE: Read. All right. Read. Hm . . . yes. "I met you in Tiananmen Square, I write to you from my little room. . . ."

KAREN: (*overlapping*) . . . Tiananmen Square. I write to you from my little room. There is no window, but I have big picture of map to show me sights of America. The Grandest Canyon and Okay Dokay Swamp. I share my room with my brother who teaches English at the high school.

Brother rises from the Chorus.

BROTHER: (*shouts out, meanly*) Hey ugly, turn out the light.

KAREN: I would like to get a new brother. Is that possible in America? I think anything is possible where you live.

The Cat sits at Karen's feet.

CAT: (*to audience*) Meeooww.

BROTHER: (*to Karen*) And get that hairball out of the room. Or I'll make kitty stew!

KAREN: (*to Brother*) You wouldn't!

BIBI: (*to Charlie*) In China, cats are not kept as pets.

KAREN: (*to Bibi*) She is not a pet. I do not own her. She is a free cat.

BROTHER: (*to audience*) Cats are functional. They eat rats. (*to Karen*) Or they are *to be eaten*. Which is it?

KAREN: (*to audience*) I put the cat outside. (*to Cat*) I say, "I sorry kittycat. So very sorry little kitty. Go on now, go to work and catch some micey mousies." (*to audience*) And then, she say in extreme irritableness. . . .

CAT: Meeooow.

KAREN: (*to audience*) I pretend to go to sleep. And when my brother starts to snore, I get up and write to you, my dear friend Bibi.

BIBI: Here it comes.

CHARLIE: Must you be so cynical, cupcake.

BIBI: Read on, *cupcake.*

KAREN: (*to audience*) It is a happy feeling I have . . . to have you for a secret friend, a special friend. I have much stupidity since I realized I never told you my name. How do you like my name? Do you think this is a good name?

BIBI: (*to Karen*) Karen? Yes. I think Karen is a good name.

KAREN: (*to Bibi*) Good. I am so glad for this. (*to audience*) I chose my new name in secret. This is my choice. Only my best friend knows about this secret. We call each other, Debbie and Karen. Where you live, you can be open about such matters. But here we must do everything in secret.

new name is a secret

CHARLIE: This is a very nice letter, Bibi. Hardly appropriate of you to be so provoked about it . . . cupcake.

Irritated by the belittling endearment, Bibi takes the letter from Charlie.

Hey!

BIBI: You aren't helping. And *don't* you cupcake me anymore . . . stud muffin. Stop patronizing me, categorizing me, labeling me like a jar of jelly.

CHARLIE: Who so miffed, love bun? I just. . . .

BIBI: You just what? A lot you know. *This*, for one, is not a nice letter. This just *sounds* like a nice letter.

CHARLIE: Cupcake, is that cynicism rearing its ugly head. Or is it bitchiness I see?

BIBI: You are not listening. This letter, stud muffin, is crafted on two predictable emotions—guilt and more guilt. I will *not* be made to feel responsible before my time.

CHARLIE: Are we not our brothers' keeper?

BIBI: I have lived in every ghetto in Los Angeles. Moved from Watts to Chinatown to Echo Park. Mom and Dad slaved so I could squander their hard work on college. And on top of everything, they got letters like this.

KAREN: Bibi, you have such freedom.

BIBI: We call them "ailment-of-the-month" letters. Dear Mr. and Mrs. Lee, my dear rich American relation, could you send us some money since life here is soooo bad, and you have it soooo good.

KAREN: I have noooo freedom. None whatsoever. Is it my misfortune to be born in my country and you were born in yours? I look at you and it is as if I look at myself in a glass.

CHARLIE: (*to Karen*) You mean mirror.

KAREN: Thank you for this correction. (*beat*) Yes, I look in mirror, yes. I think, "You are me." I was meant to be born in the United States, to live in freedom like you. Do you understand? (*beat*) Two days after I met you, my boss at the factory where I am in the accounting department, asked to speak to me.

The Cat gets up, and with an abrupt turn becomes the Boss. He approaches Karen. He has a smug, paternal smile on his face.

My boss has a kind voice, but a frown is in his heart. I am taken to a small room in the basement. This is *not* a good sign.

BOSS: Please sit down.

CHARLIE: (*to Karen*) Then what happened?

KAREN: I sat down.

BOSS: (*kindly, as if to an errant child*) You were seen talking to an American. An American student. Now, you mustn't be worried. Don't be afraid. You may talk to Westerners now.

CHARLIE: (*to Bibi*) I read about this. China is relaxing some of its policies.

BOSS: We are more relaxed under the new policies. But you must not listen to what they say. You must not get any ideas. (*pause, recites by rote*) Good citizens have only ideas that also belong to The State. The *state is your mother*. The *state is your father*. The *state is MORE* than your mother or your father. Do you understand?

KAREN: (*confused, searching*) I said, "Yes." But in my heart, I do not understand. I have never understood why I cannot speak my opinions. I only speak of my opinions to my friend, my only friend Debbie. Never to anyone else, not even my father, not even my brother. My boss talks to me as if I am but a child. I want to say, "I can think for myself. You are not my mother. You are not my father. I already have a mother. I already have a father. I do not need you." (*resignedly*) But this is China. (*beat*) I ride my bicycle home. But then . . . I see something . . . something very strange, a curious event is occurring. I must disembark my bicycle to see what occasion takes place.

The Chorus, in a semi-circle, turns their back to the audience. They crane their necks to read an imaginary bulletin board.

Very many people assemble in the street. A big man stands in my way. I cannot see. What is there to see? Something, something. . . .

CHARLIE: Extraordinary?

KAREN: No. Something . . .

BIBI: Momentous?

KAREN: No . . . no. Something . . . important.

BIBI: (*to Charlie*) Why not.

KAREN: Yes, important. I try to see for myself. I want to be a part of history. So, when a man got in my view, I used my bicycle to scrape him a little on the leg. He moved aside. Look! Look, Bibi! Do you see? A man with wire-rimmed glasses put a piece of paper with big writing on the wall. A newspaper. A poster. Many words I am shocked to read.

BIBI: (*to Charlie*) Democracy Wall.

CHARLIE: (*to Bibi*) I know, I read the papers.

KAREN: (*to audience*) Very brave to write these words, very brave to read these words. These . . . these. . . .

CHARLIE: (*to Karen*) Criticisms.

BIBI: (*to audience*) A personal favorite.

KAREN: Yes. I do not stay to read these criticisms, or else my boss would have some more to say to me. I was a little afraid. Do you understand? To be afraid of words in such a public place. I go home, thinking of freedom. How good freedom must be. What I see in the square makes me feel brave enough to write to you.

279

Elizabeth Wong

BIBI: (*to Karen*) Why me?

CHARLIE: (*to Bibi*) Stop wiggling the paper. I'm trying to read the rest.

KAREN: (*to audience*) I think Bibi I want to be having freedom like you. I think maybe I deserve a little of this freedom. So I find my pencil and a bit of paper. I try and try. I have my dictionary from a present my brother made me last year. But, I make many mistakes. Bibi, I think you must be helping me. You are my only friend.

CAT: (*annoyed*) Meeow!

CHARLIE: She's so sweet. That's what the American spirit is made of. Bring me your tired, your poor . . . et cetera, et cetera, uh you know . . . yearning to breathe free.

BIBI: I'm so glad you are such a patriot. Because she's all yours.

CHARLIE: What?

KAREN: I am thinking to accept your invitation to come to live with you in California.

CHARLIE: Ooops.

BIBI: Bingo.

KAREN: Perhaps you Bibi will pay ten thousand dollars for my airplane ticket and my living in California. Once I get to live in California, I will work and work and work and pay you back.

Does this make sense? What do you think of my idea? I know this letter is my first letter to you and I am asking you for bringing an improvement to my life.

But I know Americans have a great opportunity . . . do I say this correctly . . . for making money and for helping other people. I look forward to your favorable response. Your friend, Karen. My friend Debbie says hello too.

BIBI: Nice way to say howdy, wouldn't you say?

CHARLIE: Is she your cousin?

BIBI: I met her once . . . that is all.

CHARLIE: Chance encounter? Very interesting. Bibi cupcake, I think you will make an adorable guardian angel.

BIBI: This isn't funny.

CHARLIE: You're her sweet savior. Her fondest hope. Her nearest future.

BIBI: She's nothing to me and I'm nothing to her. And I resent that she is trying to make me responsible for her freedom. I'm barely responsible for my own. (*beat*) This is not the Promised Land and I do not have the muscle to be Moses.

CHARLIE: You most certainly do not have his beard. Kiss me.

BIBI: (*ducking him*) Oh, that will solve everything.

CHARLIE: Forget the ten commandments. How about Burt Lancaster?

BIBI: What?

CHARLIE: We have the beach. The waves are crashing. You are Deborah Kerr, or is that Donna Reed? I forget.

BIBI: *I* have a problem to solve.

CHARLIE: And *I* have to kiss you because you are lying on my beach towel and utterly available.

BIBI: What about the letter?

Charlie has maneuvered behind her to lightly explore her shoulders and neck.

CHARLIE: So headstrong and optimistic and naive—the true blue American character. Stubborn in all the right places. Naive in all the cutest spots. Hopeful sexy neck. I'm sure you'll think of something diplomatic. Now will you kiss me?

BIBI: (*genuinely impressed*) You really watched *From Here to Eternity*? Just for me?

CHARLIE: You're making me blush.

They kiss passionately.

Lights go out.

Lights up on Karen and the Cat. Charlie returns to the Chorus.

KAREN: I have no one else to tell, so I might as well tell you, my furry friend. You are my best friend. Did you catch any mice today Debbie? You better earn your keep or else.

CAT: Meeeoow.

KAREN: In America, kitty cats are friends. But we are not in America, but you *are* my friend anyway, aren't you Debbie? My good friend Debbie. Look a letter from the United States of America. Do you want to open it, or shall I? I will read it to you? Yes? Yes, I read it to you. Come sit near me. Now we begin. Spring 1980. Dear Karen. . . .

Lights up on Bibi.

BIBI: (*overlapping*) Spring 1980. Dear Karen, how are you? I am fine? How's the weather. (*to audience, crumples paper*) Too conventional. (*resumes*) Dear Karen, Happy New Year. I went to a party last night to ring in the new year 1980.

KAREN: Imagine a party in America, Debbie.

Bibi continues to write. The Chorus moves center stage to suggest a drunken, debauched tableau.

BIBI: I drank tequila shots, and someone ended up on the floor wiggling like a cockroach, and someone pulled up the rug and danced underneath it, the Mexican Hat Dance. Leroy, the skinny military guy from Camp Pendleton, ate the worm. (*to audience*) Nope. Too decadent. Bad first impression.

Bibi scratches out the paragraph. Writes anew.

Dear Karen, I am so sorry it's taken me nearly six months to write you back. (*to audience, resolutely*) Honest and direct.

KAREN: (*to Cat*) We didn't think she would write us, did we Debbie?

BIBI: I hope the new year will bring you much happiness. I would have answered you sooner, but I was unsure about how to respond to your letter. It really packed a wallop.

KAREN: What means wallop, Debbie? Do you know?

CAT: Meeoow.

KAREN: Oh.

BIBI: Karen. Two months ago, I went to the office of the Immigration and Naturalization Service. Have you ever seen that movie, "Mr. Smith Goes to Washington"? Well, we have this problem in America. It's called bureaucracy.

KAREN: Don't I have a good eye for choosing friends, Debbie?

CAT: Meeow.

KAREN: Oh, don't be jealous.

The Chorus queues up at the Office of Immigration and Naturalization. The Cat joins the Chorus.

BIBI: There were a lot of people there. Long lines. I waited in one line and they sent me to another and another and then another. It's been like that all day. Lines at the checkout stand, lines at the bank, so of course, lines at the good ole' INS. I got very frustrated.

KAREN: What did they say?

BIBI: A lady from Mexico in front of me. Bewildered, but sweetest face. She was holding up the line, you know. Her English was poor and she didn't have the right forms.

KAREN: What did they say about me?

CHORUS THREE: Hey, what's holding up this line? I've been here for four hours.

CHORUS ONE: Hey, what's holding up this line?

BIBI: (*to Chorus One*) Shush . . . be nice.

INS OFFICER: You've got the wrong form. This is an L1 Intra-company transfer I-21-B. I doubt lady you are an intracompany transfer.

MEXICAN LADY: *Pero eso es lo que me han dicho. El hombre alla . . . no se.* (But this is what they told me. The man over there . . . I don't know.)

INS OFFICER: Well, he gave you the wrong form. Look, you have to fill out another form. You want to file for permanent status? Sí? To stay in this country? Right? No deportee to the border?

abjection

MEXICAN LADY: *Huh? No, no, no. No es para mi. Es para mí hermana.* (No. No. Not for me. For my sister.)

INS OFFICER: For your sister? Why didn't you say so? Christ.

MEXICAN LADY: *Sí. Sí.* For my sister in México. *Mi hermana quiere vivir aqui.* (My sister wants to come to live here.)

INS OFFICER: Yeah, right. Everybody wants to live in America. Look, just fill out this Petition I-130, to start immediate relative status. Next!

MEXICAN LADY: *Mande usted, como?*

INS OFFICER: Jesus! Lady, look at this line. You are holding up all these people.

BIBI: (*to INS Officer*) I'm in no hurry. Help the lady out.

INS OFFICER: (*to Bibi*) Do you wanna be next or do you wanna see the back of the line.

BIBI: (*to Mexican Lady*) *Señora, este tipo es un pendejo.*

CHORUS THREE: (*to Chorus One*) What'd she say?

CHORUS ONE: She called him an asshole, asshole.

BIBI: *Este es el formulario de la Peticion E-ciento treinta.*

MEXICAN LADY: *Oh, sí.*

BIBI: *Lo tiene que llenar para reclamar a su hermana.* To claim your sister, understand? *Espere usted en esa fila.* Then you stand in line over there, *por favor.*

MEXICAN LADY: *Gracias, señorita. Muchas gracias.*

BIBI: De nada. (*to INS Officer*) Please and thank you. You should try adding them to your vocabulary.

INS Officer mimes closing window.

CHORUS (*all*): The sign says, "Closed for lunch."

The Chorus groans with annoyance. Bibi mimes opening the window.

BIBI: Wait a minute, sir. We've been here in line for hours.

INS OFFICER: Hey, I'm entitled. Jesus. What a day. Go to the next window.

INS Officer mimes closing the window. Bibi mimes reopening it.

BIBI: Look you. Some of these people can't speak up for themselves. But they deserve your respect and if not your respect, then at least some courtesy. I want to see your supervisor.

INS Officer mimes closing window.

KAREN: Bibi, did you talk about me?

BIBI: (*to Karen*) Can't you see I'm trying to prove a point here?

INS Officer exits. Bibi chases after him.

(*to Officer*) Come back here.

CHORUS ONE: Look what you did. Now we all suffer.

CHORUS (*all*): Look what you did. Now we all suffer.

BIBI: Hey. Wait a minute. Come back here. You can talk to them that way because they don't speak up for themselves. But you will treat me with respect. (*to audience*) You gotta stand up for yourself, or else your face is a doormat.

CHORUS (ALL): We're used to it.

BIBI: Well I'm not.

CHORUS ONE: Well, get used to it, Chinita.

The line dissolves. Chorus returns to upstage positions. The Cat returns to Karen.

KAREN: Will you help me, Bibi? Will you help me?

BIBI: Karen, the government told me I was *not* a suitable sponsor. To be a sponsor, I have to prove I can support you as well as myself. Karen, I'm just starting out in life. I don't have much in the way of money, just my prospects like you.

KAREN: So when you are rich, you can sponsor me, yes?

BIBI: Karen, I've gone as far as you have a right to expect. I really don't think I can do more. I mean, I don't even know you. I mean, we're not even related. I'm sorry. Sincerely, Bibi.

KAREN: (*to Cat*) Then she must get to know me. Isn't that right, Debbie? She must get to know me, and when she will get rich in America, she will send for me, and I will go to live in California.

CAT: Meeow.

BIBI: (*to Karen*) America isn't what you think it is, Karen.

KAREN: I know she will help me, when she gets to know me. Then I will go, but you mustn't be sad or jealous Debbie.

CAT: Meeow.

KAREN: No kitty cats on boats to America. But I will send you letters? Yes? Many, many letters.

CAT: Meeoow.

Lights up on Chorus.

CHORUS TWO: Karen continued to write to Bibi.

CHORUS ONE: Long letters about her life in China.

CHORUS FOUR: Her longings for America.

KAREN: While Bibi wrote detailed accounts about her new job as a newspaper reporter. Going to sewer commission meetings, the planning board. . . .

BIBI: Karen sent me letters once a month. I was developing quite a stamp collection.

CHORUS TWO: Karen would bring up the subject every now and then.

CAT: (*at Karen's side*) Karen is very "purr"sistant.

CHORUS FOUR: Bibi tried to ignore the subject.

CHORUS TWO: But finally Bibi got fed up.

BIBI: Winter 1980. Dear Karen, You may ask me if you wish. But please do not bring my parents into this. They are not rich. The streets here are not paved with gold. They are paved with concrete, sweat, hard work and struggle. My mother and father struggle every day.

KAREN: (*reads*) Bibi says her mother works in a sewing factory in the downtown. Debbie, are you paying attention?

The Cat sleeps. The Mother steps downstage.

Bibi says her mother brings home a big canvas bag filled with pieces of a shirt. Collars for five cents each and sleeves for three cents American money.

BIBI: In my mother's bedroom, there is a big shiny sewing machine.

KAREN: (*reading*) Her mother is sewing, sewing, sewing. Bibi says this is the only time they have chance to talk to each other.

Bibi joins her mother.

BIBI: (*to audience*) My mother hands me a wooden chopstick. I use the chopstick to poke and prod those collars, to make a point in the tip, you see? (*pause*) Mommy, why don't you quit for the night. You look really tired.

MOTHER: I will. I few more to go, then I stop.

BIBI: Look at that pile. We'll be up all night. Sam is a lecherous old bug-eyed man, and he's a slave driver.

MOTHER: I handle Sam.

BIBI: He gives me the creeps.

MOTHER: Sam talk about put everybody on insurance. He better. I hoping. Hospital expensive, and if something happen.

BIBI: I hate it when you talk like that. Nothing's gonna happen to you. You are still young. Forty is the prime of life. Why don't you just get another job where they have insurance?

MOTHER: Who hire me? I too old. Who want someone have no education.

BIBI: You could go to night school like you did before. Stop working all these jobs. Three jobs is for three people, not one.

MOTHER: I younger before.

BIBI: Mommy, you're still young. Look in the mirror. (*both look into audience, as into a mirror*) You got old Sam running circles around you, the old lech. Mommy, you still are pretty. You still are.

MOTHER: Before have my children, I more possibility than now. Now my life set. (*sighs*)

BIBI: (*pause, thoughtfully*) What do you mean *before* you had your children? Are we your regrets Mommy? Would it have been better if I hadn't been born? Would you have worked less? Lived more?

MOTHER: (*noise of disgust*) Aiiii.

Mother and Cat join Chorus.

BIBI: Karen, do you think my mother is sorry I was born? (*pause*) Sometimes I think it's my fault. (*pause*) Sometimes I wish I had never been born. Then she wouldn't be so unhappy.

KAREN: We can't choose to be born. In China, as in America, this is not a choice we have.

BIBI: (*ironically*) Suicide, however, is an equal opportunity. This is America.

KAREN: In China, we have only few freedoms. There is a saying. Do you know it? (*recites*) We may choose when to die, how to die and for what we will die. Yes, I think there are times for such a choice. But this is not a good choice for you, especially if you are going to help me.

BIBI: (*choral tone*) Spring 1981.

KAREN: You asked about my mother. My mother is dead.

BIBI: When did she die?

KAREN: (*pause*) When I was five years old, fifteen years ago. (*long pause*) I remember a rice field. A warm day in the rice field. Mosquitos. I am raw from the bites. (*pause, speaks slowly, remembering*) My mother is in the field. She has long black hair, not like mine. I see her. I run to her. The water from the field splashes up. The ground grabs, holds my feet as I run.

BIBI: (*to Karen, softly*) Watch out. The sheaves of rice are sharp.

KAREN: Yes. The rice sliced my legs as I ran. My legs were bloody. Warm from the blood, trickling down my legs. There is the man who watches everything.

BIBI: I see him.

KAREN: He is shaking my mother. He's shaking her. Why is he doing that? MaMa!

A gunshot is heard.

BIBI: What was that?

KAREN: I fell in the rice, and I was wet from the water. But I just watched my mother as she fell.

The Brother steps from the Chorus.

BROTHER: I had nothing to do with it. I miss Mother as much as you. It was my duty.

KAREN: (*bitterly*) My brother . . . the little red guard.

BROTHER: (*overlapping*) . . . is a good citizen of the state. The individual is not important.

CHORUS: (*whispers*) When the dust settles, the wolf stands alone.

BROTHER: The people have spoken. The individual is dead.

KAREN: Yes, our mother is dead.

BIBI: I'm sorry.

KAREN: Why?

BIBI: Something bad happens and someone should apologize for it.

KAREN: The cat eats the mouse. He doesn't apologize for doing what is in his nature to do.

BROTHER: My mother took property that belonged to someone else. She was punished. She stole food to feed us.

BIBI: That was too severe a punishment. Punishment should fit the crime.

KAREN: She was punished. Not for stealing, but for resisting. If the mouse struggles, the cat grips tighter first with one paw then with two. The only thing the mouse can do is escape, run away. As fast as you can. If you can.

BROTHER: And if you cannot, you'll be executed. Crimes against the State.

KAREN: (*to Bibi*) A common occurrence. Public execution is part of our daily lives, part of our education process. It is the one activity my brother and I do together. Lu Yan, his friend who is a teacher from the high school where my brother works, often came with us.

Lu Yan joins Karen and the Brother center stage. The rest of the Chorus enact the described scene.

BIBI: I covered an execution once. But from afar. I mean I made some phone calls to the parole board, part of a series of articles on capital punishment. And there was the time I did a piece on the Ku Klux Klan. . . .

KAREN: In the street, there is a truck.

BIBI: We have the electric chair. The cyanide capsule. . . .

LU YAN: Soviet made. Flatbed.

BIBI: We have death by hanging. No guillotine though.

BROTHER: See him there. The enemy of the people.

KAREN: Which one?

LU YAN: He is the man wearing all white.

BROTHER: There, down his back. See it?

KAREN: Yes.

BIBI: What does it say?

LU YAN: Can't read it.

BROTHER: Nature of crime. Name. A marker to identify the body.

KAREN: What is he being executed for?

BROTHER: He is an enemy of the people.

BIBI: Fascinating.

CHORUS: (*whispers*) This is what happens. This is what happens when wolves do not stay. In the group. In the pack. This is what happens.

KAREN: We all follow the truck to the stadium.

LU YAN: The man is taken out of the truck. He stands in the middle of the stadium. A loudspeaker announces his crime. Does he renounce his crime?

CHORUS (*all*): Do you renounce your crime?

A gunshot. The Chorus returns to their places.

CHORUS ONE: Karen continued in the accounting firm at the import/export factory.

CHORUS FOUR: Bibi got a job at a newspaper in the desert, hated the desert. Then she got another newspaper job and moved to the beach. Got another job, moved to the East Coast.

Bibi is standing on the tarmac of an airport.

BIBI: (*to audience*) Summer, 1982. I'm writing this quick note at a press conference at an airport, actually the National Guard Armory in Windsor Locks, Connecticut. Look on your map under . . . (*Chorus moos*) . . . . Near a Cow Pasture.

The Chorus gathers and freezes in a tableau as members of an eager press corps.

Air Force One is about to touch down and when it does the vice president is going to get a wiff of what rural America smells like. The wind has definitely shifted to the right, if you get my drift. My dress is going up over my head, no one notices, which depresses me greatly, but I'm doing a very good Marilyn Monroe impression.

Bibi freezes in a demure Monroe pose.

KAREN: Lu Yan, who is this Marilyn Monroe?

LU YAN: She was the looker with the great gams.

KAREN: Do I have great gams?

LU YAN: Maybe. Read to me the rest of the letter from Bibi.

KAREN: She says here her father got very sick recently, and that why . . .

LU YAN: (*correcting*) . . . and that *is* why . . .

KAREN: . . . that *is* why she has not . . . she did not write to me.

BIBI: My father owns a grocery store on Hope Street. I know that's corny, but it's true. It's called The Little Golden Star Market, corner of Hope and California streets in a place called Huntington Park. It's too small to be on your map.

The father rises from the Chorus and joins Bibi. He sings a few bars from "The Yellow Rose of Texas." Since he doesn't know all the words, he hums most of it.

FATHER: The yellow rose of Texas . . . ta da ta da ta da. . . . She's the only girl for me. . . . (*Tickles Bibi*)

BIBI: Oh Daddy, please I'm a big girl now. Stop that. Karen, this is my father. He likes to sing.

KAREN: He is standing in the middle of his store. Look at all the shelves. Soy sauce, oyster sauce, spaghetti sauce. So much food.

LU YAN: Cigarettes. American cigarettes. I would like to smoke this Marlborough cigarette and to wear a big hat from Texas and grow a beard.

FATHER: (*stops singing*) I feel funny. I feel a little woozy. Must have been your mother's bird's nest soup.

BIBI: Dad, you don't look so well.

Father collapses slowly to his knees.

KAREN: What's happening?

BIBI: My father, Karen, oh my God. (*pause*) My father is on the floor. I put his head in my lap. There is blood all over me.

KAREN: Yes, I know the blood.

BIBI: Thick, black, sticky. Blood, warm. On my legs. On the floor.

KAREN: Yes, the blood on my legs. Yes, the blood turned the water warm.

BIBI: Help please. Somebody call the ambulance. Get a doctor.

KAREN: Is he all right?

BIBI: Where is the ambulance? Karen, he shouldn't work anymore. But he does. Where's that ambulance? Don't they know someone is dying here. (*beat*) I don't know my father very well. He works all the time. He's always at work.

KAREN: Are you all right? Bibi? (*pause*)

BIBI: He's always at work. But he calls me his little yellow rose.

KAREN: Is everything all right?

BIBI: He used to call me his little yellow rose. He worked all the time. I didn't know my dad very well, you see.

Lights out on Bibi.

Pause.

Spotlight up on Chorus.

CHORUS ONE: Bibi and Karen continued their correspondence, but sporadically. About once or twice a year.

CHORUS FOUR: Bibi took her father's death very badly.

CHORUS THREE: In 1983, *Death of a Salesman* came to China.

CHORUS TWO: Biff. Happy. Linda. Willy Loman.

291

Elizabeth

Wong

CHORUS ONE: Willy Loman didn't know who he was. He had all the wrong dreams.

CHORUS THREE: I have those same dreams.

CHORUS FOUR: I don't know who I am.

BIBI: I don't know who I am. I'm looking though, real hard.

CAT: Meeoow.

CHORUS THREE: In late winter 1984. Debbie died. She choked on a mouse.

CAT: Meeow.

BROTHER: Shhh. Cats from the grave know too much. Yes. It was me. I turned in my mother. I confess, but I do not apologize. And I didn't tell anyone about my sister or her letters. I don't know why. Things seem a little different now. More relaxed.

CHORUS FOUR: It is Spring 1985.

CHORUS THREE: Yes, Spring 1985. By now, economic reforms. Farmers sell their surplus in the markets and keep the profit. Unheard of.

CHORUS ONE: But the more China changes, the more discontented I become.

CHORUS TWO: The more western China becomes, the unhappier I feel.

KAREN: Summer 1985. Thank you Bibi for the fashion magazines. Someday I hope to make such pretty dresses for sale.

BIBI: Fall 1985. You're welcome.

MOTHER: Spring 1986. Bibi, you not grasshopper. Stick to job.

BIBI: But mother, I don't like my job.

MOTHER: Who like job? If you quit, *aw mn yein nay* (I don't know you).

KAREN: Summer 1986. Dear Bibi, I took my first trip to the mountains. In China, you must get a permit for travel anywhere. Five years ago, I asked for permission, and now it has arrived. My brother and Lu Yan are coming with me.

Lights up on Brother, Lu Yan, and Karen who are lying on a plateau on a mountainside.

KAREN: Look at that sky. I see a dragon coiling ready to spring. I see a water buffalo. There's a big fat lumbering pig. That's you.

BROTHER: I feel restless. It's funny to feel so restless.

LU YAN: Ask Bibi to send us a copy of this Bill of Rights.

BROTHER: What is this "pursuit of happiness"? Even if I were to have it, I would not know how to go about this "pursuit of happiness."

LU YAN: I think to be on Lotus Mountain is what is meant by "life, liberty and the pursuit of happiness."

KAREN: (*to Brother*) It means even *you* would count for something, you good for nothing.

BROTHER: Oh? Who is lazy and who is not? I have written a novel.

LU YAN: So why do you hide it?

BROTHER: Because I am a bad novelist.

KAREN: Well then, your book will be very popular.

LU YAN: I think I will be a teacher in a great university. I have already applied for a transfer.

BROTHER: Impossible.

LU YAN: Maybe.

KAREN: If only I could leave my job. I hate accounting.

LU YAN: You do?

BROTHER: I didn't know that.

KAREN: Bibi sends me many fashion magazines. Only Bibi knows how I wish to be a designer of great fashion for very great ladies.

BROTHER: Burlap sacks for old bags.

KAREN: Lace, all lace and chiffon.

LU YAN: You would look beautiful.

KAREN: Not for me. For the people. I would be a dress designer and go to. . . .

LU YAN: Paris?

BROTHER: London?

KAREN: America.

LU YAN: People would clap and say, "Ahhh, of course, a Karen original."

BROTHER: People will say, "How ugly. I will not wear this in a million years."

KAREN: I would have a name. Then once I am famous as a clothes designer, I will quit and I would do something else. Maybe be a forest ranger.

BROTHER: Or a fireman.

LU YAN: Or an astronaut.

BROTHER: Or a member of the central committee.

LU YAN: Hah! You must be very old to be a member of the central committee.

KAREN: Yes, a fossil. (*beat*) Is it possible to be a somebody?

BROTHER: Yes, I am a grain of sand!

KAREN: A piece of lint.

LU YAN: Those old men on the central committee. What do they know about us? Perhaps we should all take up our books and stone the committee with our new ideas.

BROTHER: Lu Yan thinks he can change the world. But I'm telling you if we are patient, all things will come. (*beat*) Things that die allow new things to grow and flourish.

KAREN: Oh, my brother is a philosopher.

LU YAN: No, he is right. They will die off and leave us with a nation of students. No politicians. Just you and me and Karen.

KAREN: Three wolves on the mountainside, sitting in the sun.

LU YAN: Change is sure to come.

KAREN: This is changing me.

Karen indicates a small pile of books.

LU YAN: (*looks at the titles*) Hemingway. Martin Luther King.

KAREN: Bibi sent them to me. And this.

Karen turns on a tape recorder. The music is Karen Carpenter's "We've Only Just Begun." They listen.

BROTHER: Ugh. I think I will go for a walk now.

Brother returns to Chorus.

LU YAN: No good citizens of the state anywhere I can see.

KAREN: What?

LU YAN: Only clouds and insects to watch.

KAREN: Watch what?

LU YAN: This.

Lu Yan leans in to kiss Karen.

Lights out.

Lights up on Bibi.

BIBI: (*to audience*) Fall 1986. Sometimes, I wish someone would tell me. This is what you are good at Bibi, so go and do it. This is the man who is good for you Bibi, marry him. (*to Karen*) Lu Yan sounds like a very nice guy.

KAREN: Lu Yan is the only guy I've ever . . . how you say? . . .

BIBI: Slept with?

KAREN: No . . . he is the first man I ever dated. Yes, that's the word, dated. Only one to ask, only one to go out with, understand? Not much choice here in China, even though we are very many millions of people.

BIBI: Shall I regale you with tales from the darkside? Dates from hell? By my calculations, since I *was* a late bloomer, having lived at home throughout my college career, but making up for it like a fiend *after* I moved out of the house, I would say I've met a total of, or had a disastrous dinner or ahem, et cetera et cetera, with at least 127 different men—and that's a conservative estimate. Indeed, 127 men of assorted shapes and sizes and denominations. And colors. Don't forget colors.

KAREN: I am getting married next year. During the Mid-Autumn Festival next year.

BIBI: In America, we are free to choose our lovers and make our own mistakes. The most wonderful thing about freedom, Karen, is you get plenty of rope with which to hang yourself. Did you say getting married? Getting married? How wonderful. I'm jealous.

CHORUS THREE: Lu Yan and Karen were married in the fall of 1986.

CHORUS FOUR: Lu Yan's family gave as a dowry to Karen's father and brother two live chickens, eight kilos of pig's intestines, five hundred steamed buns, a sea lion bicycle, twenty kilos of fish, and ten cartons of American cigarettes.

CHORUS TWO: Karen moved in with Lu Yan's family. Lu Yan's father was a violinist with the city orchestra. There was always music in the house.

LU YAN: (*to audience*) For our wedding, Bibi sent us a box filled with books and music tapes. It was like a time capsule from the west.

With quiet enjoyment, Lu Yan and Karen listen to a few bars from Louis Armstrong's version of "Ain't Misbehavin'."

Pause.

I could eat them up. Every one, this Hemingway. This Truman Capote. This biography of Mahatma Gandhi. (*to Karen*) Look! Newspaper clippings about the New China, our new economic experiments.

KAREN: Our friends from the university come to our apartment. We sift through the box. (*to Lu Yan*) This is what Christmas must be like!

CHORUS FOUR: Tammy Wynette! Patsy Cline!

LU YAN: Mickey Spillane!

CHORUS THREE: Jonathan Livingston Seagull. James Michener!

CHORUS FOUR: *A Streetcar Named Desire!* The theory of relativity!

CHORUS THREE: Dr. Spock Baby Book!

KAREN: (*to audience*) Dear Bibi, Lu Yan would like to thank you for the book. *I'm O.K., You're O.K.*

CHORUS THREE: (*to audience*) New ideas. New dissatisfactions.

LU YAN: (*to audience*) The more she read, the more Karen grew depressed.

CHORUS FOUR: (*to audience*) Even though the sun seemed to shine very bright in China.

CHORUS THREE: (*to audience*) Politically speaking.

CHORUS ONE: Summer 1987.

KAREN: Dear Bibi, I am a bird in a cage. A beautiful bird with yellow and green and red feathers. I have a great plummage, but no one can see it. I live in a place that is blind to such wonderful colors. There is only grey and blue and green.

Mother steps forward, gets on the telephone.

BIBI: Winter 1987. Dear Karen, Do you know why I live so far from home? So I don't have to face their disapproval. My sister, my mother.

MOTHER: (*on telephone to Bibi*) Come home. It too cold in Connecticut. You not miss your mother?

BIBI: I like the seasons. I like long red coats and mufflers, iceskating on a real lake. I like snow.

MOTHER: You crazy. Come home. You warm enough?

BIBI: Yes, I'm warm enough. I'm sitting by the fireplace at what's-his-name's apartment.

MOTHER: Come home, get rid of what's-his-name. I not like him. He has frog face.

BIBI: Oh, can we please drop that subject?

MOTHER: (*reacts with disgust*) Aiiii.

BIBI: Mom. I'm thinking of quitting the newspaper and becoming an actress.

MOTHER: (*in Chinese*) *Aiii, nay gek say aw.* (You are killing me.)

Bibi silent.

There's no money in it. How you live? How you pay rent? All those actresses, all they ever do is fool around and get divorced. You want to get divorced?

BIBI: Mom, I'm not even married yet.

MOTHER: See what I mean. If you quit job, I disown you. You not special enough to be actress.

BIBI: (*to self, hurt*) I'm not special. (*beat, to Karen*) Maybe she's right.

KAREN: She doesn't mean that. She's just doing her duty. She's your mother. She wouldn't be a good mother if she didn't say those things. Threaten your children to the straight and narrow, this is written on the list for what it means to be a good mother.

BIBI: (*to Karen*) Ancient Chinese proverb?

KAREN: Fortune cookie.

BIBI: (*regains her composure*) Oh she means it all right. You watch. If I go to acting school, she'll tell everyone I'm in law school. You just wait and see if she doesn't.

KAREN: I wish my mother were alive to lecture me.

CHORUS (*all*): New age, new wave, new roads.
New thinkers, new entrees, new hairdos.
New buildings, new careers, new lives.
Who am I? Where am I going? America, always on the move!
Many choices, many roads, many ways to go.
Who am I? Where am I?

KAREN: Winter 1987. Dear Bibi, I do not know who I am.

BIBI: Spring 1988. Dear Karen, neither do I. I have changed newspapers five times in the past three years. It's easier to move up by moving out, but I'm getting a little tired of moving around. West Coast, East Coast. No place feels like home. Home doesn't even feel like home.

KAREN: Summer, 1988. Dear Bibi, I am a flower that will never open, never to be kissed by a bee. I want to open. I want to feel the sting of freedom. More and more, I feel bitter toward my life and my uselessness. I go to work, I have ideas to improve my job, and no one listens to me. I am a nobody. And I want to be a somebody.

BIBI: (*to Karen*) I think we are singing the same blues.

KAREN: (*to Bibi*) Are we?

BIBI: Well . . . you want to be a somebody. So do I. Same blues.

KAREN: No we're not. You live in a democracy, the individual can vote. You can count for something.

BIBI: That's funny. I never feel my vote counts for anything. It all happens without me.

KAREN: You have the luxury to be selfish. To think of only yourself. You live in Paradise. I live in hell.

BIBI: Well Karen, it can be hell living in Paradise.

KAREN: I want Democracy. Democracy for me. Freedom of speech. Freedom to choose.

BIBI: Freedom to be confused. But if you like America so much, join in on the national pasttime.

KAREN: What? Baseball?

BIBI: No, I'm talking retail therapy. Let's go shopping.

KAREN: Democracy is not the same thing as capitalism.

BIBI: Oh, you have the old definition.

KAREN: Bibi, you're not listening to me. Democracy is not the same thing as capitalism.

BIBI: O.K., you want to talk politics. (*Beat*) China has some right thinking. Health care for everybody. No bums bumming on the streets, jobs for everybody. Everyone EQUAL under the law. Everyone working towards the greater good.

KAREN: I think you must be a Communist at heart.

BIBI: I shudder to think what you would do with a credit card. I can see it now. You'd be mesmerized by our shopping malls. We've got mini malls, gigantic malls, also Rodeo Drive—Cartier, Yves St. Laurent—all linked by a chain of freeways stretching into infinity.

KAREN: I don't want to shop.

BIBI: All right. All right. (*beat*) I can see you now Karen—at the altar of The Church of Our Lady of Retail—Nordstroms, Lord and Taylor—kneeling beside me at the cash register as it rings up our sale. *Fifty percent off*—the most beautiful three words in the English language. Now that's America.

KAREN: I do not want to shop.

BIBI: That's downright un-American.

KAREN: There is a difference between democracy and capitalism.

BIBI: Yes. Well . . . in America, we like to *think* we're a democracy, but we're definitely a nation of shoppers. (*pause*) Ahhh, I know. You're a K-Mart Girl.

KAREN: But. . . .

BIBI: Sorry, Karen. We'll have to finish this argument later. I have a hot date with a manly man—an Adonis in a three-piece suit, a pillar of the community, and witty but in a dry outdoorsy kind of way. Yes, I think I've found the man of my dreams. I'll keep you posted. Love, Bibi.

KAREN: (*to audience*) What's K-Mart?

CHORUS (ALL): Everything happens in the mall.
We meet in the mall. We see movies in the mall.
We buy presents in the mall. We eat lunch in the mall.
We are a nation of shoppers. Attention shoppers.

Bibi and Jonathan are in the shopping mall.

BIBI: Let me get this straight . . . you think I'm too passionate, too adventurous, too enthusiastic. Jonathan, those are my best qualities.

JONATHAN: Let's not talk about it right now, o.k.? Let's just go to the movie.

BIBI: Why not? The mall is where all of America gets dumped. Let's sit right here between the Sears and the J.C. Penneys to contemplate this revelation.

JONATHAN: Don't get me wrong. I think you're terrific. But . . . it's too intense for me. You're like a pebble in my still pond.

BIBI: I can be still water too. (*beat*) Please Jonathan?

JONATHAN: You couldn't even if you tried. You don't know how to be anything else than terrific.

BIBI: You're dumping me because I'm terrific?

JONATHAN: I'll probably regret it later.

Jonathan returns to Chorus.

BIBI: But (*long pause*) I love you.

Lights up on Karen.

KAREN: Winter 1988. My ten-year-old nephew asks if you would send him a baseball glove from America. Lu Yan's mother would like the same perfume you sent me on my last birthday. The Madonna tapes must be great, but the tape recorder is broken. Can you send us another one?

BIBI: Dear Karen, I just can't afford anything right now. I'm unemployed—again.

KAREN: How can you help me, if you don't become a stable, responsible citizen?

BIBI: Stop it. Just stop. You're sounding like my mother. You are supposed to be my friend, Karen. I need a friend right now. I already have a mother.

KAREN: I'm sorry. I was being selfish.

BIBI: See already you are learning to be American.

KAREN: Did you get fired from your job?

BIBI: No, I quit.

KAREN: How lucky you are.

BIBI: What do you mean lucky?

KAREN: You get to live your own life, your way.

BIBI: But look at the price I pay. I'm totally alone in my struggles. No one I know supports my dreams. I am going to an acting school where they take your money and teach you how to pursue all the wrong dreams.

KAREN: Dreams. I have them too.

BIBI: My mother doesn't support me. The only way to convince her is to make a clean break. Everyone disapproves. My sister is the worst. You . . . on the other hand . . . have a support system—the state, your brother, your husband. You even know who your enemies are and what you are fighting against.

KAREN: Perhaps you can swallow your pride. If the support system, the harmony of your family is that important to you, then you should do as they tell you to do.

BIBI: Spoken like a true Chinese.

KAREN: I am Chinese.

BIBI: And I am American. And I will live my own life, my way. (*beat*) Even if it kills me.

KAREN: My country is changing and I no longer wish to come to be an American like you. You are too confused. (*beat*) But I will always be your friend.

BIBI: Why don't you come and visit me?

KAREN: I don't know.

BIBI: Look, why don't you come. You can meet my mother. I'm sure she'd be happy to lecture you too. Go to the consulate. Ask them for a visa.

CHORUS ONE: Karen went to the consulate.

KAREN: I have a friend in the United States who will vouch for me.

CHORUS THREE: Many people are exchanging, visiting from China to the world.

KAREN: I told them I wanted to be one of them.

CHORUS FOUR: Cultural exchanges. Ballet dancers, playwrights, artists, singers.

CHORUS TWO: Scientists, engineers, lawyers, architects, businessmen of all sorts.

301

Elizabeth

Wong

CHORUS THREE: Bringing computers and cars and Coca Cola and T-shirts.

CHORUS ONE: So many people and things and ideas flowing from west to east, east to west. Amazing.

KAREN: Since I am neither a student nor an important dignitary. I am only an accountant. A very ordinary speck of dust.

CHORUS ONE: Karen was refused a visa. No one would tell her why.

CHORUS TWO: But it all comes down to *money*. She didn't have the . . . the dinero (*attempts hip*), the bread, man.

CHORUS THREE: March 1989.

LU YAN: Karen, when you write to Bibi, thank her for the Baudelaire. Tell her I love French poetry and to send more of it.

KAREN: Lu Yan says thank you for the French poetry. Well, Bibi, I must go now. The Spring Festival is here and the students will be gathering at the university. I am going with Lu Yan. With affection, Karen.

LU YAN: We should hurry. Hu Yaobang is speaking, we don't want to miss it.

KAREN: Is it considered to be counterrevolutionary to listen to a counterrevolutionary?

LU YAN: We must be open to new ideas in order for our lives to improve.

KAREN: How can our life improve. You cannot teach at the university and I cannot quit my job to become a student. You cannot get permission for anything, so what's the point of trying to make improvements.

LU YAN: Come on, we'll be late.

Lights up on Bibi.

BIBI: Spring 1989. Dear Karen, New York City is a place you should see. I've been living here for six months now and I *love it*. Recently, my mother came to visit me for the first time since I've been on the East Coast. She *loved* it!

MOTHER: It *smell*!

BIBI: She especially loved the efficient and clean public services.

MOTHER: It *noisy*! (*grumbling*) Too many bums.

BIBI: She also thought my apartment was very cozy.

MOTHER: It so *small*! How can you live like this? Like mouse in cage. Noisy all day, all night. How you sleep?

BIBI: Happily, I took mother to see all the sights, including (*mild disgust*) the Statue of Liberty.

Mother and Bibi are at the ferry railing.

It's a grey somber day. A bit choppy out. The ferry ride to Liberty Island doesn't take very long, it just *seems* long when you'd rather be eating lunch at the Russian Tea Room.

Mother and Bibi at base of statue.

MOTHER: Look! Look!

Bibi gets caught up in her mother's emotion and excitement.

BIBI: Mother, are you all right?

MOTHER: (*laboring over the words*) Give me your tired, your poor . . .

Mother, for whom reading is a painful effort, defers to Bibi, who continues to read the poem.

Mother is inspired by the image of the statue, but Bibi finds herself moved by the words and her mother's emotional reaction.

BIBI: (*overlapping*)
. . . poor, your huddled masses, yearning to breathe free.
The wretched refuse of your teeming shore.
Send these, the homeless, tempest tossed to me.
I lift my lamp beside the gold door.

One by one, the Chorus joins Bibi. The choral tone is soft.

CHORUS ONE: (*overlapping*)
The wretched refuse of your teeming shore.
Send these, the homeless, tempest tossed to me:
I lift my lamp beside the golden door.

CHORUS TWO: (*overlapping*)
Send these, the homeless, tempest tossed to me:
I lift my lamp beside the golden door.

CHORUS THREE: (*overlapping*)
I lift my lamp beside the golden door.

Lights out.

Spotlight up on Karen.

KAREN: (*to audience*) May 1989. Dear Bibi, Here I am—sitting in a tent on Chang An Avenue in Tiananmen Square—do you know what this means—it means the Avenue of Eternal Peace. I cannot begin to describe—there is this change in the air—to be here, surrounded by my comrades—student activists and ordinary citizens—men and women, all patriots for a new China. I think this is what "pursuit of happiness" must be.

Bibi, for the first time in my life, I believe I can be a somebody, I believe my contribution will make a difference. I believe freedom will not grow out of theory but out of ourselves. We are fighting for a system that will respect the individual. The individual is not dead.

The government must listen to us. The government will listen to us. All we want is a dialogue. A conversation. We want an end to censorship. We want an end to corruption. We are the voices of tomorrow. And our voices will be heard.

There is so much power to be here together—singing songs, holding hands, listening to the speeches of our student leaders.

CHORUS ONE: "The power of the people will prevail."

KAREN: (*overlapping*) ". . . People will prevail."

CHORUS TWO: "To liberate society, we must first liberate ourselves."

KAREN: (*overlapping*) ". . . we must first liberate ourselves."

CHORUS THREE: "We must give our lives to the movement."

KAREN: Yes, I will give my life to the movement.

Karen sings the national anthem of the People's Republic of China. As she sings, lights up on Bibi. The song softly continues underneath Bibi's rebuttal.

BIBI: May 1989. Dear Karen. I'm watching the television reports. Everyone always asks me how I feel about what is happening in China. I'm torn about my own feelings, my own reaction. On the one hand, I'm envious of your power—of how you have caused your government, caused the world to take notice. I am frustrated at my own helplessness, that I am not there to participate in this ennobling event.

But on the other hand, I am concerned about your naiveté in striving toward a foreign ideal. The speech given by your premier Deng Xiaoping has a validity that frightens me. Don't be fooled, he means business.

Your efforts toward democratizaton seem like an admirable cause, and I do believe change will come, but it must be at your own pace. I am not sure America is the proper model for the new

China that you want. You should look to make a Chinese democracy, look at what you have and make the best out of it.

Please understand that I am Chinese too and I feel a deep connection to you, but what you are doing is suicide. Right now, I think that to be a somebody in China is suicide. I don't mean to dampen your spirits, but I am worried. Do be careful.

The Chorus joins Karen in singing the anthem.

Beat.

CHORUS ONE: Students. The time is now for freedom. The time is now for democracy. For six weeks, we have felt a jubilation. A celebration of spontaneity.

CHORUS TWO: I think we should shave our heads in protest. We should shave our heads like prisoners because our government turned our country into a prison.

CHORUS ONE: The time for freedom is now. The time for democracy is now.

KAREN: We are lying on the floor. Students on a hunger strike. Most of us are women. We haven't eaten in days, and I will not until I have my freedom.

SOLDIER: This is foolishness. Resolutely oppose bourgeois liberalism.

CHORUS ONE: I'm sorry, but we disagree completely.

CHORUS FOUR: Yes, we disagree completely.

CHORUS ONE: The time is now for freedom.

KAREN: A clean division between what we want and what the government stands for. A clear break.

SOLDIER: Children should not defy their parents. Harmony must be preserved. Resolutely oppose bourgeois liberalism.

CHORUS FOUR: Mothers are here.

CHORUS TWO: Workers, laborers, doctors.

CHORUS ONE: Lawyers, bakers, bricklayers.

KAREN: Accountants, teachers, writers, students.

CHORUS (*all*): We are all here. Will you hear the will of the wolf? Will you let the wolf roam free? We want to be free!

SOLDIER: The students gave me food, water. I did not want to hurt them.

305

Elizabeth

Wong

CHORUS ONE: We heard speeches.

CHORUS FOUR: We heard songs.

CHORUS TWO: We are like a small plant, tender and young, trying to reach the sunshine.

CHORUS FOUR: From this movement, which is a movement across China, free thought will grow, and from free thought a new China will grow.

CHORUS TWO: The students erected a thirty-three-foot statue called the Goddess of Democracy.

CHORUS ONE: Seven weeks of freedom.

KAREN: So this is freedom. How good it is. Seven weeks of freedom.

CHORUS (*all*): Summer 1989.

SOLDIER: Go home and save your life. This is China. This is not the West.

Gunfire. The Chorus and Karen link arms and advance slowly toward the audience. They move in military fashion, in the same way as did the real protesters—as one phlange of students was mowed down, others stepped forward to replace them.

KAREN: On June 4, 1989. Tanks, armored personnel carriers and trucks full of troops marched into Tiananmen Square.

SOLDIER: Be a good Chinese and go home. Go home and save your life. This is China. This is not the West. Be a good Chinese and go home.

CHORUS ONE: I decided to stay. Ten thousand people decided to stay. A man stood naked on the roof and shouted, "I am who I am. I am me."

SOLDIER: Go home and save your life.

CHORUS FOUR: Change is coming. We will all march forward.

CHORUS TWO: Bricks, rocks.

SOLDIER: This is not the West. Be good Chinese and go home.

CHORUS ONE: Run! Get out of the way. Get out of the way.

KAREN: Run! Get out of the way. Run!

CHORUS FOUR: This is the Avenue of Eternal Peace.

CHORUS TWO: The Goddess of Democracy is crushed.

KAREN: Lu Yan, watch out! Lu Yan!

SOLDIER: Troops pouring out of the gate.

CHORUS FOUR: The Gate of Heavenly Peace.

CHORUS ONE: Bullets riddle the crowd.

KAREN: Beatings. Bayonets.

CHORUS TWO: Blood.

KAREN: Blood everywhere.

CHORUS ONE: Tanks. March forward!

SOLDIER: Tanks. Blood. March! Be good Chinese and go home.
This is China. This is not the West.

CHORUS TWO: A black curtain.

CHORUS ONE: A black curtain.

CHORUS FOUR: Over the entrance.

KAREN: A black curtain.

CHORUS FOUR: Blocking the view.

CHORUS ONE: Of blood and bodies.

CHORUS FOUR: A black curtain falls over China.

KAREN: Lu Yan? Where are you? Lu Yan.

SOLDIER: Be good Chinese and go home.

KAREN: The statue fell. Everyone was running.

CHORUS TWO: Everyone was falling.

CHORUS ONE: Everyone was pushing.

CHORUS FOUR: Blood. Everywhere. Screaming.

KAREN: (*screams*) You animals!

Lights out.

Slides of the Tiananmen Square massacre flash in rapid fire succession on a backdrop. The final image should be the famous photograph of the lone man standing in front of a line of tanks.

Black out.

Spotlight on Bibi.

BIBI: (*composing a letter*) Spring 1990. Dear Karen, It's been several months since . . . (*scratches out*) . . . since the massacre. I

307

Elizabeth

Wong

haven't heard from you. Are you and Lu Yan all right? Why haven't you written me? (*scratches out*) Don't write to me. I know you will write to me when it is safe. I hope this letter doesn't cause you any trouble. . . . I know your country has started a campaign to erase what happened in Tiananmen Square. But I want you to know I haven't forgotten you. I want you to know I am thinking of you and Lu Yan. Somehow, let me know if you are all right. Love, Your Good Friend, Bibi.

Long pause.

Bibi, shaken, tears up the letter.

Lights out.

THE EPILOGUE

The Chorus speaks nonchalantly.

CHORUS TWO: According to newspaper and television accounts . . .

CHORUS THREE: . . . immediately following the massacre in Tiananmen Square . . .

CHORUS FOUR: . . . the Chinese authorities have arrested, tortured, and killed some of the student leaders of the Democracy Movement . . .

CHORUS ONE: . . . and as many of their supporters as could be rounded up. . . .

CHORUS TWO: . . . Remarkably, some students were able to escape.

CHORUS FOUR: The world has turned its attention to other events. Other struggles, other tragedies.

CHORUS THREE: And China has begun a policy of selective historical amnesia.

CHORUS ONE: And fast-food America has gone back to shopping and the concerns of everyday living.

BIBI: . . . I don't know whether Karen was among those who were killed or among those who got away. . . .

Lights out.

THE END

A P P E N D I X

❀

P L A Y S B Y A S I A N A M E R I C A N

W O M E N

This is a partial listing of plays by Asian American women, which will both serve as a resource for those interested in doing research in the subject and give the reader a sense of the larger body of literature.

Haruko Nakata Akamatsu
The Only Hope (1944)*

Mary Akimoto
By and By (1950)*
Strangers (1950)*

Rosanna Yamagiwa Alfaro
Barrancas (1989)
    Staged reading: New Play Cafe, Lyric Stage, Boston, 1 May 1988
    Production: The Magic Theater, Multicultural Playwrights Festival, San
    Francisco, 9–20 Aug. 1989
Behind Enemy Lines (1982)*
    Staged reading: Nucleo Eclettico, Boston, 8 Aug. 1980
    Staged reading: East West Players, Los Angeles, 27–29 Aug. 1982

*Plays marked with asterisks are in the archives at the University of Massachusetts library under Roberta Uno Asian American Playwrights' Script Collection 1924–1992. Further information on Asian American Hawaii playwrights can be found in *An Index to Original Plays in Sinclair Library 1937–1967*, by Edward A. Langhans and Fay Hendricks (Honolulu, 1973) which lists plays in the following collections in the Hamilton Library at the University of Hawaii at Manoa: *College Plays 1937–1955*; *University of Hawaii Plays 1958–1969*; *Theatre Group Plays 1946–1969*. Additional unindexed plays can be found in *University of Hawaii Plays 1970–1992*, *Theatre Group Plays 1970–1981*, and *Kumu Kahua Plays 1982–1984*, ed. Dennis Carroll.

Production: People's Theatre, Cambridge, Mass., 12 Feb.–8 March 1981

Production: Pan Asian Repertory Theatre, New York City, 24 March–14 April 1982

Production: School of Contemporary Arts, Ramapo College of New Jersey, Mahwah, N.J., 8–11 Dec. 1982

Fresh from Detroit (1987)

Production: Playwrights' Platform, Cambridge, Mass., 21–22 Nov. 1987

Going to Seed (1989)*

Staged reading: Playwrights' Platform Fall Festival, Cambridge, Mass., 30 Sept., 7 Oct. 1989

Workshop production: Seattle Group Theatre, Seattle, 8, 10 June 1985

If the Truth Be Told (1989)

Staged reading: Theater in Process, Cambridge, Mass., 22 Feb. 1987

Staged reading: Twelfth Night Club, New York City, 11–20 Nov. 1987

Martha Mitchell (1988)

Production: Playwrights' Platform, Somerville, Mass., 8, 16, 21 July 1988

Production: Theater Center, Philadelphia, 13 Oct.–13 Nov. 1988

Production: Calton Studios, Edinburgh Fringe Festival, Edinburgh, Scotland, 20–26 Aug. 1989

Matters of Life and Death (1987)

Staged reading: Theater in Process, Cambridge, Mass., 2 March 1986

Staged reading: New Voices, Boston, 5 June 1987

Staged reading: Theatre in the Works, Amherst, Mass., 10–11 June 1987

Mishima (1988)

Staged reading: Pioneer Square Theatre, Seattle, 14 May 1985

Production: East West Players, Los Angeles, 7 April–14 May 1988

Over the Hill (1986)

Production: Playwrights' Platform Workshop One-Act Festival, Boston, 10, 18 July and 16–18 Oct. 1986

Pablo and Cleopatra (1990)

Workshop production: Cleveland Public Theater, 18, 20 Jan. 1991

The Second Coming (1990)

Staged reading: Writers' League of Boston, Lyric Stage, Boston, 3 Feb. 1991

Lynette Amano (Lisa Inouye)

Ashes (1972)

Published in *Kumu Kahua Plays*, ed. Dennis Carroll (Honolulu: University of Hawaii Press, 1983)

Hotel Street (1970)

Brenda Aoki

Obake! Tales of Spirits Past and Present (with Jael Weisman) (1988)

Production: At the Foot of the Mountain Theatre, Minneapolis, 23–25 Sept. 1988

Production: Ventura High School Little Theatre, Ventura, Calif., March 1990

Production: Climate Theatre, San Francisco, Sept. 1991

The Phoenix and the Dragon (with Jael Weisman) (1988)

The Queen's Garden (1993)*

Whisperings (with Jael Weisman) (1989)

Jeannie Barroga

Adobo (1988)

Staged reading: The Seattle Group Theatre, Seattle, 21 Jan. 1988

Angel (1987)

Staged reading: Playwright Forum, Palo Alto, Calif., 5 Feb. 1987

Batching It (1985)*

Staged reading: Playwrights' Center of San Francisco, 5 Dec. 1985

Staged reading: Playwrights' Center of San Francisco, San Francisco, Jan. 1986

Production: Path Channel A-10 Mountain View, Calif., 1986–87

The Deli Incident (1984)*

Production: Teletheatre Channel 60, San Jose, Calif., 3 Dec. 1984.

Donato's Wedding (1983)

Staged reading: Playwrights' Center of San Francisco, 4 Oct. 1983

Eye of the Coconut (1987)*

Staged reading: Playwright Forum, Palo Alto, Calif., 16 Jan. 1986

Production: Northwest Asian American Theater, Seattle, 14 Oct.–11 Nov. 1987.

Staged reading: Asian American Theater Co., San Francisco, 2 April 1987, 8 Aug. 1989, 21 May 1990, 6 June 1990, 30 Jan.–14 Feb. 1991

Staged reading: East West Players, Los Angeles, 4 March 1991

Family (1988)*

Staged reading: Northside Theatre Co., San Jose, Calif., March 1988

The Flower and the Bee (1983)

Staged reading: Playwrights' Center of San Francisco, 4 Oct. 1983

The Game (1988)

Staged reading: Playwright Forum, Palo Alto, Calif., 1988

Gets 'Em Right Here (1982)

Staged reading: Playwrights' Center of San Francisco, 30 Oct. 1982

In Search Of . . . (1984)

Staged reading: Playwrights' Center of San Francisco, Calif., 30 Oct. 1984

Kenny Was a Shortstop (1990)*

Staged reading: New Traditions Theatre Co., San Francisco, 5 Sept. 1990

Production: Brava! Women for the Arts, San Francisco, 10 May 1991

Kin (1990)

Production: Teatro Ng Tanan, San Francisco, 12, 28 Feb. 1991

Letters from Dimitri (1992)

Staged reading: American Conservatory Theater, San Francisco, 27 July 1992

Staged reading: TheatreWorks, Palo Alto, Calif., 22 Nov. 1992

Lorenzo, Love (1986)*
   Staged reading: Playwrights' Center of San Francisco, 2 April 1985
   Production: Foothill College, Los Altos Hills, Calif., 12 March 1986
Musing (1989)*
   Staged reading: Asian American Theater Co., San Francisco, 1989
My Friend Morty (1989)*
   Production: Playwrights' Center of San Francisco, 20 Oct. 1989
Night before the Rolling Stones Concert (1985)
   Staged reading: Playwrights' Center of San Francisco, 11 June 1985
Older . . . Wiser (1984)
   Staged reading: Playwrights' Center of San Francisco, 30 Oct. 1984
Paranoids (1985)
   Staged reading: Playwrights' Center of San Francisco, 5 Feb. 1985
Pigeon Man (1982)*
   Staged reading: Playwrights' Center of San Francisco, 28 Sept. 1982
   Production: Teletheatre Channel 60, San Jose, Calif., 3 Dec. 1984
Reaching for Stars (1985)*
The Revered Miss Newton (1990)*
   Staged reading: New Traditions Theatre Co., San Francisco, 10 Feb.
   1991
Rita's Resources (1991)
   Workshop production: Pan Asian Repertory Theatre, New York City,
   20 Feb. 1992
Sistersoul (1986, 1988)*
   Staged reading: Playwright Forum, Palo Alto, Calif., 12 June 1986
   Production: Crystal Springs Uplands School, Hillsborough, Calif., 24
   Sept. 1987
   Production: San Jose State University, San Jose, Calif., 25 Sept. 1987
   Staged reading: Playwrights' Center of San Francisco, 9 Oct. 1987
   Production: Inner City Cultural Center, Los Angeles, 29 Sept. 1987
   Production: TheatreWorks, Palo Alto, Calif., 28 Jan. 1988
   Production: Playwrights' Center of San Francisco, 19 Feb. 1988
   Production: Bay Area Playwrights' Foundation, San Francisco, 22 Aug.
   1989
Talk-Story (1990)*
   Staged reading: Asian American Theater Co., San Francisco, 12 March
   1990
   Staged reading: Bay Area Playwrights' Foundation/Magic Theatre, San
   Francisco, 28 July 1990
   Staged reading: TheatreWorks, Palo Alto, Calif., 24 March 1991
   Production: TheatreWorks, Palo Alto, Calif., 3 April–2 May 1992
   Staged reading: Philippine American Heritage for the Arts/Pacific The-
   ater Ensemble Los Angeles, 25, 26 Oct. 1992
   Staged reading: Mark Taper Forum, Los Angeles, 9 Nov. 1992
   Staged reading: Perseverence Theatre, Douglas, Ala., 22 Nov. 1992
Walls (1989)*
   Staged reading: Playwright Forum, Palo Alto, Calif., 14 Jan. 1988
   Staged reading: Asian American Theater Co., San Francisco, 1988

Production: Asian American Theater Co., San Francisco, 26 April–4 June 1989

Production: Stanford University Drama Department, Stanford, Calif., 9 April 1991

Production: New WORLD Theater, University of Massachusetts, Amherst, Mass., Oct. 1991

Published in *Unbroken Thread: An Anthology of Plays by Asian American Women*, ed. Roberta Uno (Amherst: University of Massachusetts Press, 1993)

Wau-Bun (1983)

Staged reading: Playwrights' Center of San Francisco, 10 May 1983

When Stars Fall (1985)

Staged reading: Playwright Forum, Palo Alto, Calif., 17 Oct. 1985

Production: Playwright Forum, Palo Alto, Calif., 25 April 1986

Bernadette Cha

Salted Linen

Shee-Jhyak (*Begin*)

Eugenie Chan

Emil, a Chinese Play (1991)*

Rancho Grande (1991)*

Leilani Chan

Mama (1991)*

Production: Hampshire College Department of Theater, Amherst, Mass., April 1991

Kitty Chen

Eating Chicken Feet (1986)

Staged reading: Summer Solstice Theater Conference, New York City, July 1986

Rosa Loses Her Face (1989)*

Staged reading: Manhattan Theatre Club, New York City, 24 Aug. 1989

Staged reading: Hudson Guild Theater, New York City, 13 Nov. 1989

Staged reading: Double Image Theater, New York City, 24 March 1990

Margaret Chinen (Lee Mei Ling)

Aftermath (1948)*

All, All Alone (1947)*

Diana Chow

An Asian Man of a Different Color (1981)

Published in *Kumu Kahua Plays*, ed. Dennis Carroll (Honolulu: University of Hawaii Press, 1983)

Eileen Choy

*Sidney Bernstein**

Wai Chee Chun (Wai Chee Chun Yee)

For You a Lei (1936)*

Reading: "Lucky Come Hawaii: The Chinese in Hawaii" conference, East West Center, Honolulu, 20 July 1988.

Reading: Honolulu Academy of Arts Focus Gallery, 28 Jan. 1990.
Published in *Paké: Writings by Chinese in Hawaii*, ed. Eric Chock
(Honolulu: Bamboo Ridge Press, 1989)
Marginal Woman (1936)*

Marina Feleo Gonzales
Once a Moth (filmscript, 1976; play, 1990)
Rice Stalks (1983)
The Seed (1973)
A Song for Manong (1987)*
  Recited as narrative for dance performance by Alleluia Panis, Kennedy
  Center, Washington, D.C. (date unknown)
  Staged reading: Word of Mouth Theater (date and location unknown)

Jessica Hagedorn
The Art of War: Nine Situations (1984)
  Production: Dance Theater Workshop, New York City, 1984
Holy Food (1988)
  Radio version: commissioned by WNYC-FM for "Radio Stage" series,
  taped before a live audience and aired nationally, 1988
  Production: Cornell University, "An American Festival," Center for the
  Performing Arts, Ithaca, N.Y., 1989
Mango Tango (1978)
  Production: New York Shakespeare Festival Public Theater, New York
  City, May 1978
Petfood (1981)
  Staged reading: Pan Asian Repertory Theatre, New York City, 1981
  based on *Pet Food and Tropical Apparitions*
Ruined: A Beach Opera (1985)
  Production: Art on the Beach, New York City, 1985
Teenytown (with Laurie Carlos and Robbie McCauley) (1988)
  Production: Franklin Furnace, New York City, 1988
  Production: Danspace Project, New York City, 1988
  Production: L.A.C.E., Los Angeles, 1990
  Production: The Intersection, San Francisco, 1990
  Published in *Out from Under*, ed. Lenora Champagne (New York: The-
  atre Communications Group, Inc., 1990)
Tenement Lover: No Palm Trees/In New York City (1981)
  Production: The Kitchen, New York City, 1981
  Published in *Between Worlds*, ed. Misha Berson (New York: Theatre
  Communications Group, Inc., 1990)
Where the Mississippi Meets the Amazon (with Ntozake Shange and Thu-
  lani Davis) (1978)
  Production: New York Shakespeare Festival Public Theater, New York
  City, 1978

Linda Faigao Hall
Americans (1987)*
  Production: Catskills Reading Society, Ellenville, N.Y., July 1991
  Production: Chelsea Theater Arts Center, New York City, March 1987

And the Pursuit of Happiness (1991)
Burning Out (1991)
Manilla Drive (1992)
   Staged reading: Working Theater, New York City, 8 Feb. 1993
Men Come and Go (1987)*
   Production: The Actors' Institute, New York City, Oct. 1987
Requiem (1986)*
   Production: Henry St. Settlement House, New York City, Oct. 1986
   Staged reading: East West Players, Los Angeles, 1990
   Staged reading: Pan Asian Repertory Theatre, New York City, 1989
Sparrow (1990)
   Staged reading: Dramatist's Guild, New York City, June 1987
   Staged reading: Henry St. Settlement House, New York City, May 1988
   Staged reading: Catskills Reading Society, Ellenville, N.Y., July 1991
State without Grace (1984)*
   Production: Pan Asian Repertory Theatre, New York City, Oct. 1984
   Production: Asian American Theater Co., San Francisco, Oct. 1985

Lionelle Hamanaka

Adrian's Wish (1984)
Blues Around the World (1988)
   Production: Safari East, Lincoln Center Out-of-Doors, New York City,
   Aug. 1988
Last Night at the Morosco (1984)
   Staged reading: Actors' Creative Theater, New York City, June 1984
Nikkei (with Philip T. Nash and Kuni Mikami) (1990)
Nobody Knows His Name (1986)*
   Staged reading: Basement Workshop, New York City, April 1986
Pawns (1985)
   Production: Henry St. Settlement House, Asian Writers Series, New
   York City, April 1987
   Staged reading: Actors' Creative Theater, New York City, June 1985
Rohwer (1982)
   Production: Pan Asian Repertory Theatre, New York City, March 1982
Strokes (1987)
Trump and Emi (1982)

Amy Hill

Beside Myself (1992)
   Production: Mark Taper Forum "Out in Front Festival," Los Angeles,
   October 1992
   Production: Northwest Asian American Theater, Seattle, Jan. 1993
   Production: East West Players, Los Angeles, July–Aug. 1993
Reunion (1993)
   Production: Japan America Theatre, Los Angeles, June 1993
   Production: L.A. Festival, "Crossing L.A.," Crossroads Theater, Los
   Angeles, Sept. 1993
Tokoyo Bound (1991)*
   Production: Northwest Asian American Theater, Seattle, Jan. 1991

Production: Asian American Theater Co., San Francisco, April–May 1991

Production: East West Players, Los Angeles, Aug.–Sept. 1991

Production: New York Shakespeare Festival, New York City, Dec. 1991

Mary Hirakawa
Blood Is the Victor (1951)*

Velina Hasu Houston
Alabama Rain (1992)*
Albatross (1988)*
    Staged reading: The Playwrights' Theatre, Los Angeles, Sept. 1988
    Staged reading: The Playwrights' Theatre, Los Angeles, Nov. 1988
    Staged reading: Manhattan Theatre Club, New York City, Oct. 1989
    Workshop and staged reading: Old Globe Theatre, San Diego, Jan. 1990
    Staged reading: Arizona Theater Co., Phoenix, June 1991, Tucson, May 1991
    Staged reading: Theatre/Theatre, Los Angeles, June 1992
Amerasian Girls (includes *Petals and Thorns* and *Father I Must Have Rice*) (1983)
    Production: Ensemble Studio Theatre, Los Angeles, Feb. 1987
American Dreams (1983)*
    Production: The Negro Ensemble Co., New York City, Jan.–Feb. 1984
    Produced for radio by L.A. Theatre Works and National Public Radio/KCRW, 1991
Asa Ga Kimashita (*Morning Has Broken*) (1980)*
    Production: Studio Theater, U.C.L.A., Los Angeles, Dec. 1981
    Production: East West Players, Los Angeles, Jan.–Feb. 1984
    Production: Pacific Rim Productions, San Francisco, Feb.–March 1985
    Production: Kumu Kahua Theatre, Honolulu, Jan. 1991
    Production: University of Southern California, Los Angeles, Oct. 1991
    Production: State University of New York at Geneseo, Feb. 1992
    Published in *The Politics of Life: Four Plays by Asian American Women*, ed. Velina Hasu Houston (Philadelphia: Temple University Press, 1993)
Broken English (1991)
    Workshop and staged reading: Odyssey Theatre Ensemble, Los Angeles, May 1991
Cactus Bloom (1990)
The Canaanite Woman (1990)
Child of the Seasons (1984)
Christmas Cake (1990)
    Staged reading: East West Players, Los Angeles, May 1991
    Workshop production: Kumu Kahua Theatre, Honolulu, Dec. 1992
The Confusion of Tongues (1990)
    Production: St. Augustines By-the-Sea Episcopal Parish, Santa Monica, Calif., June 1991
Ka'piolani's Faith (1990)
    Staged reading: Kumu Kahua Theatre, Honolulu, Dec. 1991
Kokoro Kara (*From the Heart*) (1989)*

The Legend of Bobbi Chicago (1985)
  Staged reading: Mark Taper Forum, Los Angeles, Feb. 1987
Lysistrata's Peace, an adaptation (1992)
The Matsuyama Mirror (1979)
The Melting Plot (1990)
My Life a Loaded Gun (1988)
  Workshop and staged reading: Old Globe Theatre, San Diego, Sept. 1988, May 1989
  Staged reading: Old Globe Theatre, San Diego, Calif., June 1989
Necessities (1990)*
  Workshop and reading: Old Globe Theatre, San Diego, Calif., Oct. 1990
  Production: Old Globe Theatre, San Diego, Calif., July 1991
  Production: Purple Rose Theatre, Los Angeles, March 1993
O-Manju (1989)
Once Every Christmas (1992)
A Place for Kalamatea (1989)
Plantation (1991)
Princess Kaiulani (1990)
The Sky Is Falling (1992)
Tea (1983)*
  Rockefeller workshop production: Asian American Theater Co., San Francisco, March 1985
  Staged reading: East West Players, Los Angeles, June 1985
  Staged reading: The Seattle Group Theatre, Seattle, Oct. 1986
  Staged reading: First Stage, Los Angeles, Feb. 1987
  Staged reading: Manhattan Theatre Club, New York City, June 1987
  Production: Manhattan Theatre Club, New York City, Oct. 1987
  Production: Old Globe Theatre, San Diego, Calif., March 1988
  Production: Interstate Firehouse Cultural Center, Portland, Oreg., April 1988
  Production: Whole Theater, Montclair, N.J., Oct. 1989
  Production: Philadelphia Theatre Co., Nov. 1989
  Production: TheatreWorks, Palo Alto, Calif., Jan. 1990
  Production: Kumu Kahua Theatre, Honolulu, Jan. 1990
  Staged reading: University of California at Santa Barbara, June 1990
  Staged reading: Japan America Theatre, Los Angeles, Aug. 1990
  Production: Odyssey Theatre Ensemble, Los Angeles, Aug. 1990
  Production: Kumu Kahua Theatre, Honolulu, May–June 1991
  Production: Syracuse Stage, Syracuse, N.Y., Oct. 1991
  Production: Horizons Theatre, Washington, D.C., Oct. 1991
  Production: Mount Holyoke College Department of Theatre, South Hadley, Mass., Dec. 1991
  Published in *Unbroken Thread: An Anthology of Plays by Asian American Women*, ed. Roberta Uno (Amherst: University of Massachusetts Press, 1993)
Thirst (1981)*
  Staged reading: The Lee Strasberg Creative Center, Hollywood, Calif., April 1984

Production: Asian American Theater Co., San Francisco, March–May 1986

Tokyo Valentine (1991)*
   Staged reading: East West Players, Los Angeles, Oct. 1992
Word for Word (1992)
Zyanya (1979)

Karen Huie
*Across Division Street**
   Production: Drama Ensemble, New York City, June 1978
   Staged reading: Western Addition Cultural Center, San Francisco, 1980
*Columbus Park**
   Staged reading: Los Angeles Theatre Center, Festival of New Plays, Los Angeles, March 1989
*Maiden Voyage**
   Staged reading: Los Angeles Theatre Center, Festival of New Plays, Los Angeles, March 1989
   Staged reading: East West Players, Los Angeles, 1991
*Songs of Harmony**
   Staged reading: East West Players, Los Angeles, 1985
   Staged reading: UCLA Conference on Asian American Families, 2 March 1991
   Production: East West Players, Los Angeles, Oct. 1990
*What Did You Say?**
   Production: Los Angeles City College, El Camino College and Orange Coast College, 1981
*What's Wrong with Him?**
   Production: Los Angeles City College, El Camino College and Orange Coast College, 1981
*The Widow Lai**
   Staged reading: LA Actors' Theatre, Los Angeles, 1980
   Staged reading: AmerAsia Bookstore, Los Angeles, 1981
*Yasuko and the Young Samurai**
   Production: Pasadena City College, Pasadena, Calif., 1979
   Production: Inner City Cultural Center, Los Angeles, 1980
   Production: Japan America Theatre, Los Angeles, 1983

Miyoshi Ikeda
Barrack Thirteen (1951)*
Lest We Forget (1951)

Momoko Iko
Boutique Living and Disposable Icons (1987)
   Production: Pan Asian Repertory Theatre, New York City, 1988
Flowers and Household Gods (1975)*
   Production: Pan Asian Repertory Theatre, New York City, 1981
   Production: Northwest Asian American Theater, Seattle, 1984
Gold Watch (1970)*
   Production: Inner City Cultural Center, Los Angeles, 1972

Produced for TV by PBS, Visions series, KCET, Los Angeles, 1975
Production: University of Washington, Seattle, 1976
Production: Stanford University, Stanford, Calif., 1977, 1982, 1987, 1988
Published in *Unbroken Thread: An Anthology of Plays by Asian American Women*, ed. Roberta Uno (Amherst: University of Massachusetts Press, 1993)
Hollywood Mirrors (1978)
Production: Asian American Theater Co., San Francisco, 1978
Old Man (1972)
Second City Flat (1976)*
Production: Inner City Cultural Center, Los Angeles, 1978
When We Were Young (1973)
Production: East West Players, Los Angeles, 1974
Production: Asian American Theater Co., San Francisco, 1976

Akemi Kikumura
The Gambling Den (1983)
Production: East West Players, Los Angeles, 1987
Production: Northwest Asian American Theater, Seattle, 1988–89

Leigh Kim
Da Kine (1979)

Jean Sadako King
Confetti (1964)
Production: The Kennedy Theatre, University of Hawaii, Honolulu, 1965
Encounter or *The Way It Really Was* (1964)
Whither Thou Goest (1964)
Production: University of Hawaii Theater, Honolulu, 3–7 March 1965

Victoria Nalani Kneubuhl
Conversion of Ka'ahumanu (1988)
Production: Arts Council of American Samoa, tour of American Samoa, June–Aug. 1990
Production: Edinburgh Festival, Scotland, Aug. 1990
Emmaleha (1986)
Production: Kumu Kahua Theatre, Honolulu, 1986
January 1893 or *Overthrow in Five Acts* (1992)
Production: Hui Na'auao, Honolulu, 1993
Just So Stories (1992)
Production: Honolulu Theatre for Youth, Spring 1993
Tofu Samoa (1991)
Veranda Dance (1985)
Production: Kennedy Lab Theatre, Honolulu, 1986

Clara Kubojiri
Country Pie (1953)
Hale O Olelo Nane (*House of Fable*)

Margaret Kwon
Mama's Boy (1937)*
I Fear Not Péle (1937)*

Cherylene Lee
Arthur and Leila (1991)*
　　Staged reading: Mark Taper Forum, Los Angeles, 7 Oct. 1991
The Ballad of Doc Hay (1987)*
　　Production: Marin Playhouse Theatre, San Anselmo, Calif., March 1987
　　Production: Chinese Cultural Center, San Francisco, March 1987
Bitter Melon (with Jeff Gillenkirk) (1989)*
　　Staged reading of Act III excerpt: New Traditions Theatre Co., San Francisco, 13 Jan. 1991
Delta Pearl (with Jeff Gillenkirk) (1989) [first two acts of *Bitter Melon*]*
Memory Square (with Cynthia Leung) (1988)*
　　Staged reading: P.F. Flyer Productions, San Francisco, 3 Feb. 1991
　　Staged reading: Asian American Theater Co., San Francisco, 3 Feb. 1991
Overtones (1984)*
　　Staged reading: Bay Area Playwrights' Festival VII, San Francisco, July 1984
　　Production: Kumu Kahua Theatre, Honolulu, Nov. 1988
Pyros (1983)*
　　Staged reading: Bay Area Playwrights' Festival VII, San Francisco, July 1984
　　Video: American Folk Theater, Seattle, June 1984
Wong Bow Rides Again (1985)*
　　Production: East West Players, Los Angeles, Jan.–Feb. 1987
Yin Chin Bow (1986)*
　　Staged reading: Pan Asian Repertory Theatre and Basement Workshop, New York City, 30 June 1986
　　Workshop production: Asian American Theater Co., San Francisco, March 1987
　　Staged reading: Third Step Theater, New York City, June 1990

G. M. Lee
One in Sisterhood Asian Women
　　Published in *Asian Women's Journal*, ed. Emma Gee (Berkeley: University of California at Berkeley, 1971)

Gladys Li (Ling-ai Li)
The Law of Wu Wei (1925)*
　　Production: Arthur Andrews Theatre, University of Hawaii, Honolulu, 1928
　　Published in *Hawaii Quill Magazine*, 1927
The Soga Revenge (1930)
　　Production: McKinley High School Auditorium, Honolulu, 1930
The Submission of Rose Moy (1924)*
　　Production: Arthur Andrews Theatre, University of Hawaii, Honolulu, 1928

Reading: "Lucky Come Hawaii: The Chinese in Hawaii" conference, East West Center, Honolulu, 20 July 1988
Published in *Hawaii Quill Magazine*, June 1928
Published in *Paké: Writings by Chinese in Hawaii*, ed. Eric Chock (Honolulu: Bamboo Ridge Press, 1989)
The White Serpent (1924)*
Production: McKinley High School Auditorium, Honolulu, 1928
Production: Arthur Andrews Theatre, University of Hawaii, Honolulu, 1929
Published in *Hawaii Quill Magazine*, 1932

Loretta M. J. Li
The Bridge (1952)*
Painting on Velvet (1925)*

Genny Lim
Bitter Cane (1989)*
Staged reading: Seattle Group Theatre, Seattle, July 1989
Workshop production: Bay Area Playwrights Festival XII, San Francisco, 17 Aug.–3 Sept. 1989
Published in *Bitter Cane and Paper Angels: Two Plays by Genny Lim* (Honolulu: Kalamaku Press, 1991)
Published in *The Politics of Life: Four Plays by Asian American Women*, ed. Velina Hasu Houston (Philadelphia: Temple University Press, 1993)
Faceless (1989)
Production: The Magic Theater, Multicultural Playwrights Festival (in collaboration with Persona Grata Productions), San Francisco, 2–19 Aug. 1989
The Magic Brush (1990–91)
Paper Angels (1978)*
Production: Asian American Theater Co., San Francisco, 12 Sept.–26 Oct. 1980
Production: New Federal Theater, New York City, March–April 1982
Production: Chinese Cultural Center, San Francisco, June–July 1982
Production: Asian Theater Group, Ethnic Cultural Center, Seattle, May 1983
Television production: American Playhouse, PBS video broadcast, July 1985
Published in *Bitter Cane and Paper Angels: Two Plays by Genny Lim* (Honolulu: Kalamaku Press, 1991)
Published in *Unbroken Thread: An Anthology of Plays by Asian American Women*, ed. Roberta Uno (Amherst: University of Massachusetts Press, 1993)
Pigeons (1980)*
Production: Paper Angels Productions, Chinese Cultural Center, San Francisco, Sept. 1983
Production: New WORLD Theater, Amherst, Mass., Nov. 1985
The Pumpkin Girl (1987)
Workshop production: Artists of Marin, Bay Area Playwrights' Festival X, San Rafael, Calif., Aug. 1987

The Sky Never Stops (1987)*
Winter Place (1988)
    Production: Hatley-Martin Gallery, San Francisco, Dec. 1988
XX (1987)
    Staged reading: The Lab, XX Theater, San Francisco, June–July 1987

Sharon Lim-Hing
Superdyke, the Banana Metaphor and the Triply Oppressed Object (1990)*
    Published in *Piece of My Heart* (Cambridge: Sister Vision Press, 1991)

Nikki Nojima Louis
Breaking the Silence: Japanese Voices in America (1985)*
    Staged reading: University of Washington, Seattle, May 1985
    Production: Northwest Asian American Theater, Seattle, Feb. 1986
Changing Faces (1987)*
    Production: Seattle Group Theatre, Seattle, Jan.–Feb. 1988
Gold! Gold! Gold! (touring adaptation of *Winds of Change*) (1990)
    Toured Centennial Celebration, Seattle Public Library, King County
    Public Middle and High Schools, Seattle, April 1991
Living the Turn of the Century [later entitled *Winds of Change*] (1990)
    Production: Museum of Science and Industry Theatre, Seattle, Sept.–
    Nov. 1990
Made in America (1985)
    Production: Pioneer Square Theatre New Works Festival, Seattle, Aug.
    1985
Most Dangerous Women (with Jan Maher) (1990)
    Staged reading: Museum of Science and Industry Theatre, Seattle, Sept.
    1990
    Production: Bryn Mawr College, Bryn Mawr, Penn., June 1991
Our Mothers' Stories (1989)
    Staged reading as work-in-progress: Kent Arts Commission, Kent,
    Wash., March 1989
    Production: Seattle Group Theatre, Seattle, May 1989

Charlotte Lum
Mistaken Nonentity (1948)*
These Unsaid Things (1948)
    Published in *Paké: Writings by Chinese in Hawaii,* ed. Eric Chock
    (Honolulu: Bamboo Ridge Press, 1989)

Louise Mita
For Sale (1992)
Let It R.I.P. (1990)*

Nobuko Miyamoto
A Grain of Sand (1992)
    Production as work-in-progress: Highways, Santa Monica, Calif., Dec.
    1992
Talk Story (1987)
    Production: Japan America Theatre, Los Angeles, 1987

Production: Dept. of Education, State of Hawaii, Kauai, and Maui, 1988
Production: Theatre Artaud, San Francisco, March 1989
Production: Los Angeles Theatre Center, June 1989

Karen Morioka
Echoes (1975)*

Maybelle Nakamura
Asa Wakuru [*Tomorrow Will Tell*] (1954)*
Production: University of Hawaii Theatre Group, Honolulu, 29, 30 Oct. and 4–6 Nov. 1954

Jude Narita
Coming into Passion/Song for Sansei (1985, 1987)*
Production: Powerhouse Theater, Santa Monica, Calif., 27 May–28 June 1987
Production: Fountain Theater, Los Angeles, 9 July 1987–3 Sept. 1988
Production: Theater 6111, Los Angeles, 16 June–5 Aug. 1989
Production: People's Playhouse, New York City, 5 Oct.–2 Dec. 1989
Production: Whitefire Theater, Sherman Oaks, Calif., 23 Feb.–1 April 1990
Production: Vancouver East Cultural Center, Vancouver, B.C., 23–28 Oct. 1990
Production: Storefront Theater, Portland, Oreg., 4–7 Sept. 1991
Production: Mamiya Theatre, Honolulu, 30 July–8 Aug. 1992
Stories Waiting to Be Told (1991)
Production: Stages Theatre, Los Angeles, 26–28 June 1992

Judith Nihei
Intake-Outtake (with Marc Hayashi) (1978)
Production: Asian American Theater Co., San Francisco, 1978
Intake-Outtake Take 2 (with Marc Hayashi) (1979)
Production: Asian American Theater Co., San Francisco, 1979

Barbara Noda
Aw, Shucks (1981)*
Production: Asian American Theater Co. in cooperation with The People's Theater Coalition, San Francisco, 5–8 Feb. 1981
Production: Asian American Theater Co., San Francisco, 15 May–28 June 1981

Sandra Oshiro
Someone's Drowning

Patsy Saiki
The Return (1959)*
Second Choice (1959)*
The Return of Sam Patch (1966)*

Lillian Sakai
The Family Tie (1958)*

Canyon Sam
*The Dissident**
Production: Green Gulch Zen Farm, Marin, Calif., 14 Nov. 1991
Production: La Pena Cultural Center, Berkeley, Calif., 21 Nov. 1991
Production: The Phoenix Theatre, San Francisco, 17, 24 Nov., 1 Dec. 1991
Production: Asian American Theater Co., San Francisco, 29 Jan.–2 Feb. 1992
*Taxi Karma**
Production: Green Gulch Zen Farm, Marin, Calif., 14 Nov. 1991
Production: La Pena Cultural Center, Berkeley, Calif., 21 Nov. 1991
Production: The Phoenix Theatre, San Francisco, 17, 24 Nov., and 1 Dec. 1991
Production: Asian American Theater Co., San Francisco, 29 Jan.–2 Feb. 1992

Amy Sanbo
Benny Hana
Staged reading: Northwest Asian American Theater, Seattle, 6, 7 Jan. 1984
Lady Is Dying (with Lonny Kaneko)*
Workshop production: Asian American Theater Co., San Francisco, 1977
Production: Northwest Asian American Theater, Seattle, 16 April–10 May 1981

Molly Tani Shell
In the Tide of Times (1953)
Where Dwells the Heart (1953)*

Naomi Sodetani
Obon (1982)

Emiko Tamagawa
Living in Infamy (1992)
Production: Old South Meeting House, Boston, 30 May 1992
Production: Brandeis University Intercultural Center, Waltham, Mass., 3 Oct. 1992

Besse Toishigawa (Inouye)
Nisei (1947)*
Reunion (1947)*
Production: University of Hawaii Theatre Group, 7–10 May 1947
Production: Kumu Kahua Theatre, Honolulu, May 1974
Published in *Kumu Kahua Plays*, ed. Dennis Carroll (Honolulu: University of Hawaii Press, 1983)

Mary Tomito
Dear Kay (1948)*

Motoko Tsubokawa
Bran in the Sun (1981)*

D. A. Tsufura

Origami (1987)*
  Production: Pan Asian Repertory Theatre, New York City, 1987
  Staged reading: Playhouse 46, New York City, 7 Nov. 1987
  Staged reading: Seattle Group Theatre, Seattle, 21 June 1988

Alice Tuan

Coast Line (1992)*
Dim Sums (1992)*
Four O'Clock Two (1989)*
General Yeh Yeh (1991)*

Alyce Chang Tung

The Age of Personality (1930)*
  Published in *Hawaii Quill Magazine*, Feb. 1930

Roberta Uno

Falling Through (1993)*
  Staged reading: Department of Theatre, Amherst College, 6 May 1993
In the Rock Garden (1977)*
  Production: Mainstage, Hampshire College, Amherst, Mass., 30 May–
  2 April 1978
  Production: Hallie Flanagan Studio Theatre, Smith College, Northampton, Mass., 13, 14, 18 Oct. 1978
  Production: Hampden Center for the Performing Arts, University of Massachusetts, Amherst, 29 April and 2, 3 May 1979

Denise Uyehara

Hobbies (1992)
  Staged reading: Senshin Buddhist Community Hall, Los Angeles, 30 March 1991
  Staged reading: Los Angeles Theater Center, Los Angeles, July 1991

Ermena Marlene Vinluan

The Frame-up of Narciso and Perez (with members of Sining Bayan) (1977)
Isuda ti Immuna (with members of Sining Bayan) (1973)
Tagatupad (with members of Sining Bayan) (1976)
Ti Mangyuna (with members of Sining Bayan) (1980)
  Production: Five-island tour sponsored by the International Longshoreman's and Warehouseman's Union Local 142, Hawaii, 1981
Visions of a Warbride (1979)

Nancy Wang

If We Only Knew (with Robert Kikuchi-Yngojo) (1990)*
  Production: Bay View Opera House, San Francisco, 20 Oct. 1990
  Production: New Performance Gallery, San Francisco, 8, 9, 15, 16 March 1991
  Production: Chicago Cultural Center, Chicago, 30 May 1991
  Production: Berkeley Arts Center, Berkeley, Calif., 8 June 1991
  Production: The Stage, San Jose, Calif., 7, 8 July 1991

Production: University of California at Santa Cruz, Santa Cruz, 21 Sept. 1991
Production: Colorado State University, Fort Collins, 7 March 1992
Production: Edge Festival, San Francisco, 1–3, 8–10, 15–17 Oct. 1992
Leave Me My Dreaming (1980)*
Production: Asian American Theater Co., San Francisco, Feb. 1981

Elizabeth Wong

The Aftermath of a Chinese Banquet (1988)*
Assume the Position (1990)*
Published in *Script Magazine*, New York University, 1990
China Doll (1990)*
Kimchee & Chitlins (1990)*
Staged reading: Primary Stages, New York City, June 1991 and June 1992
Staged reading: The Women's Project, New York City, April 1992
Staged reading: The Actor's Institute, New York City, Oct. 1992
Staged reading: Mark Taper Forum, Los Angeles, May 1992
Workshop production: Chameleon Productions, Chicago, Sept. 1992
Letters to a Student Revolutionary (1989)*
Staged reading: Theatre Works, Colorado Springs, Colo., March 1989
Staged reading: Henry St. Settlement and Pan Asian Repertory Theatre, New York City, May 1989
Staged reading: Theatre in the Works, Amherst, Mass., July 1990
Production: New WORLD Theater, Amherst, Mass., March 1991
Production: Pan Asian Repertory Theatre, New York City, 7 May–1 June 1991, Singapore Arts Festival 1992 (only North American entry),and national tour 1993
Published in *Unbroken Thread: An Anthology of Plays by Asian American Women*, ed. Roberta Uno (Amherst: University of Massachusetts Press, 1993)
Published in *Women on the Edge* (New York: Applause Books, 1993)

Karen Tei Yamashita

Godzilla Comes to Little Tokyo (1990)*
Gilawrecks (1989, 1992)*
Production: Northwest Asian American Theater, Seattle, 1992
Staged reading: Japan America Theatre, Los Angeles, 1992
Hannah Kusoh: An American Butoh (1989)*
Production: Japan America Theatre, Los Angeles, 1989
Production: Highways, Santa Monica, Calif., 1990
Hiroshima Tropical (1984)
Production as play-in-progress: East West Players, Los Angeles, 1984
Noh Bozos (1990)
Omen: An American Kabuki (1977)
Production: East West Players, Los Angeles, 1977
Tokyo Carmen vs. L.A. Carmen (1990)*
Production: Taper Too, Los Angeles, as part of the Thirteenth Hour: Celebration of Performance, June 1990

Wakako Yamauchi

And the Soul Shall Dance (1974)*
  Production: Northwest Asian American Theater, Seattle, 1974
  Production: East West Players, Los Angeles, 1977
  Production: University of Hawaii at Manoa, Honolulu, 1978
  Production: Kauai Community Theater, Kauai, Hawaii, 1979
  Production: Pan Asian Repertory Theatre, New York City, 1979
  Production: Asian American Theater Co., San Francisco, 1980
  Production: Cal State Asian American Theatre, Los Angeles, 1985
  Production: Pan Asian Repertory Theatre, New York City, March–April 1990
The Chairman's Wife (A Gang of One) (1988)*
  Staged reading: East West Players, Los Angeles, 1989
  Production: Kumu Kahua Theatre, Honolulu, Oct. 1990
  Production: East West Players, Los Angeles, Jan.–March 1990
For What
A Good Time (1983)*
The Memento (1983)*
  Production: Pan Asian Repertory Theatre, New York City, Feb.–March 1984
  Production: East West Players, Los Angeles, Jan.–Feb. 1986
  Production: Yale Repertory Theatre, Winterfest, New Haven, Conn., Jan.–Feb. 1987
The Music Lessons (1977)*
  Production: New York Shakespeare Festival Public Theater, New York City, 30 April–18 May 1980
  Production: Asian American Theater Co., San Francisco, 1982
  Production: Cal State Asian American Theatre, Los Angeles, 1982
  Production: East West Players, Los Angeles, Feb.–March 1983
  Published in *Unbroken Thread: An Anthology of Plays by Asian American Women*, ed. Roberta Uno (Amherst: University of Massachusetts Press, 1993)
Not a Through Street (1981)*
  Production: East West Players, Los Angeles, 1991
Shirley Temple Hotcha-Cha (1977)*
Songs That Made the Hit Parade (1988)*
Stereoscope I: Taj Mahal (1988)*
The Trip (1982)*
12-1-A (1981)*
  Production: Kumu Kahua Theatre, Honolulu, March–April 1990
  Production: East West Players, Los Angeles, 1982
  Production: Asian American Theater Co., San Francisco, 1982
  Published in *The Politics of Life: Four Plays by Asian American Women*, ed. Velina Hasu Houston (Philadelphia: Temple University Press, 1993)
What For? (1992)

Holly Yasui

Unvanquished (1990)
  Workshop production: Seattle Group Theatre, Seattle, July 1991

Violet Yee (Yap)
The Moon Goddess (1930)

Gerri Igarashi Yoshida
Adventures of Momotaro, the Peach Boy (1984)*
    Production: Any Place Theatre, New York City, 1984
    Staged reading: Puerto Rican Traveling Theatre, New York City, 1985
All the Way (1983)*
    Staged reading: Dragon Thunder Arts Forum, New York City, 1983
    Staged reading: Rainbow Coalition for Jesse Jackson, New York City,
    1983
The Baptism (1988)*
I Remember Papa-San (1986)*
    Staged reading: Asian American Dance Theatre, New York City, May
    1986
    Staged reading: Universal Jazz Coalition, New York City, Aug. 1986
    Staged reading: Long Island Chinese Circle, New York City, Oct. 1986
Sisters Matsuda (1985)*
    Staged reading: Basement Workshop, New York City, 1985